Members of our senior community talk about writing and the activities of Ageless Authors.

"Ageless Authors captures the best offered by seasoned writers—and no other contest does that! I'm grateful to be judged against my peers. We may be the fine aged wines of the writing world!"

—Jean Yeager

"Good luck on the contests and anthologies. This is a great venue for us old guys! (I am 82, by the way.)"

—Gordon Smith

"Thank you Ageless Authors, Ginnie Bivona and Larry Upshaw, for encouraging all of us to voice our experiences."

—Sandy Hill

"I just turned 65! Never ever thought I would be looking forward to this significant age, but so far the perks and opportunities are good."

—Sherry Mills

"The only old fogey writer I ever knew was Kurt Vonnegut. None of you is a Vonnegut, of course, but don't quit trying. He was a man of few words. Just used them over and over again to produce better stories. So it goes."

—Kilgore Trout

"My interest in writing began a few years ago before my grandmother died at 96 years of age. She saved all the letters I sent her from Vietnam. My memories of actual events and the interesting people from my early life…are stories that I've never been able to tell until now."

—Larry Sanders

"Ageless Authors is the only writing contest I'm aware of exclusively for writers over the age of 65. For all you younger folk who can't participate in this yet, just keep writing! Maybe after you reach age 65, your work may have come up to the level of some of the things you'll find in this anthology."

—Bill Pitts

"At age 70, my biggest fear is that I'll run out of time before I write all the poems from the ideas scribbled on the paper scraps that cover my desk."

—Norma Bernstock

"I am so excited about this venue for mature writers! I recently retired after teaching for 27 years…I absolutely loved my job, but I also enjoy the time I now have for writing."

—Rebecca Sandifer

"This is my first venture into non-academic publishing, and it certainly is more fun to write than research papers! I'm looking forward to reading your publication."

—Marilyn Boemer

"We haven't gone to our rocking chairs in old age! We stay active and love it!"

—Carol Smith

Well, my friends are gone and my hair is grey,
I ache in the places where I used to play.
And I'm crazy for love but I'm not coming on.
I'm just paying my rent every day in the tower of song.

—Leonard Cohen

AGELESS AUTHORS

Anthology

FIRST EDITION 2017

A collection of the best work from the first
Ageless Authors Writing Contest
for people age 65 and older.

Compiled by

GINNIE BIVONA
LARRY UPSHAW

Ageless Authors Anthology
Published by
Ageless Authors
10844 Meadowcliff Lane
Dallas, Texas 75238
214.405.5093
info@agelessauthors.com
agelessauthors.com

Copies of this book may be purchased at the website, agelessauthors.com,
from Amazon.com and many other retail book outlets. If you should have any
problem purchasing from the website, please contact Larry Upshaw by email:
publishing@agelessauthors.com.

ISBN 978-0-692-98164-1

To all those late bloomers
who had other things to do when they were young
but are now reaching their creative heights.

TABLE OF CONTENTS

Poetry

Essays

Short Stories

Contest Judges

INTRODUCTION

"Okay, so you've seduced me with this ageless thing. It's a great idea and I'm all in."

That's how Ageless Authors began, with author and poet Ginnie Siena Bivona's unique vision and the aquiescence of her friend and fellow author, Larry Upshaw. Ginnie had the entire concept in her head—to offer encouragement and incentives that would coax the creativity out of people in their senior years.

Nothing bothers Ginnie more than depicting people over 65 years of age as physically and mentally broken, unable to think straight or keep up with the youth culture. Cartoons of men all hunched over their walkers and block-shaped women with boobs hanging to their waist come to mind.

Ginnie will have none of it, and she takes a back seat to no one. She is 86 years old at this writing, with an energy level of people half her age. After many years as a housewife, Ginnie indulged her creative side by starting to write. And that opened the floodgates to a rush of words and images that obviously had been fighting to get out for decades. One of her novels has been the basis for a made-for-TV movie. She has written an X-rated cookbook for couples who enjoy food and, uh, each other. As acquisitions editor of a regional press, she became a leading publisher of Texana. All of this happened after age 50.

Today, Ginnie is firmly within the Greatest Generation. She takes pride in her ability to seduce a younger man, even if it's just for a business venture. Larry is at the leading edge of the Baby Boomers. In fact, he claims to be THE Boomer Baby.

"My dad was in the occupation forces in Japan during and after the war," he said. "He was mustered out of the Army on December 1, 1946 in San Francisco. It took him two days to get home on a train, (and, as they say, twenty minutes to get his shoes off) and I was born August 3, 1947, exactly nine months later. You could say I was his first DIY project when he made it home."

Larry established his career in journalism, writing for newspapers and magazines before initiating a service offering marketing and public relations services to law firms and other professional businesses. In this capacity, he has ghostwritten a dozen nonfiction books along with hundreds of essays and white papers on business, law and the professions.

Helping people publish their own works is a mainstay of Ageless Authors. Ginnie is on a quest to document the lives of her generation for their children and grandchildren.

"Not everyone has a book in them," she says, "but everyone age 65 and older has something to say, experiences to write about. They can expound upon their lives. We've lived in very interesting times, and it would be a shame if those memories were lost forever."

And that's what could happen as the world goes digital. Every time the industry standard on document retention changes, information is lost. People discarded floppy discs without converting them to CDs. Now many computers won't even accommodate a CD. Books, on the other hand, are always readable and never need to be converted to a newer medium. Ginnie works with older folks from all walks of life, helping them fashion their memoirs into books.

One of Ginnie's clients is 91 years old, had never used a computer and certainly had not written a book before. This lady helped her husband generate his memoir, then worked with Ginnie to publish two volumes of her own. She didn't believe her life had so much meaning until Ginnie encouraged her to find her voice.

And finding that voice, for those who just went through life doing what they thought was expected of them, is the mission of Ginnie Bivona. For Larry Upshaw, the mission is to simplify information so that most people can understand it.

Ageless Authors began the process of helping older people find a voice with our first writing contest late in 2016. This initial contest had no subject or focus. We simply asked people age 65 and older to submit short stories, essays and poetry they had written. At first, there was a concern that these people would not be able to navigate a computer or submit their work on a website, but Ginnie set them straight.

"If you have trouble with the technology," she said, "ask your kids to help. After all, you taught them how to use a spoon."

The number and quality of submissions to our first contest was a pleasant surprise. We honored writers and awarded cash prizes, and from the hundreds of entries we selected the best submissions for publication in this anthology.

This is quality literature, and we are proud to present it for the 65+ submitters, their families, friends and other lovers of words and ideas. We plan to continue with our contests each year and select the best entries to publish. It is our sincere hope that whatever your age, you, too, will be seduced to enjoy the many facets of Ageless Authors.

The Editors
agelessauthors.com
larry@agelessauthors.com

Age is like climbing a mountain.
You are so involved with the scenery
that you don't notice the terrain.
You can handle the climb with ease.
Life is beautiful. But going down the other side,
when you are tired and not so steady,
can be perilous if you don't take it slow.

—**Barbara Mott**
92-year-old author

Poetry

First Prize

COME HERE

Sherry Mills

Sit down.
Wait a minute.
Turn it off.
Tell me.
Come down from there.
Don't do that.
Hold this.
Don't make a mess.
Pick it up.
Hold on.
Listen to me.
Don't touch it.
Stop that.
Give it to me.
Put that down.
Hurry up.
Did you do that?
Bring it here.
Stand still.
Don't come in here.
Put this on.
Be quiet.

Get out of there.
Don't drop it.
Move over.
Leave it alone.
Go get it.
Come here.
Give me a hug.
I love you.

❧

Sherry Mills is an award-winning (retired) filmmaker who makes unusual jewelry from hardware, plumbing parts, antique fishing lures, "junk" and "found" objects; paints and creates multi-media, collage, and fabric art, and writes. Her geographic circle took her from Texas to Mexico, to Texas again, California, Hawaii, and back to Texas. Her professional work life included hotel management, the film business, and the nonprofit educational world. Last year, she and her husband didn't have a good knee between them, but after replacements their plan is to be back to two-steppin'.

Second Prize

PROCRASTINATION

Greg Rogers

I kept putting off writing this......

Oh shucks! I'm late for the meeting
At Procrastinators Anonymous
There's probably no one there quite yet
That would be neither odd nor ominous
If someone did show up on time
We'd probably refund their dues
If anyone bothered to pay them
Well, the treasury has nothing to lose
I think I'm on the committee
To write the bylaws and such
In fact, I think I'm the chairman
Go figure, we haven't done much
In fact, that's the meeting I'm late for
I've postponed it nine times this year
And now I am late, I'll miss the debate
If anyone shows up to hear.

Greg Rogers is a retired musician and programmer in Farmers Branch, Texas.

9

Third prize

LONG TERM CARE

Norma Bernstock

As I age, with no children of my own,
I worry about how I'll manage.

My friend Sharon says:
That's why I live in town,
I can walk to everything.

Joyce has long-term health insurance:
My kids would hate me, she says,
if they were responsible for my care.

Michael's plan is to take himself out
while he's still in control:
Wheel me onto Pond Eddie Bridge
with a bag of pot, he tells me.
I know he wants George Harrison's "My Sweet Lord"
played at his funeral but I refuse to put him on the bridge.

What if there were a home for aging poets?
We'd have readings every night,
loud speakers and microphones,
cushioned chairs and a high stool
with a lighted lectern for the feature.

Bedrooms furnished with writing tables,
stacks of yellow pads and sharp pencils,
user-friendly computers and printers that work,
a staff available 24/7 to critique every writers' first drafts.

And even if the poems were rejected for publication elsewhere,
The Aging Poets Printing Press would publish them
in a collection of final works.

Norma Ketzis Bernstock writes and creates art in her studio in the woods of Pennsylvania. Her poetry has appeared in journals and anthologies including *Connecticut River Review, Paterson Literary Review, Lips, Stillwater Review, Exit 13, Edison Review* and the anthology, *Voices From Here.* Previous achievements include a Geraldine R. Dodge Scholarship to the Fine Arts Work Center in Provincetown, Massachusetts, and recognition by the Allen Ginsberg Poetry Awards.

Honorable Mention

A WINTER TREK ALONG EAST BRUSH CREEK

Robert Robeson

Clouds shroud distant mountain peaks, like a flimsy silk curtain, above the icy flow of East Brush Creek near Eagle, Colorado. Surreptitious silence envelops each inch of the frigid terrain while angled light falls across its forested face helping to illuminate a cloak of new-fallen snow.

My breath rises in this austere isolation, in puffs of white vapor, reminiscent of a bird aware of its freedom. The lustrous landscape garnishes this winter scene, as a sprig of parsley on a chef's culinary delight, with a frosty image having the power to calm both mind and spirit.

Far from the din and traffic of city life, my senses focus on this idyllic scene while experiencing the shivering grasp of an arctic chill. Patches of glistening and colorful ice frame this remote stream mirroring stained glass windows in a cathedral. They provide their own distinct artistry...compliments of God.

This unspoiled terrain proves that it can't always be summer in life. Seasonal changes force its visitors to endure the fatigue and burden of winter's freezing breath. It's a transformation that can only make one stronger. A panorama of untamed mountain grandeur, with East Brush Creek flowing through its heart in serpentine fashion, stretches across this landscape.

A white jacket of snow is pulled tight around the riverbanks. It hugs the ground and water in a chilling embrace. Time seems to be frozen in place while overhead clouds appear as though white paint has been splashed onto nature's canvas against a colorful blue background. They extend their wispy, milky fingers in all directions.

The only sound comes from a whisper of wind and water rippling softly as it courses along an ancient streambed sheltering brown, brook, and rainbow trout in its depths. It provides a mesmerizing snapshot of tantalizing beauty. This high country amphitheater has the power to command attention and invigorate one's spirit, even in the dead of winter.

❦

Robert B. Robeson is a 74-year-old who has been published 880 times in 320 publications in 130 countries, in addition to 47 anthologies. After retiring with more than 27 years of military service on three continents, he served as a newspaper managing editor and columnist. He has a BA in English from the University of Maryland-College Park and has completed extensive undergraduate and graduate work in journalism at the University of Nebraska-Lincoln. He lives in Lincoln, Nebraska with his wife of 47 years.

Honorable Mention

BOX PURSE

Michael Owens

Summer brought me to live with county cousins
Without television, telephone or electricity
Aunt Reba locked us outside in the heat
With our imaginations, we sought devilment

Squawking and feathers flying from the chicken coop
We three boy cousins ran to investigate.

In the coop we found ourselves a chicken snake
Stuffed with eggs, coiled up digesting dinner.
Boyce Ray grabbed it and held it by the head
Now where do we put it? was the question.

He spied my sisters' small black box purse
On the back porch by my pile of things.
Six hands stuffed the snake into the purse
Quickly closed it up and schemed
What to do with the angry thing.

Out front on the asphalt road from town
We placed the purse on the centerline
Hid in the tall grass, out of sight and watched.

Our hearts pumping with anticipation
When an old black car came cruising down the road
We could see six high school boys packed inside.

It slowed down and passed, stopped and backed up
A back door opened out came a hand and snatched the purse
The doors slammed shut the car took off.

Before we could count to three
All four doors flew open and six bodies flew
Yelling and a shouting as they radiated out.

Within a second they paused to see the car
Four doors wide open, rolling down the hill
Six young men now running close behind
The rolling crash was silent about a quarter mile away.

Michael Owens writes from his home in Cypress, Texas. A native Texan born in Galveston, Mike takes inspiration from overheard conversations. Married for 48 years to his wife, Peggy Sue, he retired as a school administrator and now fills his time visiting his granddaughter, woodworking and writing.

Honorable Mention

MORNING VISITOR

Linda Mohr

Unexplained lightness on bed
One week after your passing
Spot where you used to snuggle.

Did you return to your beloved home?
Is this the sign I asked you to send?
A sign that you are safe.

My life is so different without you
My life is so rich because of you
Ten years my fur baby, my muse.

Unexplained lightness on bed again
Ten days after your passing
I whisper Lexie Lee.

I turn over to look at you
Lightness is gone in an instant
But you are forever safe in my heart.

My welcome home greeter
My napping buddy and lap kitty
My kindred spirit.

Linda A. Mohr is an educator, entrepreneur and author. She is the author of an award-winning memoir, *Tatianna Tales and Teachings of My Feline Friend*. Her poetry and essays have received Cat Writers Muse Medallion awards and state Pen Women awards. Her work appears in *laJoie, Catnip* and numerous anthologies. She lives in N. Palm Beach with her cats Grace and Chauncey. http://amzn.to/1I10vQi and www.lindamohr.com.

Friends are like the diamonds in a ring.
You know they are special because they reflect their
importance in your life. Each one is a
beautiful jewel that can make you proud.
Be careful not to lose them.

—Barbara Mott
92-year-old author

WEATHER
WHETHER YOU LIKE IT OR NOT!

JOHN K. PROBST

It's really not as though we had a choice,
within this matter, we humans have no voice.
But like it or not, it has its effect,
on us, whether it; we accept or reject.
We do have the technology to make a prediction,
as to whether the weather will be to us
a blessing or an affliction.

And predictions have improved as have communications,
giving us far more knowledgeable weather interpretations.
In the old days a newscaster would or could, only say,
 A storm is coming there is no delay,
it will arrive, sometime, tomorrow or maybe today.

Today's technology allows all predictions we seek,
with accuracy and dependability for the length of week.

And what about people who are conversational killers,
you can always use weather talk as conversation fillers.

So!
Weather the weather
whether you like it or not.
For the weather we weather,
is the only weather we've got.

In 2005, **John K. Probst** retired as Professor Emeritus of Humanities from Feather River College in Northern California and now has time to write novels and poetry. He has self-published five novels and a booklet of poems on a variety of subjects. For further bio information, view his web page www.worldofjohnkprobst.com.

TIME PIECE

James Stewart

Old clocks get tired.
Nothing seems random.
There is no rest while the spring
grips taut intent,
or the electrons keep moving
across potential in constant current,
or the sun casts a shadow
on a face as old as humanity.
The heart knows this:
it reads shadows and rides
an electronic pendulum arc.
This journey of flesh carries
until the spring is slack
and the energy of who
we are finds a ghost,
wholly or in part.
My clock will not get tired,
it will just stop
in a quantum moment.
Warm and Round
The night is still and round.
An ocean rises from city traffic
as my skin rejoices the fan

whirling from the ceiling.
I sit where the dog sleeps
when he's here.
I can almost hear
his stir and stretch
as he dreams his dreams,
but he is far away,
farther than the train
blaring an intersection
on the other side of the river.
The clock ticks as it has
for two hundred fifteen years.
My clock has ticked
for sixty-five years plus
one hundred and three days.
I have a lot to learn.
I am blessed:
this warm round night will teach.

James Stewart's past credits include *The Alembic, The Licking River Review, Orange Willow Review, Orion Magazine, The Blue Hour, The Progenitor, Rattapallax,* and *Tulane Review.*

THE TIMELESS STREAM

Gordon Smith

I came to the brook at dawn one day
Among the sound and sight
Of rippled shallows, leaves at play,
And rainbows bending light.
A bird beside the water's edge
Stood frozen staring still,
Its eye upon a muddy ledge
Where sunned a breakfast fill.
Too soon it lunged and missed its aim.
The prey was gone too fast;
Its plan destroyed, no meal to claim,
It flew away at last.
I came to the brook at noon one day
To cast among the reeds,
To find the lair where fishes stay
And mimic Walton's deeds.
My spoil was wiser, quicker far
Than I could ever be
And swam and tagged and cleared the bar
To make a game of me.
I came to the brook at dusk one day,
My heart was full of woe,
My soul so bruised I could not pray,

My every thought a foe.
I sat beside its azure pool,
My mind I emptied there,
And let its gentle soothing cool
Relieve my load of care.
The moon that rose all full and white
Its beams a shimmer gave,
The breeze that stirred the balmy night
Caressed each pulsing wave.
The stars burst through in air so clear,
Their pictures slowly teaching,
That once for Jacob made a scene
Of heaven's ladder reaching.

The heavenly lights are old each night,
The bird and fish each day,
The stream that runs with haste and might
Has flowed its course always
The world renews in every age,
Our God gives mercy blest;
And we must claim each clean new page
To write upon our best.

My soul, my will, my spirit healed
I left this holy place,
Eternal truths to me revealed,
The morrow's hours to face.

❋

Gordon Smith is a retired public school teacher who lives in Hot Springs, Arkansas, with his wife, Carol, who is a retired public school English and journalism teacher.

THE JOY OF A BIRD

Gloria Casey

I was dark and brooding
Distracted and concerned
When suddenly a dove appeared
And all my worry cleared.

I focused on its beauty
How it enjoyed the day
And knew it came to pray with me
And lighten up my way.

It sat down in the sunlight
And looked around in peace
I followed its example
And let my worries cease.

Gloria Casey's interest in writing began in high school when she was a feature writer on her school newspaper. She is a former grade school teacher and later earned an MBA. As a consultant and business writer, her experience included writing advertising, marketing materials, studies for government agencies and clients, articles for business periodicals, and speeches for executives. Now, in retirement, she is switching to creative writing with a special interest in short stories and poetry.

SOME SWEET DATE

Suresh Shridharani

We were young then, in our twenties and dating.
This one weekend we were hiking a little known hill
Somewhere north of Atlanta.

The trail was pleasant under the cool canopy
Of tall trees with their tangled web of exposed roots
In the pathways preventing or causing a fall,
Depending on one's focused footing.

An incident occurred half way up the hill where
A young girl slipped and fell hard. All her peers
Laughed and jeered at her. Teased and tormented
Her. We both truly empathized with her.

When we got to the top it was beautiful.
Cool summer breeze and vast tranquil vistas
Embraced us, calmed us and gently erased out
The maddening humanity down below.

On our way down I pointed where earlier
The sweet girl had her sad tumble. Before I knew I
Also slipped and fell at the very same haunted spot.
All I remember next was a scream of laughter

Shot out by my sweet date. Empathy? None.
I might as well be rain dancing in Death Valley!
Contrary, she made me feel like a pompous fool and
Thought I deserved what I got—at that spot.

This story she has narrated ever since then
Many, many a time, with the same carefree
Killer laughter I've known—while all along very
Earnestly holding my hand ever so tenderly.

I have long since forgotten that old summit,
The cool summer breeze and its scenic vistas,
But the true treasure I found when I slipped and fell
On that hill there then . . . is still around.

Suresh Shridharani is a 71-year home builder. His wife always has fun telling this story, which he says is a true story.

SALUTE

Launa Fackrell

I salute America, the land that I love
I salute my flag waving proudly above.

I salute the people who fought all the wars
For my freedom—my future—my journey to the stars.

I salute as our beautiful flag unfurls and think of a child
    with golden curls
Laughing, teasing, full of fun who was six years old
    in World War I.

Daddy was gone and uncle too! Off to war for the red,
    white and blue
She stands at the tracks and dances and cheers. The soldiers throw
    flowers and hide their fears.

The big engines hiss and grind to start
She keeps on waving as they depart.

This charming child dressed in red and white
Blows them all kisses as the trains pull out of site.

There she is! Bea's her name!
Our red, white and blue girl, the soldier's proclaim.

Where's the blue? she teased as she ran alongside
Why, the blue—little sweetheart's—right there in your eyes!

World War I passed, then World War II
The red, white and blue girl served her county, too.

Her husband went off to defend the nation
And she worked as a clerk in the Army station.

Life went on and the gleam in her eyes
Dimmed just a bit as she grew more wise.

A son was born. He grew strong and bright
The red, white and blue girl sent him off to the fight.

The years march on. There's sadness and glory
The red, white and blue girl continues her story.

She loves this country—the mountains, the sea—
The wide open spaces, the land of the free.

The red, white and blue girl—Bea's her name
Still honors her country just the same.

She salutes America watching the flag unfurl
That's my mom—the red, white and blue girl.

❧

Launa Fackrell earned a bachelor's degree in English and Theater in 1975 and always wanted to write. She wrote this poem as a tribute to her mom. She would like to find someone to illustrate it and consider putting this into a children's book.

Pause and Ponder...

Phyllis McKinley

pause and ponder
how the profile of a hand
shows through
a translucent china plate,
make that an X-ray plate,
the bones gleam
bleached and sharp

see against a winter sky
white as paper,
charcoal branches of oaks,
penciled sketches
of tree-bones sleeping

watch how a dapple of sunlight,
colorless, flits scarlet
off a cardinal's wing,
beams emerald
on a trembling leaf

look how the darkness
of a December street
is swept back

by Christmas lights
and children's eyes,
big with wonder

pause and ponder
how light,
depending on its source,
and how porous we are,
can change
what we see,
and how...

Phyllis McKinley has authored four books of poetry and one children's book. Her poems have received multiple first place awards in Florida's Royal Palm Literary Awards. Her nonfiction has been published in several *Chicken Soup for the Soul* books and FWA annual Collections. She hopes to live to be 100 so she can keep on writing!

More Peas, Please!

Rebecca Sandifer

"I need more peas upon my plate!
I need them quick, it's getting late!
More mashed potatoes, too please.
Put them here, right by my peas."

I didn't know peas could be so much fun,
But, yes they can, and one by one...
I loaded them on the tip of my spoon,
Mixed in potatoes, and shot them all over that room!

Peas on the floor, peas on the chairs,
Peas on the ceiling, peas even in the new kid's hair!
But, hey, what's this?
That new kid has his eyes on me.

Oh my, does he have a pea?

He shot it straight.
He shot it true.
It landed right upon my plate.
Flipped in the air and in MY hair!

"HURRY, MORE PEAS, PLEASE!"

Rebecca Sandifer recently retired after teaching for 27 years. "I absolutely loved my job, but I have also enjoyed the time that I now have for writing," she said. She often draws upon her experiences as a teacher for her pieces. "More Peas, Please!" came into her head one day as she walked through the cafeteria and spied those green peas on the students' plates...untouched. She quickly went to her classroom and wrote this poem and had a good laugh as she shared it with colleagues and students.

Marital Bliss

Zandra Mink-Fuller

I've been married for over forty years.
Not to one man, several in fact.
Well, maybe a few more than that…
I like men.
What do you suppose I've learned from all
these years of marital bliss?

I am thinking how adept I am with a paring knife.
Peeling at least a million potatoes has taught me this skill.
My hand fits a mop handle better than Mickey Mantle's
on a Louisville Slugger.
The sweetest music is the whirring of a washing
machine loaded just right.
My pies, cakes and cookies baked to perfection,
would make Martha Stewart cringe with envy.
Sparkling windows cleaned without streaks is
a secret, I will not share.
Ironing with precision, making every crease a statement,
took time to master.
Keeping a clean house, fresh linens on every bed
with folded clothes in drawers nice and neat is
simple for this pro.
Clipping coupons, shopping for bargains

loading my precious purchases into the trunk
of my well-kept car is a weekly chore.
Tending a plentiful garden of sumptuous yields,
makes calloused hands of little worry.
Remembering, wiping tears from three-year-old faces while
kissing boo boos, made the warp speed ride through the
teen years bearable...almost.
Lying next to a man who just bent my heart, trying to
warm the cold covers of pain is a most brutal task.

Watching with silent wisdom, after forty years is
a talent I have yet to achieve

So, what have I learned?

I have learned, I am a maid, a cook, a chauffeur, a gardener,
a financial wizard, a lover, a jack of all trades and
a master of one...myself...and as sure as I'll be clipping
coupons from Sunday's paper, I will be looking for
the next Mr. Right if this one goes wrong!

***

Zandra Mink-Fuller writes from a small country house in rural Texas, which gives her ample opportunity to contemplate her life and those of many four-legged critters. She is grateful for being previously published and is excited as a senior writer to open her to this challenge. Sometimes as we age, we get discouraged and feel a bit "out of the loop." This opportunity made her get to thinking and typing.

Long-Lost Friend

Joyce Schmid

Amazingly, she was as old as I was.
She told me that she'd blown her mind
with acid in her hippy days, her happy days,

her giddy, free, frizzante days,
but still she treated me the way she did
when we were girls, and she

was magical to me,
my junior high school deity
in pixie haircuts, turned up collars,

whistles everywhere she walked,
rock n' roll and lindy in her steps,
and flecks of brilliance in her eyes.

Joyce Schmid's poetry has been published or is forthcoming in *Atlanta Review, Chautauqua, Canary, Blueline,* and other journals, and she won an Honorable Mention in the 2016 Robinson Jeffers Tor House Foundation Poetry Contest. She lives with her husband of almost 50 years in Palo Alto, California.

LIFE OF THE UNIVERSE

James Livingston

Fifteen dimensional nothing
slowed by vibrating strings
swallowed by black holes
held together by
the fifth force of empty space
accelerating
to smooth distribution
empty nothing
infinite nothing
total nothing
time alone

Non-existent

Light Mystery

Information on Light
travels
faster than itself
arriving
before it's left.
Is Now a refracted wave of then?
Is Now only a moment ago?

Does Future form Now and Past?
Formerly measured
jumping rapidly
universe and energy now
variations
strings
Maya, a stressed material ripped
from   gravity
gravitons
gravity waves
to quarks and gluons,
to strings and colors

by energy change
in atomic clocks
out of tune
on a broken melody
from a chaotic mirage

Born in Winnipeg, **James B. Livingston** was raised with five younger sisters in Minneapolis. He has a master's degree in philosophy from Bryn Mawr College and a master's in education from the University of St. Thomas. He continues to live, love, and influence in Minneapolis. He has more than 175 poems published in more than 75 journals including *The Best of Mage, Xpressions Journal, Aoife's Kiss, Beyond Centauri, Penwood Review, Timber Creek Review, Blue Collar Review, Love's Chance,* and *Writers Journal.* He also has a poem on MNArts.org and two on TowerofBabel.org.

BY THE SEA

Michael Morawey

By the sea,
a child went walking,
barefoot, wiggling cool sand between his toes,
footprints filling and disappearing in the watered
boundary of ocean and sand.
He watched a crab scuttle from its sandy hole to
the water and wondered—why does the crab go to the sea?

By the sea,
a boy went walking,
clogs slapping heels down the lonely beach,
kneeling, he dug into the firm wet sand, foamy water
sweeping up in a wide curve lapping at his feet.
Forming battlements with his bucket, moat filling
then draining,
a Crackerjack flag surmounting all,
he raised his defenses, but the sea lashed at the castle's
foundations and collapsed his dream.

By the sea,
a young man walked,
hand in hand with a girl, laughing, hair free in
the wind, eyes sparkling with life.

In silence, their hearts spoke of love and their future,
dreaming as the young must,
and when their sun-warmed arms touched,
they held each other close, while a sleek clipper,
white sails billowing, cut the horizon behind them.
The young man's eyes left the girl and filled
with the image of the ship.

By the sea,
a young girl walks alone.
Sweatered against fall's first chill wind,
she sits on the rising swell of a grassy dune,
her eyes searching the sea, swelling blue then deep green,
foamy waves shredded by the wind, scudding from crest to crest.
Hugging herself warm, she remembers his embrace, his love,
and the ship sailing in the reflection of his eyes,
knowing somehow that in him, the sea, the ship and she were
one and the same.

By the sea,
she waited and watched as a crab scuttled from its
sandy hole into the water and she wondered—why does the crab
Go to the sea?

Born in Chicago, **Michael Morawey** earned a bachelor's degree in so-cial sciences from Loyola University in 1961. He served twenty years as a Naval officer, with tours around the world including three tours of duty in Vietnam. In 1965, he married his wife Mary Ann and in 51 years of marriage they had four children. He retired from the Navy in 1982 as a Lieutenant Commander. He worked as an appeals hearing judge with the Texas Workforce Commission until he retired in 2007.

BLUEBONNETS AND OIL

Margaret Anderegg

We live under a giant bowl—this Texas sky,
rising high and wide and reaching to forever.
Davis Mountains swell o'er grey mesquite and sage
on plains once bottom to the Permian Sea.
Before hills rose sea creatures fell to fossilize,
to render fossil fuel for modern America.

Winds whip through The Basin like a train,
with roar and whistle, swooping desert dust
to take your breath away,
and muddy meager waters, which are trapped,
transformed to lakes and reservoirs,
against the failing rain.

Cliffs of marble flank the Colorado,
cause hearts to sing, exalting "Hills of Home!"
Look to these hills, feel strength rise up within you.
Here, Roadrunners run, Scissor-tails alight,
Golden Eagles sail, and Hummingbirds make tiny nests
at the base of Cedar branches.

Morning sun greets dense pine forests
in black earth by The Bay,
where, across the Sabine River, early settlers came
to make their homes in Texas,
on lands able to sustain them and be worth fighting for.

Texas, our Texas, so rich in history, be our home forever.
Anchor us with your diversity, and make us one-
with office towers, spacecraft towers,
wind farms, shrimp farms, cotton, cattle,
home-made quilts, bluebonnets and oil.

Margaret Daphne Anderegg lives in Odessa, Texas. As a retired widow, she writes, publishing poems in anthologies, *Noble Generation II, Poetry Society of Texas Book of the Year* (2012), *Best of Austin Poets* (2011-2012) *Wildflowers, Oil and Water,* and *Chaos West of the Pecos.* Her own book of poetry is *These Faces of Love* (2006) about the dynamics of family relationships.

As the Night Falls

Suresh Shridharani

Sounds of the crazy streets
Fading, ebbing, receding and
The cackles, coos and caws
Of the busy birds all around
Have simmered down.

All the shady trees and their
Zillion shaking leaves are filtering
And smearing the good earth
With the onslaught of darkness.

I am sitting by the picture window
Soaking in the slow swelling silence
After the long day of purposeful,
Purposeless, purported work—

Industry needed to pass the time,
To feed the fire in the belly,
To maintain my sanity, dignity,
Equity, sobriety and the family.

At last the evening is turning
Into a solid veil of dark wall
And much sought after serenity
Is wafting here after all
And it is tenderly soothing
My tired and achy soul

As the night falls.

Suresh Shridharani is a 71-year home builder.

I WILL, ONE DAY

Del Cain

You ask me why I never sing love to you
the way I do to the land that formed me.
You ask me why I never celebrate
our chiming together in hot breezes
the way I rattle those causes that draw my ire or joy.

How can I convince you that in all my
bags and boxes of words,
in those I carry in my pocket
and those picked up from foreign curbs,
I have not yet found that word
that would trace the shape
of my greatest passion.

One day,
when I have delved the secrets
of the mine of perfect words,
I will write my love for you.

Del Cain is author of *Lawmen of the Old West: The Good Guys; Lawmen of the Old West: The Bad Guys;* and two books of poetry—*Songs on the Prairie Wind and Voices of Christmas* from Words and Music Press as well as poems and stories in various journals and anthologies.

In the Face
of Yet Another Storm

Scott Lennox

The brute shouldered its way across the land,
its deep voice threatening, its fists snatching
and twisting even strong trees from their roots,
then flinging them aside, wasted, useless now,
its diluvial rain outflowing creeks and streams
and washing away what had rested beside them.
It's not that I am careless, but refusing to be bullied,
painfully aware of the hard miles I have come,
and grateful for the grace that daily gives me breath,
I blew out the candle, said a prayer, and went to bed.

Scott Lennox is a poet, writer, and fine art painter in Fort Worth, Texas. He is currently developing an English and Spanish version of his first book of poetry, *In Brazos River Country*. His artwork is found in private and commercial collections throughout the country, as well as traveling abroad through the US Department of State's program, Art In Embassies.

STILLBORN

Lee Elsesser

Just off the train from Colorado,
the cowboy asked, "Is it a boy or girl?"
"The child is dead," the doctor said,
"I am trying to save the mother."

The doctor laid the tiny body
on a table and covered it with a towel.
"Stillborn," was all he said.

The new mother screamed.
Her sister, sitting at the bedside,
sobbed, "Oh, no. Oh my God, no."
"I'll be outside a minute," the doctor said,
and turned to leave without looking back.

He did not see the mother's mother
lift the still form from the table,
rip away the towel and plunge the body
into the washpan of fresh hot water
she had just brought from the kitchen.

He did not hear the clatter
of his instruments on the table
as the woman dumped them from

a second pan, or hear that pan filled
from a cold pitcher of drinking water.

He was stepping outside when
she pulled the baby from the hot bath,
rubbed it briskly with the towel
and splashed it into the cold, then
out into the towel, and back into the hot....

He had just answered the cowboy's question,
and was lighting up a Chesterfield,
when through the door came the cry,
not of a grieving mother or sobbing aunt,
but of a wet and angry infant.

The cowboy, shocked to immobility,
by the news of his firstborn's death,

pulled his face from his hands,
slammed the doctor aside and burst
through the door and into the house.

His mother-in-law stood, babe in arms,
to welcome him. "It's a girl,"
my great-grandmother told my grandad,
"It is a girl."

Former TV newsman **Lee Elsesser** grew up on his parents' farm outside the small town of Rocky Ford in southeastern Colorado. Lee developed early interests in western history, writing, fly fishing and cooking. He worked for Channel 5, the NBC affiliate in Dallas-Fort Worth, from 1967 to 1984. As an adjunct professor at Southern Methodist University in Dallas, he taught radio-TV newswriting for a decade. Lee divides his time among cooking and teaching cooking, writing and fishing.

Age is just an accumulation of years. Without it you couldn't have acquired all of that stuff. You might not have moved up in your company. You probably wouldn't have had that big adventure. You might not have married the love of your life, had kids and grandkids. And you wouldn't be eligible for Medicare. Sounds like a pretty good deal to me.

—**Barbara Mott**
92-year-old author

Essays

First prize

THE KITE OF OUR GENIUS— SAIL ON

Jean Yeager

Age twelve is one of those tension-filled crossing points in life. It is a time when the tenderness of childhood is waning and we are beginning to test our growing bodies, to create our intellect. Our genius arrives in a "do-it-yourself kit." But, there are no specific instructions; we must struggle to form it. We wrestle with this unique "higher self" and fashion all kinds of challenges, inner and outer, large and small. Our gifts seem to emerge from our engagement in, or our fleeing from life.

When I was twelve my family lived in a particularly windy part of Colorado just east of the Rocky Mountains out on the prairies in a bedroom community named Broomfield just between Boulder and Denver. The wind blew so much out there that the metallic threshold on our front door vibrated whenever the wind velocity topped 40 miles an hour, which was frequently, at all hours of day or night.

My mother had been a young woman in the "Dirty 30s" in the Midwest and Texas. That was the era of drought and giant clouds of dust which would blow up, become storms and roll across the open prairies engulfing farms and lives. So, she knew the tragedy borne by ill winds of the Great Depression and World War II. In 1961, when I was twelve, my father was in the midst of a political "dust up" in his job which would eventually lead us to being blown off the Colorado prairies and tumbling toward a new life in San Antonio, Texas.

Age twelve is also the age of grandeur. Grand ideas, big challenges are just the thing for learning life lessons. In my case, life gave us wind, lots of wind; we foolhardy boys seeking a thrill made "bike boats." "Bike boats" were a way for us to test ourselves, our creativity and seek lofty adventure.

Two kids would ask our mothers for an old, worn-out bedsheet then get on our bikes, holding the sheet between us so it caught the wind like a sail and propel us. We would ride our bicycles holding the sheet with hands off the handlebars rocketing down dirt farm roads, whooping and hollering.

When we crashed, and we did crash, we got the tragedy we apparently wanted to experience. The world, life, gave us feedback on our "great and adventuresome ideas." We would limp home, trying not to cry, practicing swear words aimed at the wind, dragging along our busted bikes, sprains and bruises and composing great lies about our adventures and daring one another for our next even grander exploit.

My father may have saved me from further damage when he gave me one of the best, yet perhaps most modest gifts that a father could ever give a boy—a bundle of raw, balsa wood kite sticks.

"Look what I found at the Army surplus store!" he said with sparkling eyes as he physically radiated glee.

There must have been 100 pre-made sets of kite sticks without the cheap paper covering that was typically found in that era's 10-cent drugstore kites. A broken kite stick was less threatening than a broken limb. So, for the next several weeks, while our bruises healed, my friends and I (and my Dad) made kites, dozens of kites of all configurations.

We became kites.

Genius will work with whatever it has at hand in order to fashion you. At age twelve, through your imagination and inspiration, your genius will take whatever you give it to a higher level.

A stick becomes a wand and you become a Harry Potter. A basketball and a plastic box nailed to a telephone pole and you become LeBron James. A homeless little girl named Ella Fitzgerald transforms a neighborhood talent contest into the launch pad for a lifetime singing career. Slavery, neglect and horrific abuse spins George Washington Carver into the heights of scientific insight.

The greater the headwind challenge of youth, the higher the potential to rise. Twelve year-olds are the holy boys (*puer aerternus*) or the holy girls (*puella aerterna*); the genius we ride in our lives to great grandeur is the kite of our selves.

Kites are all about capturing the tension between two dynamic sets of polar opposites in two bent sticks. Each of the two kite sticks is like a different aspect of our genius. Both must be put under tension and bent into an arc and both are joined together. The vertical stick represents our upright self which stands between the spiritual and the earthly poles. The horizontal stick represents that which goes between our self as an individual and the world.

If we put too much pressure on any stick, it might crack. In kite making, you have to risk in order to have enough arc to generate lift. Adding tension in life is risky because genius is both positive and negative, there is always the danger of unbridled egoism, hubris, anger or violence; or fear, depression and brooding.

The sticks are bent to create a wing shape and high flyers are the ones who can create more than enough draft to create lift well in excess of the weight of their situation. It's a mix of wing span, angle of the wing and velocity of the wind.

Genius inspires all arts, transforms all effort into art, and all people into artists. The configuration or the form of the art is the wingspan. For a writer, a haiku, for example, is a short, intense form with high imaginative velocity. Meaning, inspired in the reader, gives lift (or not). The angle of the message rises above culture and makes use of the headwinds. Genius inspires all the arts.

Genius can be craft, all hand work, or earth focused and inspired as well—contractors, carpenters, mechanics, farmers, or gardeners. We all have connections with the spirit and with our communities.

Kites can spin out of control if the genius is too intense and one sided. A kite can spin in a strong wind and won't rise unless there is counterbalance. A kite, a genius, requires a counter balance—a tail.

Kite tails are bits of fabric, usually cast aside fabric, torn up and tied together and attached to the earthly end of the spirit / earth pole. Separate bits of life brought together. Each is like a memory perhaps of attempts, failures, regrets, embarrassments, tragedies. Bike boat crashes. Gravity. These are what give weight to our souls. Our shame adds heaviness. We are glad they have sunk down beneath our consciousness, but they are not gone, never gone. They balance out our enthusiasm. They are the fruits of our lives. Our seasoning. Our tempering. Our scars. The tail of the kite of our lives.

Some wise high flyers with special genius to see into the spiritual world have said that when we die, and we look behind ourselves as we ascend into the spiritual world, we see that our egoism, failures, misdeeds, sins and errors stream behind us like the tail on the kite of our genius. They are the tail of the kite of our genius.

The memorial services which I have attended for friends have a public portion in which we speak and honor the genius of the dear-departed friend. And at the same time, we sit in unspoken silent remembrance of their flight, including the choices which held them back.

The headwind of life continues to blow no matter how old we are. There is a chance to rise even higher than before. Are we able to rise with it? Do we still struggle? Do we risk failure? Bike boats of elder-age? Are we still in contact with the source of the good and holy of our genius?

Our final years are tension-filled crossing points in life. We wrestle to free ourselves from what we have created during our life in order to rise again. This is another "do it yourself kit."

Sail on.

Jean W. Yeager has been an award-winning writer since the 1970s. You may find his complete work history, client list and sample radio comedy ads at: http://www.the-three.com. In 2013, Duke University Libraries accepted Jean's collected works into a special collection of the Rubinstein Library. http://library.duke.edu/rubenstein/findingaids/yeagerjean/.

Jean has worked for spiritually based, progressively oriented nonprofits. His recent activities are on his Linkedin page: http://www.linkedin.com/in/jeanyeager2.

Jean's book *Th3 Simple Questions: Slice Open Everyday Life* has been published by WestBow Press. Find out more at: http://www.Th3SimpleQuestions.com.

Alternate First Prize

LET ME TELL YOU HOW MY FATHER DIED

Michael Coolen

Dad was killed by whales.

Hundreds of whales.

They began killing him in 1919, soon after he started working at a whale-blubber rendering plant on the Seattle waterfront. My father was only thirteen years old.

It was a job his alcoholic dory fisherman father got him supposedly to help out with finances at home. Most of the pay went to support his father's addiction.

Dad worked twelve hours a day loading dozens of one-hundred pound barrels of whale oil onto waiting trucks. He worked amid a stench of rendered blubber so potent that an arriving whaling ship could be smelled over the horizon long before it could be seen.

> [The whale's] *smoke is horrible to inhale ... it has an unspeakable, wild, odor about it ... It smells like the left wing of the day of judgment; it is an argument for the pit.*
> —*Moby Dick,* The Try-Works

Dock workers smoked cigarettes all day to keep from choking and gagging. Like his older co-workers, my young father began smoking pre-packaged unfiltered Camel cigarettes R.J. Reynolds introduced to America in 1913. Instead of having to roll a cigarette, all he had to do was pull one out of a pack and inhale that lethal combination of Turkish and Virginia tobacco. The Camels began destroying Dad's body while keeping him from vomiting.

"The smell was awful," Dad once told me. A man who normally kept his own counsel, he'd once described the death of his newborn baby in the 1930s as "awful," and the suffering of World War II as "awful." In his hospital bed, he described the pain from the pancreatic cancer caused by a lifetime of inhaling unfiltered Camels as "awful."

Dad became a two-plus-pack-a-day smoker for 62 years. During those decades, he smoked close to eight hundred thousand cigarettes. Laid end to end, that many cigarettes would stretch thirteen miles, about the height of 38 Empire State Buildings stacked vertically.

I could just as easily have begun this story by writing, "My father was killed by Camels."

Six decades after Dad left the docks, his journey from health to illness to death was a short one. Just six weeks.

I was living in Oregon when I got a call late one night in June from my mother.

"He came up to me last week," she said, "and he told me he felt sicker than a dog. We went to the doctor yesterday, and your dad went through some tests." She was quiet for a few moments. "Dr. Olson recommended exploratory surgery as soon as possible. And it doesn't look good."

Two days later my sister Theresa called me less than an hour after Dad had gone into surgery.

"We'd barely had our coffee," she said, "when my name was paged and Dr. Olson wanted to meet with us."

"Your father has pancreatic cancer," he said. "It has metastasized all over. There is nothing we can do, so we've just sewed him up again."

After I hung up, I sat on the deck of my cabin, looking out at the moonlight reflecting on the dark water of the Willamette River. I tried and failed to remember a single instance Dad was ever sick or had complained that he didn't feel well. I drove through the night to

Seattle, and by early morning I was sitting next to him in his room at Providence Hospital.

He was still a little groggy when Dr. Olson came into the room. He had been Dad's primary care physician for decades, and the two were good friends.

"I've never kept anything from you, Harvey," he said. "We found pancreatic cancer, and it has spread everywhere. There's nothing more we can do except make you comfortable. I'm truly sorry."

Dad didn't seem to understood the diagnosis. He just stared at the doctor and didn't say a word. But shortly after the doctor left, I saw a single tear flowing down his right cheek. I had never seen my father cry. Never.

Mom once said she'd seen him cry twice. The first time was after a car slammed down on his left hand while he was changing a flat tire. Dad was a violinist, and the damage to his pinky finger was so bad he lost the flexibility he needed to play as well as he had for years. He struggled with the sorrow of that loss the rest of his life.

The second time Dad cried occurred in the mid-1930s, when he had to tell Mom that their newborn daughter, Patty Jo, had just died from the influenza that was sweeping the hospital. She was two days old. Over a hundred other fathers and mothers cried over their dead babies during those terrible two weeks at Providence Hospital. And now, 40 years later, we were back in that same hospital knowing there would be months of tears ahead for our family.

After the doctor left, Dad stared at the ceiling for several silent minutes.

"What a revoltin' development this is," he finally said.

I smiled as he quoted the television show *The Life of Riley* starring William Bendix. It had been one of his favorites in the 1950s, and we had watched it as a family. Bendix played Chester Riley, a blue-collar worker with a gift for turning small problems into catastrophes.

At some point, Bendix would sum up what had happened by saying "What a revoltin' development this is." Dad always chuckled at that phrase.

When my brother Pat came to sit with Dad, I wandered down the hall to a room that had been set aside for the family. There were coffee and donuts and a collection of magazines and books to distract us from the antiseptic smell and death watch we were experiencing. I picked up a book of poetry. It opened immediately to *Do Not Go Gentle into That Good Night*, a villanelle by Dylan Thomas. Four kinds of men inhabit the poem's world—wise, good, wild, and grave—and each in turn is urged to resist death, to not go gentle into that good night. Life is not over just because you are old and ill.

> *Though wise men at their end know dark is right,*
> *Because their words had forked no lightning they*
> *Do not go gentle into that good night.*

Realizing that although death is inevitable, even the wise man fights on in the hope that he will have the time for his words to fork lightning, part the seas, raise the dead, say goodbye one more time. My father was a wise man who felt that the success of a life should not be measured through forked lightning, but in being a good husband and father and devout Catholic.

When I returned to his room that evening, we talked about some of his favorite violinists. He thought Jascha Heifetz was a genius, but he was particularly partial to Zino Francescatti. After he went to sleep, I read that poem to myself as if it was a kind of cosmic prayer with the power to heal him—or ease both his death and my sorrow.

The next morning, the hospital chaplain came by to give him Holy Communion.

"I am not worthy," Dad said, so quietly I almost missed hearing it.

"I will come back to take your confession later," replied the priest, using his right hand to bless Dad with the sign of the cross.

I sat in raging silence—furious that Catholic doctrine could make such a good man ever think he was unworthy; a doctrine that urges its members to pray and give thanks while devouring them from the inside. Much like the whales that started Dad on this voyage.

Here be it said in a whaling voyage the first fire in the try-works has to be fed for a time with wood. After that no wood is used...the crisp, shriveled blubber, now called scraps or fritters...feed the flames. Like a plethoric burning martyr...once ignited, the whale supplies his own fuel and burns by his own body.

—*Moby Dick,* The Try-Works.

Dad had the reputation of being a quiet man. I discovered the reason for his silence the previous fall, not knowing he would be dead in nine months. Trying to learn more about this quiet man, I had told the folks I wanted to tape-record an oral history of them after Thanksgiving dinner. The result was a three-hour tape of my Dad talking about his life. About fifteen minutes into my interview, I asked him about his reputation for being quiet.

"You know, everybody says I'm quiet, but with a wife, three daughters and three sons I haven't been able to get a word in edgewise for about thirty-five years! It was just easier not trying to talk. Anyhow, I was never any good at talking unless I thought about something before I opened my mouth."

In his hospital room nine months later, Dad was even quieter because there were so many agonizing blisters inside his mouth from the medication. I returned to the poem as I sat with him.

Wild men who caught and sang the sun in flight
And learn, too late, they grieved it on its way
Do not go gentle into that good night.

A wild man my father was not. Dad's idea of "wild" was to show us how he could partially eject his upper and lower dentures and make them dance and click around in his open mouth. When we were kids, it was hilarious, but it became a little sadder as we got older and understood why he had dentures to begin with. For most of his early life, he couldn't afford to go to a dentist; not to mention what the cigarettes had done to the teeth he no longer had.

60

Grave men, near death, who see with blinding sight
Blind eyes could blaze like meteors and be gay
Rage, rage against the dying of the light.

As Dad's condition worsened, the oncologist prescribed chemotherapy, in this case intravenous fluorouracil to fight the growth of cancer cells so that Dad might have a few more days...of awful. Known as 5FU, it is toxic poison whose side effects include nausea, vomiting, diarrhea, and sores in the mouth. In Dad's case, it probably eventually killed him. Ironically, 36 years later, I use a topical cream containing 5FU to seek out and destroy cancer cells on my face.

Three days after going on chemotherapy, Dad's breathing became more labored. Whenever I was alone in the room with him, I tried to breathe louder, hoping he could still hear me and breathe more easily. By this time, I knew the poem by heart, and I spoke it to him and whispered it to him and yelled it to myself, frantic to see him improve.

"Rage Dad, rage!" I said. "Don't go yet!" Children have so many questions they would like to ask their parents when it is too late for answers.

And you, my father, there on the sad height,
Curse, bless me now with your fierce tears, I pray.
Do not go gentle into that good night.
Rage, rage against the dying of the light.

Fierce tears flowed down my face when Dad died. My mother could barely walk because of the damage to her hip, but she hobbled over to his bed using her walker and threw herself on his body and howled like an animal caught in a trap. I don't remember who was in the room, although I remember one was a hospice nurse that my brother Pat eventually married (and who eventually was the hospice nurse for him when he died from prostate cancer 36 years later). I'm sure there were other siblings there, but I can't recall who. But I do remember that the anguish in the room was palpable.

Dad died on August 15th, the Feast of the Assumption of the

Blessed Virgin Mary. It was Dad's favorite feast. It commemorates the ascension of the mother of Jesus directly into heaven without being buried. There is no Biblical citation or proof of any kind that this ever happened, but Pope Pius XII formally declared it was true in his *Munificentissimus Deus* ("the most bountiful God") published on November 1st, 1950. Since Pope Pius IX had declared in 1870 that popes were infallible (in large part as a response to Darwin's publication of *Origin of Species*), the Assumption must have happened like XII said it did.

The funeral was a few days later at St. Patrick's Church, just a few blocks from the folks' house. Knowing I wouldn't be able to speak at it, I composed a piece for organ combining the tunes "Road to the Isles" and "Simple Gifts." Over a decade later, I revised it for my Mom's funeral, adding a fragment of "Little Boy Blue," the song she sang to all of her children at bedtime.

I have read "Do Not Go Gentle" often over the years. With the arrival of YouTube, I have also listened to its recitation by Dylan Thomas, Richard Burton, and many others. One performance by Rodney Dangerfield sticks in my mind. Toward the end of the film, *Back to School,* Dangerfield delivers a powerful recitation of the poem to prove he's a good student. When he finishes, his girlfriend asks him what the poem means.

"It means...," he responds, "I don't take shit from no one."

Words to live by. Or die by, especially if a life lived passionately becomes so unbearable that death is preferable.

I know I would not purchase a few more days of breath at the price of "awful." I would not go gentle into that good night. I would rip the scythe from the Grim Reaper's hands.

"I don't take shit from no one!" I would spit at him, just before turning off the light and leaping into the abyss.

Michael Coolen is a pianist, composer, actor, performance artist, and writer living in Oregon. He has been published in *Ethnomusicology, Western Folklore, Oregon Humanities, 50wordstories Online, The Gold Man Review, Best Travel Stories, The Fable Online, Kalnya Language Press, Twisted Vine, Clementine Poetry Journal, Creative Writing Institute, Rats Ass Review, Solarwyrm Press, Synesthesia Magazine, Broken Plate Poetry Magazine, WalkWriteUp,* and *StoryClub Magazine.*

Michael is also a published composer, whose works have been performed widely, including at Carnegie Hall, New England Conservatory of Music, Museum of Modern Art, and the Christie Gallery.

Second Prize

WEATHERING

Karen Mastracchio

The open front door frames a snapshot image: the gray-striped cat curled asleep on the mat near the porch railing. Plenty of cats curl up on a tattered porch mat and sleep deep and hard, waiting for owners to call them to dinner or into the safety of their home. The picture is not uncommon, but touching. For this cat, though, there is no home; there is no owner.

Little Mama is one of many feral and abandoned cats who grace our porch seeking food. Our apartment complex stands alone on a dead end street, small and peaceful at this wooded edge of civilization. At the north end of the complex, trees and vines advance and push the wooden fence barrier into disrepair. Winds and storms bring dead wood tumbling onto the walkway several times each year. One bad storm last year dropped a tree limb right against Miles' downstairs window, not a pane of glass shattered. We who live on the "backside" of Building 1700 are people not too concerned about tree limbs falling or raccoons rummaging. Miles, Andrea and Salem, Elizabeth and I have chosen this most remote part of the complex because each of us in our own way is a bit less socialized, old enough to be disenchanted with busyness and noise. We have weathered failed relationships or failed expectations. We are comfortable with solitude, a small wave of a neighbor's hand or brief "hey." We hold privacy to be sacrosanct, preferring the company of jays, raccoons, and homeless cats.

Homeless cats abound, yet there is a distinct difference between the abandoned, and now homeless cats, and the feral cats. The few cats periodically abandoned by transient apartment-dwellers will mainly wander within the complex searching out, not only food, but also some human interaction, a kind word or a rub behind the ears. Careless owners don't consider that these former pets will ceaselessly pace perimeters waiting for some door to open and welcome them in. They will sleep under cars hoping their owner will return. They will rely on handouts that may or may not come their way. They congregate around the gated dumpsters where, unspayed and unneutered, they yowl and procreate. Concerned apartment residents are reluctant to call animal control because it's never quite clear whether these cats have negligent or non-existent owners. While the question of ownership remains vague, the challenge to the care of roaming cats is ever present. Not only are food and shelter an issue, but the abandoned homeless have the feral cats to battle.

Alley Cat Allies explains that a feral cat is an unsocialized cat, born outside or never in contact with a human family. Feral cats can rarely be socialized and are most content living outdoors in colonies. It is estimated that in North America, there are tens of millions of feral cats; approximately four million are euthanized in animal shelters yearly as they are not adoptable. In the last decade, several organizations including Alley Cat Allies and ASPCA have implemented programs to trap, vaccinate, neuter/spay, and return feral cats to colonies where caregivers can oversee the stabilized population. Still, the problem is monumental. In our area, like most urban/suburban areas, too few organizations can cope with the innumerable homeless, especially the ferals.

Most cats around the back end of this apartment complex are feral, born in the wild from a cat sometime abandoned who lately or generations ago retreated to the woods. They're mini tigers, panthers, and cougars that live by their instincts and have little trust of humans. They are magnificent in their wildness—and hungry, neglected, plagued by parasites, mange, and all the other diseases that owners must inoculate and groom against. Rarely do they live beyond four years. From season to season, two or three will become temporary regular visitors to the back porches of Building 1700, vying with raccoons and possums for handouts. Although Miles, Andrea, Elizabeth, and I feed these cats, we cannot pet them, hold them in our laps, or nuzzle in their fur. At best, they may stretch out on the concrete or the porch mat for a brief viewing.

The gray-striped "Little Mama" cat has been with us since late fall. She came reluctantly, fearfully, starving, and seldom in the beginning. We all took note when the yowls rose up, and some of the snarly, big gray males hissed and followed her relentlessly. We knew to expect kittens that we might never see. By mid-March, we watched Mama grow hungrier, rounder, and slower. One day she actually stepped a few feet into our apartment while our door was ajar, perhaps contemplating a better, more domestic life for her babies. Neither she nor we were quite prepared for that possibility.

Her kittens were born in early April during a week of loud thunderstorms with heavy rains. One day she didn't come for food, then another. Because she had become such a regular visitor, Elizabeth and I watched for her and worried. The third day she returned, lean and very hungry. We knew a litter of kittens was carefully tucked away somewhere nearby.

I silently asked, "How many, Little Mama? Are you doing okay?"

She had no time for questions. Four, five giant greedy gulps and she was gone. Like all new mommies, she had to balance her needs with the needs of her newborns. So for the first few weeks, it was always eat and run. No time to lounge; no time to visit. There was no daddy, aunt, or grandma to mind these babies. They were hers and hers alone in a woodlot feral jungle. She took her responsibility seriously.

Elizabeth and I waited patiently to get a peek at these new little felines. From previous experience, we knew feral mothers would bring kittens to their feed stations when they were old enough. Hoping Little Mama would bring them out to feed, we encouraged her, offering

Star-Kist and other canned delicacies. Mama appreciated the spoiling, but the kittens did not appear.

Near Mother's Day, we heard loud, unfamiliar "meows." Andrea had caught one of the babies, four according to her. Her thoughts paralleled ours: capture the kittens early enough and Volunteers for Animal Protection can domesticate and place them. Rarely can feral kittens beyond eight or ten weeks be socialized enough for adoption. But that little tiger wanted loose, and even red-haired Andrea, our bravest wildlife aficionado, could not hold on. Out of her grasp and back under the fence raced the kitten. Little Mama was relieved and much more cautious about bringing her children to Building 1700. Two weeks passed before we saw them again, this time all five, much bigger already, frolicking downstairs in the shadow of the fence-line while their mama came upstairs to eat.

As May ended, Little Mama relaxed more, lounging about the porch, separating herself without guilt or concern. However, she always had an eye or ear to the fence, her invisible line of connection clear and open. The young ones apparently had instructions to remain beyond the fence, out of human reach. When any of us put food out downstairs, like tasters who protected royalty in olden times, she sampled the food before calling the kittens to dinner. After sharing the family meal, the kittens tumbled with each other, chased blades of grass, and investigated civilization this side of the fence. Although concern about this feral population hovered in half-hatched plans, the delight at seeing such a healthy, wild brood prompted smiles and covert peekings even from the gruff and skeptical former veteran, Miles.

Then the long week of the June flood intervened. Rain always meant that we would see less of our forest friends. Following their own protective instincts, the animals vanished into whatever cover nature offers. Days went by watching footage as Tropical Storm Allison pelted the Houston area. Roads were flooded; life was locked in or washed out. Abandoned cars littered roadways which were impassable, unnavigable for days. Residents in houses only a few blocks away became victims, and four miles down the road, Mercer Arboretum and the public library were inundated. Hospitals were compromised; the downtown tunnel system flooded. The fragility of life was omnipresent whether looking out the door or at a television screen. Ultimately, about 30,000 were left homeless in and around Houston as neighborhoods staggered under rising water. No one had much time to worry about the "wildlife," one of the least concerns when these natural disasters occur.

On the Monday after the storm, Mama came back for a meal, but no sight of the kittens-turned-adolescents. We waited and watched. By Thursday, it was clear that Little Mama was looking for her kids. Could the high water have scattered them as it had so many Houston residents? Perhaps those hormone-driven males who again stalked Mama scared off the young ones like some whip-toting stepdaddy. Maybe something subtler occurs in those wild breeds and instinctively sends the adolescents on their way when Mama mates again.

Days later, curled up on this mat, Little Mama sleeps the sleep of one exhausted. When I put a dish of food down and she eats a few bites, verifying its safety, and opens her whiskered mouth in a plaintive meow that communicates maternal distress, my heart aches. Her meow voices what every human mother feels about absent children. Her meow reflects the sound of the near frantic mom whose five-year-old has strayed too far out of sight at the mall. Her meow recollects the reticence as mommy leads that firstborn into kindergarten on the first day of school and walks away, afraid to look back. Little Mama represents every mother letting go and hanging on to those precious, precious children that have given her life purpose and richness. Her meow echoes the loss and trauma of the past two weeks. I stand two feet away remembering my own children, remembering the families torn apart by the storm and suffering separations. In sisterhood, wishing I could embrace her as I would a neighbor or a friend, I look into her green-flecked eyes. I look over the railing. I whisper, "It's okay, Little Mama, you've done well. They'll be fine."

Karen Mastracchio is a retired high school creative writing and English teacher. Karen is currently programs chair for Poets Northwest, and member of Poetry Society of Texas, part of National Federation of State Poetry Societies, Inc. Karen divides her writing time between poetry and memoir, with a few essays thrown in, sometimes merging the forms.

We are not masters of our fate. If we could know
the future, we would not make mistakes.
We would know that if this event had happened, that better
plan wouldn't have happened. Call it chance or coincidence,
but we can marvel at how fate redirected our life
and we were saved from some questionable choices.

—**Barbara Mott**
92-year-old author

Third Prize

MY "GO DAU HA" PUPPY
I promised I would never forget her

Larry Sanders

We had just arrived in the middle of the village of Go Dau Ha after returning from a day long trip to Tay Ninh for supplies. It was only about 30 miles away but traveling in Vietnam always took twice as long as it should. The roads were bad from all kinds of traffic, hidden mines, and occasional sniper fire along the way. Go Dau Ha was located near the Cambodian border on the banks of the Song Vam Co Dong River. It was where Highways #1 and #22 crossed, creating terrible traffic jams of military convoys, motorcycles, mopeds, and bicycles. Everything had slowed down to a creeping standstill. The deep potholes full of water from the monsoon rains the night before were now covered with soot and dust and god knows what else. This corner was where we regularly turned left down a narrow dirt road toward our small compound in the "boonies." I lived with four other military advisers sharing this compound with soldiers from the Army of the Republic of Vietnam (ARVN) and their families. We all lived together in bunkers, hootches and huts, in a barricaded area about half the size of a football field, surrounded by a moat, concertina wire, and claymore mines.

There were three of us in the jeep that afternoon. Sgt. Smith and Lt. Conner were in front with me in the back. I had my M-16 rifle across my lap and medical bag at my feet. As we sat there waiting for the dozens of local motorcycles and bicycles to pass, I spotted a little puppy in a ditch. It was drinking dirty black water while trying its best to stay out of everybody's way on this busy road.

"Wait a minute and don't move," I shouted at Smitty, who was driving. "What's wrong?" he said. "Nothing, I see something I need to do quickly!" I jumped out in a flash still holding my weapon in one hand while reaching down into the ditch and grabbing the pup with my other hand before it had time to run. I leaped back into the jeep just as fast as I had jumped out, but now I had a skinny runt of a puppy under my arm. When I looked down, I noticed it was a little female. We had left early that morning, joining the safety of a military convoy, before making several stops to collect provisions near the village of Tay Ninh. On the return trip, all alone and no longer with the security of the convoy, we rushed to go back to the safety of our compound before the sun went down. None of us wanted to be on these roads after dark when the area was no longer secure. There were more chances for mines, sniper fire, and the enemy to move around after dark. So we were in a hurry.

We finally turned left through a break in the dusty traffic and headed northeast and back to the place we called home. The small barricaded ARVN compound was about eight miles down a secluded dirt road, surrounded by rice paddies and dense jungles. It was just outside the tiny village of Suoi Cao, so small it was not on most maps.

I had what I wanted and hung onto her in my lap in the back of the jeep as we hurried those last few miles. She was a dirty, little floppy-eared mutt with short light brown hair, almost the color of a jar of mustard, only mixed with dark dried mud. I could tell she was no more than six weeks old, maybe even younger. Lost, frightened, and hungry, she would not have made it another day without getting run over or starving to death. Looking into her little face and those big black eyes, I immediately named her Deros.

DEROS was military abbreviation for Date of Expected Return from Overseas. It was the most important day all soldiers waited for in Vietnam!

Every GI spoke or bragged of their individual "special date of departure" as a badge of courage and hope. It was as important as the town you grew up in or the life you left behind.

"Where are you from?" "What did you do back there in the real world?"

"When is your DEROS date?" "How long do you have before you DEROS out of Nam?"

From the moment we arrived, "it" was the most important and, hopefully, lucky date we all looked forward to! It meant we were still alive, and to prove it, we had a date.

It also meant that you had put in your year of duty and had survived!

It meant you would be leaving this "god-forsaken country and screwed-up war" far behind you!

It meant you would be returning home alive all in one piece!

It meant you were still one of the lucky ones!

Deros was also one of the lucky ones! She was a lucky pup. I made sure of that. She was now going to her new home.

I grew up with pets around me my whole life: small turtles, ducks, hamsters, cats, puppies and, of course, dogs. I left my favorite dog, a mixed Cocker mutt named Curly, back home when I was drafted. I got him when I was in the third grade from a neighbor whose dog had a litter of too many pups. I named him for his long black curly hair.

Curly and I grew up together, going everywhere on foot or him following my bicycle. We had great adventures around the world. We explored nearby neighborhoods which took the place of strange far-away lands I had seen on television or at the drive-in movies. Curly loved following me into isolated wooded areas near my house that turned magically into the far off African jungles, where Tarzan swung from the trees. Small creeks full of tadpoles changed automatically into wild Amazonian raging rivers full of man-eating piranhas that we both tried crossing without getting wet. If we were lucky enough to get some snow during winter time, we both found ourselves high in the Himalayan Mountains, searching for tracks of the Abominable Snowman. Much of the time, Curly and I just ran errands together for my mother. We knew all the short cuts to the nearby small Mom & Pop grocery store where we usually picked up a loaf of bread and sliced bologna for school lunches. We made most of our trips to an even closer nearby liquor store to buy cigarettes for my mother, who seemed always to be out. Curly even followed me on my hunt for empty soda bottles for extra money. I collected the bottles after school, stashing them in the backyard until I could cash them in at the end of the week for candy, comic books and Saturday matinees at the neighborhood picture show. Those bottles added up fast and were as good as money.

Yes, Curly and I were a team. We went everywhere together. If you saw Curly, you knew I was somewhere nearby and, if you saw me, you knew Curly was not far away. Some family members even joked that we were like Larry and Curly of the Three Stooges, always searching for our third member, Moe.

During the school week, I locked Curly in the small backyard behind our rent house just inside an unpainted picket fence. My father and I built it just for him out of scrap wood. On cold mornings my mother, who had old fashioned ideas, and was always declaring, "dogs belong outside and not in the house," would bend her rules. She allowed Curly inside as my sister and I set off on our long walk to school until we were totally out of sight. My mother would then let Curly outside where he patiently waited until I returned home at the end of the school day, greeting me with his wagging tail. We would then pick up where we last left off, playing or running or going on new adventures or just running more errands for my mother. Curly and I were best friends who just liked being together.

By the time I entered high school, Curly was growing older and slowing down. Age had mixed his black hair with gray, and he preferred to sit at my side, seldom leaving the safety of his yard.

Soon after graduating from high school, I was drafted into the

Army. I spent almost six months in two different states training to be, first, a soldier, and then, a combat medic, without seeing my faithful dog, Curly. Returning home on military leave, briefly, before leaving for Vietnam, I bent down on my knees and hugged my favorite black curly dog with all my might, and whispered into his ear. "I'll be going away soon and want you to be a good boy while I'm gone. I love you very much and will be home soon. I will never forget you," I promised him.

That was the last time I ever saw Curly.

A year later on my return home, I discovered Curly had passed away while I was in Vietnam. My mother didn't want to inform me of his death while I was in Vietnam. "I wanted to tell you in person because Curly was so special to you and you were so special to him," she said. "I could tell Curly was sad when you left. He had slowed down from age and always stayed close to the house, waiting for you to return soon. One day Curly just got up and walked away while everyone was gone, and we never saw him again. We searched everywhere for him but never found him," she said. "That's what old dogs do when their time is up and they know they're dying. They just get up and walk away to die."

So, without knowing about Curly, my little pup Deros was as important to me in Vietnam as I was to her and as important as Curly had been to me all those years growing up long ago.

⁂

I introduced my new puppy, Deros, to her new home in our small barricaded ARVN compound and she was never alone again. She made friends with all of the South Vietnamese soldiers, their families and especially the kids. My four other MACV team members accepted her into our family as well. Deros loved all the attention and the scrap food. She was becoming not just my pet, but everyone's pet. She loved playing and running with all the children. No matter what she did or who she visited within the small compound, she always returned to me in the evenings to sleep at the foot of my cot or guard the door of our hooch. On the days we went out on distant patrols, Deros stayed behind within the small compound. She usually waited near the guard tower on piles of sandbags, protecting her new home and looking out over the distant rice paddies, waiting for our safe return. Deros was also now safe.

About five months after rescuing my puppy, Deros, I received orders for my military DEROS. The date I had anxiously waited for was here. Soon, I would be returning home and finally leaving Vietnam. My emotions were mixed. I was excited and happy but also very sad to leave my new pup. Deros was by then fat, sassy, and very happy. She was no longer a puppy but growing into the dog she was meant to be. Knowing how much she loved her new extended large family made my leaving a little easier for both of us.

The morning I left, after packing my duffel bag of memories, I went around saying my goodbyes to everyone I had lived with on the compound. First, to the South Vietnamese soldiers and their families, especially all the children. I shook hands, saluted, and hugged each one. "Please take good care of Deros, after I'm gone," I asked the four members of my advisory team that had been like a family to me. "Make sure she is always happy and fed regularly because she now belongs to all of you. Deros is part of your family now."

The long journey back would take many days and nights before I arrived home. I traveled from the small village of Suoi Cao by way of Go Dau Ha, where I had first found Deros, onto Tay Ninh then Saigon, before boarding a plane and flying over the Pacific, arriving in California and then on to Arkansas.

Just before climbing into the jeep I bent down on my knees to hug and squeeze Deros as hard as I could. She knew something was up as she nuzzled into me while looking at me with her sad black eyes. I whispered into her floppy mustard colored little ear that I loved her very much and wished her a continued long and good life with her new large family. "I will never forget you, my little Go Dau Ha puppy," I promised her.

That was the last time I ever saw Deros.

Larry Sanders' memories of actual events and the interesting people from his early life, as well as his time in Vietnam, are stories that he had never been able to tell until now. Larry was born in Little Rock, Arkansas in 1947 and served in the U.S. Army during the Vietnam War (1967-1969). He holds a bachelor's degree in fine arts, spent 20 years as an art director and sixteen years as owner of a Mexican folk art store. He is recently retired.

What do you think when you see a middle-aged guy driving down the street in a sports car with a beautiful babe? Gee, is that one of the rewards of getting older? Can't wait.

—Barbara Mott
92-year-old author

Honorable Mention

CHISELED IN MEMORY

Murli Melwani

Some days, like birthdays and anniversaries, are chiseled in memory.

September 17, 2008 is one such day for me. That was the day I became an American.

September 17 is also commemorated as Citizen's Day, a day on which America recognizes those who have become U.S. citizens. At the naturalization ceremony, I allowed myself the excusable vanity of believing that the coincidence was a personal honor.

My trivia-loving mind also signaled that the U.S. Constitution was signed on Sept. 17, 1787. Was that august document being handed down to me as a personal gift, a precious one? Was I being told to be a humble custodian in a long line of impressive guardians stretching over history and time?

When all 350 of us, from almost every part of the world, were asked to stand and take the oath of allegiance, the experience took the form of emotion. I felt as a child does when he tells his mother, "Of course, I'll do all this for you—and more."

The keynote speaker, Lynden Melmed, chief counsel of the U.S. Citizenship and Immigration Services, had brought his parents, naturalized citizens of long standing, to sit among us. He lauded their vision in moving to this country when he was a child. He held them up as models of the opportunities this country offered.

With the Pledge of Allegiance, the emotion became an intellectual experience, the watershed of a consciously arrived-at decision: the desire to live in a place where one is allowed to give full play to one's gifts, talents, skills and abilities freely, while respecting similar rights of others; where one is not treated as a foreigner in a part of one's own country because one comes from another county or state; where punctuality, civic responsibility, honesty, political accountability are upheld; where the rule of law deals fairly but firmly with terrorists who see violence, not negotiation, as a solution to problems.

The president of the United States, George W. Bush, came on the screen and welcomed us. "Our country has never been united by blood or birth or soil," he said. "We are bound by principles that move us beyond our backgrounds, lift us above our interests and teach us what it means to be citizens."

By the time "America the Beautiful" started to play, I felt the red carpet had been laid out especially for me. I imagined there were many in the hall who thought exactly as I did. Had I turned around to look, I knew I would have seen tears barely held back.

An old story flashed into my mind. In the eighth century, a community from Iran, the followers of the prophet Zoroaster, fled persecution by fanatical Muslim invaders. They arrived on the coast of India. Before these pilgrims set foot on the shore, their leader sent a glass of milk to the Indian ruler. The ruler returned the glass after adding more milk, topping the glass right up to the brim. His action sent the signal that the country couldn't accommodate any more people. The leader of the pilgrims, a sagacious man, added a spoonful of sugar, without spilling a drop, and sent the glass back to the Indian ruler. The ruler understood the significance of the gesture: sugar blends with milk and sweetens it without changing its composition or qualities. The ruler allowed them to settle in India. This community came to be known as Parsis. This minority has flourished in India, in manufacturing and professions like teachers, writers and doctors.

I fully understand the sincerity of the emotion behind the hand that added the spoonful of sugar to the glass of milk. Because I, too, will add sugar to the ingredients melting in the American pot.

Murli Melwani taught English Literature at Sankardev College, Shillong, India, before making a career change to head an export office in Taiwan. His business required him to travel to various parts of the world and his travels gave him ideas for stories. His short stories have been published in magazines in various countries, including the U.S.A., Hong Kong and India. Retirement coincided with his son and daughter in the U.S. making him a grandfather. He lives in Plano, Texas.

A FEW MINUTES WITH...

Don Johnson

I think a lot about romance novels.

Yeah, you read it right. Romance novels.

It's hard NOT to think of them nowadays. You can't swing a cat without hitting a display rack full of the things just about any place you go. They're on sale everywhere. But due to recent events, I've decided that romance novels are the key to a new direction in my career. I'm going to start writing and selling them.

My closest associates, of course, have always known that I have a natural bent in the romantic direction. They don't call me "Mister Chock Full O' Hot Monkey Love" for nothing. But my career direction took a radical turn toward the romance genre just a couple of days prior to this writing.

A colleague and I were attending an afternoon conference at one of the swankier convention hotels in Dallas, when we walked through an atrium area filled with people dressed to the nines. It felt like we had walked through a time warp. The crowd was predominately women in their thirties and older (some MUCH older) who looked like they were getting ready to attend a Washington reception being put on by the AALWROTBIP ("American Association of Lobbyists Who Really Ought to Be in Prison"). I had to look at my watch to assure myself that it was only two o'clock in the afternoon. My watch didn't give me any assurance that I was still in Dallas, though. I had to go ask a bookie.

Almost all of these women looked like Joan Collins on her way to

J.R. Ewing's wake. Millions upon millions of sequins had given their lives to outfit this group in floor-length outfits like you'd see at an inaugural ball, and I haven't seen so much eye shadow and mascara since my Senior Prom.

To borrow a phrase from a well-known syndicated humor columnist who gets paid a lot more for his columns than I do for mine: I am not making this up.

As you may have guessed by now, we had stumbled into the annual national convention of the Romance Writers of America, meeting in Dallas to exchange ideas for plot lines and to share patterns for applying Retin-A in industrial strength. We spoke briefly with one of the convention participants, an elegantly groomed and coiffed lady of indeterminate years who looked like Jackie Collins (heck, for all I know, it was Jackie Collins). She had eyebrows drawn higher than flying buttresses on a medieval cathedral, and she was wearing an outfit that was so covered with shimmering glass beads that she appeared to be in the final stages of being beamed aboard the starship Enterprise.

This lady told us the convention offered sessions on everything from standard plots (there are apparently only five or six basic ones, with varying subthemes), to software for researching historical periods and events, to the art of conducting interviews and plugs on early-morning television, to marketing tips for movie rights and mini-series, and finally to investment advice and negotiating residuals. It's quite an industry, and I started feeling its pull. I figured, hey, how hard could it be?

The clincher for me was the lady's jewelry. I can recall seeing only one other person wearing more gold and precious stones. She was the mummy of an Aztec princess on display at the British Museum.

That's when I determined that romance novels are a financial gold mine, just waiting to be claimed. The way I figured it, most of that gold and those precious stones just had to be real. I mean, even the American Military-Industrial Complex couldn't produce that much fake jewelry. So I decided then and there to enter the field of romance novel writing, at least on a pilot basis.

But I need your help.

To date, my sole experience with romance novels has been looking at their covers while standing in the Express Checkout line at the supermarket. From this, I've gleaned that the most consistent feature of romance novels is a cover featuring a young guy with shoulder-length hair who doesn't wear shirts. This young man is always carrying or embracing a young woman who also has long hair and who is wearing some type of nightdress, regardless of the time of day or night depicted in the cover art. These nightdresses are often torn, in almost (but not quite) strategic places. As a final note, these young women are invariably "statuesque" (if you get my meaning), yet have no apparent need for foundation garments.

One of my female colleagues has pointed out (and I'll take her word for it) that horses figure prominently in these novels, since the long-haired shirtless young men are never far from a fast means of escape. (These guys are evidently big on relationships, but not so big on commitment.) The horse motif allows the use of terms such as "fiery," "steaming," "pounding," and the like. I can see some common themes here: horses, like the guys on the book covers, usually have long hair in the form of tails and manes, and I've never seen a horse wearing a shirt.

Anyway, I'm confident in my ability to write these novels, since I can correctly spell "wet," "warm," "torrid," "sweaty," and "passion."

What I need is material for plots. This is where you come in.

This inquiry is directed primarily at those of you of the female persuasion, but if any of you guys out there have any thoughts along these lines, I promise that I will protect your privacy and anonymity until such time as it would inure materially to my benefit to spill the beans on you.

My question is: If you had the opportunity to pair up with a young, muscular guy with a flat stomach and long hair who never wears shirts, or with a statuesque young woman with long hair wearing a torn nightdress, where would you prefer to go and what would you prefer to do? I don't mean the "obvious," of course; I mean an activity that would provide a setting and a historical backdrop for the "obvious," like being a double agent for the Sultan of Turkey or captain of a tramp freighter smuggling auto parts into Togo. Or something. You get the idea.

If I use any of your plot ideas, I won't share any royalties with you, but I will include you in the book dedication. I might also consider using you as a model for the book cover. Maybe. It will depend largely on your apparent need for foundation garments.

So keep your eyes open in the checkout line of your supermarket. Until I become a rich and famous novelist (and it's only a matter of time), just keep this thought in mind:

Behind every successful man, there is an amazed mother-in-law.

Don Johnson is 67 years old and a Dallas native, now living in McKinney. He has retired after practicing law for over 35 years.

BARGAINS

Karen Mastracchio

When asked by my children what I wanted for my 58th birthday, I requested money toward the purchase of a bicycle. They snickered—one more whim of Mom's, but I had decided it was time to buy a bike and commit to riding again. I knew I needed more activity for my health. If there were anything akin to a sport in my early life, it would have been bicycling. I'm not talking about thirty-mile competitive rides from the center of Chicago to outlying suburbs; I'm talking about jumping on the bike and riding ten miles just to discover other neighborhoods, for the sheer joy of reaching Western Avenue from Kedzie which felt, at eleven, comparable to a Lewis and Clark expedition. It was time to recapture that sense of exploration and physical vigor, so I went bicycle shopping.

I had recently reconnoitered the Wal-Mart bicycle inventory. Having browsed sale flyers as well, I believed about a hundred dollars would do it. With limited income, I generally have a ceiling for purchases based on the item's worth in my day-to-day routine. Even though gift money would cover most of the cost, the same philosophy of value applied. I selected Academy as my first stop because that store offered a fine array of makes and models. I looked at all the models on display regardless of price.

Traditional brands like Huffy and Schwinn offered several options, but I eyed a Pacific. It was a rather streamlined silver-gray bicycle with acceptable seat and tires, selling for $89. I called over the saleswoman and asked about purchasing that model. Just my luck…there were none in stock. Furthermore, Pacific was replacing that particular model with an updated version. Telephone calls to all surrounding Academy stores disclosed that none of that current model was available. How discouraging! It was comparable to finding the perfect dress and then discovering it is unavailable in your size. I looked once more at the lineup on display, taking mental notes of cost and features. I would have to reassess and continue the search.

I began to focus more clearly on what I really wanted in a bike. Mainly, I listed what I did not like about the bicycles I had seen: too many gears, too narrow a seat, oddly angled handbrakes, poor assembly, wrong tire tread. I simply wanted a vehicle that would provide twenty recreational minutes around the subdivision, at most a five-mile push to Mercer Arboretum. This was about comfort and maneuverability, yet the root of my selectivity went much deeper. This search wasn't just about a bike. It was about a memory. I wanted back the bicycle I received for my eleventh birthday.

In 1959, many children were given bikes by the age of seven or eight. Most bicycles were simple contraptions—no gears or handbrakes then, usually twenty-inch wheels and coaster brakes. I, too, had received such a bike when I was nine. Somehow, though, I longed for a machine that would take me farther, wind rushing through my hair as I glided down inclines on Chicago's far south side. I needed a bigger, faster bike. I made my desire known as my eleventh birthday approached.

Our family had little money, so the cost of every gift was limited. I don't really know why Dad paid any attention to this request of mine; perhaps he had similar dreams of freedom and adventure. Even used, it would not be cheap. Dad undertook the quest to find a used English racing bicycle. I was hopeful when he found one in the newspaper ads.

The drive to see the bike was my first inkling of how this gift would open new worlds to me. I knew Chicago's south side well because we traveled regularly to my grandparents' homes. I could trace the streets from 103rd to about 50th running south of downtown. However, the north side of Chicago was beyond the boundaries of my experience. I was still a child in many ways, so the drive seemed endless, especially since my mother and sister remained at home. Dad and I had long since passed not only the limits of conversation, but the flashing orange Jay's Potato Chips' factory sign and the big green head of the Turtle Wax turtle. There were no recognizable landmarks to help me judge distance. I unexpectedly realized how vast and truly unknown Chicago was to me, a new view of what I had believed a familiar city.

It was late afternoon when Dad and I arrived at an apartment on Chicago's near north side. A rather reserved young woman in thick glasses invited us into her apartment. No one had much to say. Dad and I were anxious to see the bicycle. While Dad asked a few relevant questions about the bicycle's age and the young woman's reason for selling, I waited to see and touch the bike. It was a metallic blue Raleigh English racer with three speeds, handbrakes, and a headlight powered by a tiny bottle-shaped generator. There was even a rear leather saddlebag, slightly worn. I was sold, more than sold—I was enchanted. Its mechanical condition—gears, brakes, and tires—passed Dad's scrutiny. I have no recollection of the price, but Dad was also sold. The bike was mine, and we began the long trek home.

I don't recall many words exchanged as we drove home in that dusky twilight that soon turned dark. Dad wasn't much of a talker, but I am certain he spoke to me of my responsibility: lock the bike, ride safely, don't let other kids borrow the bike. Ten years later he would share similar advice about my first automobile. Dad had earned a living as a truck driver at various times in his life, so he loved vehicles and expected owners to care well for those marvelous machines that conveyed us beyond the confines of our front yard. Perhaps he invested that English racer with his vision for me of moving out into the world with independence and confidence. I doubt that any gift could have been more meaningful for me at age eleven.

I logged in hundreds of miles before I "outgrew" that English racer. It took me north to 95th Street and as far south as 111th Street. It took me to far-away friends' homes, distances that earned lectures and punishments from Mom. When we moved to the suburbs two years later, I could ride west to the forest with its winding trails and tree-scented air or east three or four miles beyond the drive-in theater and the public elementary school to the nearest shopping center. I rode alone as my sister rarely found joy in such excursions. I learned directions and traffic patterns, early rules of the road. Most of all, though, I learned to enjoy the wind, the sun, neighborhood sights and sounds, the physical pleasure of exertion, the beginnings of independent exploration, and solitude. Whatever that bicycle had cost, it was a priceless bargain.

Suddenly, the search for my bicycle went a whole different direction. I hit the computer and typed in the magic word: Raleigh. Indeed, Raleigh still made bicycles. However, I would have to go to a bicycle shop, and the cost would be greater than $100. Fate favored me—the bicycle shop was only five miles from my home. I even recognized the name because I had passed it so often. A tingle of anticipation crept under my skin.

I entered Bike Lane in the same way that I walked expectantly into that distant apartment forty-seven years ago. A well-dressed, gray-haired woman, a bit older than I, greeted me. I told her I was looking for something like the simple three-speed model of my youth. I also needed a wide, comfortable seat. She immediately pointed out the Raleigh Venture. I would have to be measured and the correct frame determined. The cost would be $232. Bike Lane would service the bike for as long as I owned it.

I angsted over the justification of such indulgence: two hundred and thirty-two dollars for a bicycle that with some commitment I would likely ride only a few times a week around the subdivision. Still, this was the best bicycle I had seen. It was simple; it was well constructed; it was backed by service. Like my father decades ago, I was deciding not on the cost of a gift, but on the worth of an experience. I was sold.

It was not metallic blue; it had no light generator; it had no rear saddlebag. It was an opalescent white with straight handlebars and simple handbrakes. It had manageable gears and a nice wide seat. It carried the same heraldic emblem that I recalled from those many years ago, a sort of Raleigh coat of arms. It would take me to the nearest shopping center and on to the library and the arboretum. I would feel the wind flapping my shirt sleeves and reacquaint myself with the rasping screech of squeezed handbrakes. Early on a sunny Saturday morning, I would, for just a little while, feel a bit like that eleven-year-old coasting along Rambling Brook believing that the world was an open road still offering so much.

***

Karen Mastracchio is a retired high school creative writing and English teacher. She is currently programs chair for Poets Northwest, and a member of Poetry Society of Texas, part of the National Federation of State Poetry Societies, Inc. Karen divides her writing time between poetry and memoir, with a few essays thrown in, sometimes merging the forms.

Deputy Barney and Sheriff Andy Battle Terrorists

Jean Yeager

"I am your Deputy Barney self. I'm your built-in system for thought, emotions and behavior. I'm on guard and on patrol 24/7. With my quick reactions you are hyper-vigilant! Nothing gets by me, I mean, you. You are armed and ready! I have a dash-cam in my squad car; I mean you, have a... <grin> you know what I mean. I, you have a Taser on my, your hip. I am quick thinking and fearless!"

"And your Deputy Barney self quickly jumps to conclusions 100% of the time, don't you, Barney?"

"Yeah." <grin> "I'm a machine for jumping to conclusions, aren't I Sheriff Andy?"

"And statistically, 80% of the time, your intuitive conclusions are wrong, aren't they Barn? Your conclusions lead to contusions." *

"Oh, Sheriff Andy! You know I don't like statistics!"

"The Sheriff Andy self is not impulsive. Sheriff Andy thinking slows you down. The Deputy Barney self wants you to believe quick action is the way to go, right Barn?"

"Well," <grin> "I don't have time for reflection! I'm a doer, I see and I do." (Pointing a finger), "Click-bang!"

"Click bang, huh?! So, tell 'em, why did you un-holster your TAS-ER in the squad car?"

"It's my job to be ready for bad guys. I was practicing my quick-draw."

"TASERed your crotch, huh?"

"It was an accident."

"Thousands of people in our country get shot accidentally each year? That's why I made you unload the bullets from your service revolver."

"But, Andy! I can't be courageous with an unloaded gun! I gotta be a winner."

"You haven't re-loaded, have you!?"

"No." <moping> "I got my bullets right here!" (Pats shirt pocket.) But, Sheriff Andy, that TASER shot was not my fault."

"The Barney brain will never admit it made a mistake."

"Why should I? Live and learn is my motto, Andy."

"Learn? Don't think the Barney brain is strong on forethought, are you Barn. Tell 'em about eating chili with beans in the squad car."

"I hate dash-cams with audio. Not fair. Ought to be banned from squad cars. We deputies are professional!"

⁂

"Sheriff Andy, after what happened in France, Orlando and Dallas, Mayberry's finest needs body armor."

"Oh, really? The Barney self wants body armor?"

"Yeah with "POLICE" stenciled on the back. And a black sweater! 'N black paratroop pants, and a really nice black belt with lots of holsters 'n pockets to put stuff in! And a black truncheon in case it gets hand-to-hand! Oh, and storm trooper boots! 'N a black balaclava, so only my eyes are visible. And, of course, a black euro-style helmet stenciled with 2-inch high letters reading: "MAYBERRY SHERIFF DEPARTMENT—M.S.D.—SWAT TEAM—B. FIFE, DEPUTY"."

"You really thought that out well, didn't you Barney."

"Yeah." <grin

"2-inch high letters? SWAT? As in fly-swatter? That's the kind of SWAT we need around here."

"Mark my words, Andy, there are rumors of foreigners. Strangers coming to Mayberry! It's all over the social media!"

"Barney, this is fear talking. I'm gonna have to ask you to turn off your wi-fi tablet in the squad car. You've been sitting in the squad car watching the internet and FaceBooking with Gomer."

"But Andy....!"

"Apparently it makes you afraid of our new neighbors. So, as Sheriff, I want you to turn off the social media! I want you to talk to people. Just do your job. We don't have to be paranoid here."

"Oh, come on, Sheriff Andy! I heard a new Falafel Restaurant may come into town. I gotta investigate!"

"Yes, go investigate. Meet the new owners. It's Aisha, the wife of Ali, the new math teacher at the high school. Don't over-react, Barney."

"Can I get anti-terrorist gear?"

"The Deputy Barney brain likes to snoop around at night, dressed in black. Right Barney?"

"I gotta be suspicious 24/7. It's my job!"

"Aunt Bea would be scared out of her wits to see you sneaking around at night dressed all in black! Why do you want to scare Aunt Bea or anybody?"

"But, you can't prove we're safe!"

"Barney, settle down! If you scare the Gomer, Goober, or the Floyd the Barber brains, one of them might accidentally shoot you! You don't want that and neither do I."

"Aw An-dy!"

"We don't need terrorists in our souls. Do we Barney?"

*Sheriff Andy and Deputy Barney" are inspired by Pulitzer Prize Winning Psychologist Daniel Kahneman's book, *Thinking, Fast and Slow* which describes the two systems within us.

Jean W. Yeager has been an award-winning writer since the 1970s. You may find his complete work history, client list and sample radio comedy ads at: http://www.the-three.com. In 2013, Duke University Libraries accepted Jean's collected works into a special collection of the Rubinstein Library. http://library.duke.edu/rubenstein/findingaids/yeagerjean/.

Jean has worked for spiritually based, progressively oriented non-profits. His recent activities are on his LinkedIn page: http://www.linkedin.com/in/jeanyeager2.

Jean's book *Th3 Simple Questions: Slice Open Everyday Life* has been published by WestBow Press. Find out more at: http://www.Th3SimpleQuestions.com.

Fear: A Writer's Worst Four-Letter Word

Robert Robeson

You gain strength, courage and confidence by every experience
in which you really stop to look fear in the face...
You must do the thing you think you cannot do.
—Anna Eleanor Roosevelt,
You Learn by Living (1960)

Many struggling scribes find themselves enveloped in the classic combat pilot's mind-set and one which I experienced innumerable times during nineteen years in U.S. Army aviation. This is a state of consciousness wracked by uncertainty and fear, torn between the compulsion to fly every insecure mission under enemy fire or entertaining some excuse in your mind for not taking off.

This latter act most often creates a strong desire, in short order, to identify what degree of commitment you do possess. The alternative is to deny your manifest destiny. Do that and it will be difficult to look in a mirror again and you'll never know what it is to be a fulfilled pilot and writer.

Trust me, I've known the all-encompassing fear that Captain Yossarian—a U.S. Air Force bombardier—displayed in Joseph Heller's classic novel *Catch-22*. Yossarian made a habit of checking himself into the hospital during WWII with fake maladies in an attempt to avoid bombing runs. In my case, I flew 987 medical evacuation combat missions for over 2,500 patients from both sides of the action as a helicopter pilot in South Vietnam (1969-1970). I had seven aircraft shot up by enemy fire and was shot down twice in one year. So the statement, "You're really not crazy if you continually believe someone is trying to kill you in war"—in conjunction with significant aviation experiences—has a special connotation for me. Perhaps this meaning was similar in Yossarian's world, too.

Through my 27+ years of military service on three continents and 48 years of intertwined freelance writing, including time spent as a newspaper managing editor and columnist, I've discovered what separates doers from the dreamers in life. Doers have the courage and determination to do whatever it takes to reach a goal or complete a mission. Dreamers are in the initial planning phase.

I remember my first dreams at the tender age of six, as the second son of a small-town Protestant minister in 1948 in Truesdale, Iowa. This was a sleepy hamlet encompassing about 125 souls in the northwestern corner of the state that even maps barely acknowledged. At that time, I wanted to be three things when I grew up: a pilot, army officer, and writer. A yellow, single-engine airplane that often flew low over our parsonage—so low I could see the pilot wave back when I waved—may have been a contributing factor to this order.

Then I recalled an event that happened the previous year. My parents had left me with one of our church farm families so they could attend a ministerial convention in another state. While they were gone I was taken to the top of the newest and tallest building in Storm Lake, seven miles away, to see the view. The man I was staying with picked me up and set me atop a four-foot wall that encircled the roof's viewing area. With my stubby legs dangling over the edge of this dramatic precipice, numerous times he pretended to push me off with fake shoves as he grasped me around the waist.

It's a crisis moment that has stayed with me for 69 years. I began crying and fought to get down. He would never be aware of how his prank terrified me. I had intense fear of heights from that moment in time. This "secret" was never revealed to anyone, not even my parents, until I mentioned it to my wife when I was over 50 years of age.

As I was growing up, there were still those dreams of becoming an adventurous aviator, defying gravity, leaping tall buildings with a single bound, and exploring cloud canyons like Superman. Yet, even then, I believed that one couldn't be a pilot and be afraid of heights. So flying remained a mere fantasy.

One Sunday in the late '50s, during my high school days in La Grande, Oregon, my father preached a sermon about Moses. Dad mentioned that when God informed Moses he'd been chosen to lead the Israelites out of Egypt, he begged God numerous times to send someone else. Moses had a speech difficulty and didn't feel he could speak well enough to confront the Egyptian Pharaoh. But God told Moses, "...I will be with thy mouth, and teach thee what thou shalt say" (Exodus 4:12, KJV).

This story made me aware that some people are overwhelmed by their fears while others are challenged by them. It was then that something deep within impressed me that somewhere in aviation there was a job for me to accomplish, regardless of my fear of heights.

In May 1960, I enlisted in my hometown Oregon Army National Guard infantry unit as a medic. After basic training, 2 1/2 years of college in Oregon and California, and being promoted to sergeant, I applied for and completed Army Infantry Officer Candidate School at Ft. Benning, Georgia and was commissioned a second lieutenant.

With the Vietnam conflict heating up in 1967—and a desire to do my part—I applied for U.S. Army helicopter flight school as a medical evacuation pilot. This emotional decision was akin to diving into the middle of a frigid, shark-infested ocean without a life jacket. Just about any height above sea level was still a scary proposition for me. But, at the time of application, I vowed that this weakness and fear—even if the cause wasn't my fault—wasn't going to rule or dictate my future.

My one-hour orientation flight in a flimsy-looking, open-door,

OH-23D observation helicopter at Ft. Wolters, Texas in Mineral Wells in 1968, was an unnerving experience. It mirrored undergoing brain surgery by an inebriated doctor with a rusty chainsaw and no anesthetic. Yet I believed people who win great battles of the mind, body, or spirit must first have a dream or vision of what's required for victory. By motivating oneself to move in that direction, a person can provide a realistic way of helping to make that dream come true.

On March 25, 1969, I graduated from Hunter Army Airfield in Savannah, Georgia as an army aviator with an instrument rating. For ten trying months my fear of heights was like chronic arthritis; it can encompass great pain and anxiety every day, yet the only logical remedy is to press on anyway.

Having already volunteered for combat duty, I was in the right place, at the right time, the right age, and had the right skills. In less than three months, I married my fiancée and then found myself 10,000 miles from home in my first aviation assignment as a captain and operations officer for the 236th Medical Detachment (Helicopter Ambulance) in Da Nang, South Vietnam.

The more hours I flew the less altitude mattered to me. After my first months of combat, additional confidence was gained in mastering the UH-1H ("Huey") helicopter under hazardous conditions. This life and death flying also helped calm my fear of heights. There was less thought about myself and more about preserving lives. I learned, as Moses had, that from the wells of my deepest fear can spring water capable of refreshing oneself and those in desperate need. It soon became apparent to me that love for others can conquer fear and that courage is measured by one's deeds and not by the amount of fear one has.

In 1967, at the age of 25, my first freelance article had been submitted to Bee Nelson, the editor at *Straight*. It was accepted the first time out, and she later reproduced it in pamphlet form, as were the succeeding two articles written for other religious publications. This early success provided incentive to continue writing about other personal experiences and those things that were important to me.

Sports throughout my high school, college, and military years had taught me the value of teamwork, taking risks, tenacity, persistence, discipline, hard work, and a never-say-die philosophy of life. These attributes were carried over into my writing life.

In combat I learned that overcoming fear leads to worthwhile achievement and that you have to take risks if you're going to do anything of value in life. A wealth of Vietnam experiences has been part of over 880 articles, short stories, and poems I've published in 320 different magazines and newspapers in 130 countries, in addition to being featured in 47 anthologies. These stories have reached a readership of millions. They include the *Reader's Digest, Positive Living, Frontier Airline Magazine, Vietnam Combat, Soldier of Fortune, Official Karate,* and *Newsday,* among others.

In less than 24 hours, during August 21-22, 1969, my flight crew had two helicopters shot up. Our medic, Specialist Five John Seebeth, III, was wounded in the larynx by AK-47 small arms fire. After we limped back from this final mission to the battalion aid station at Landing Zone (LZ) Baldy, with two of our three radios shot out, I held John's legs while a tracheotomy was performed without anesthetic by Dr. George Waters. His wound had swollen so fast that it had cut off his airway. He survived. After twelve subsequent operations an army surgeon's skill gave him back a voice. But it wasn't the one we'd been familiar with.

Even with a 100% Veteran's Administration disability, John later ran marathons and was elected student body president of his college in Ohio where he subsequently graduated. He bicycled to the Arctic Circle, around Europe, and from Seattle, Washington through Baja California, in addition to kayaking on the open ocean, among other things. He was my inspiration and motivation for publishing his personal story and the story of that mission in six publications, including the English and Russian editions of *Soldier of Fortune.* I've met and flown with a host of other unique and heroic individuals like him and have done my best to share their stories with others, too.

On September 13, 1969, I was shot down for the first time after we evacuated four American infantrymen from a landing zone encircled by enemy forces. Although our jet engine, both cyclic controls, and various oil lines had been shot up or shot away, our bird refused to die easy. The instant I greased our skids onto the bumpy ground, a few minutes later, in an emergency running landing at LZ Ross, our Lycoming engine's 1,100 horses died en masse. The story of this mission has been published five times and won a $1,000 international Amy Writing Award in 2006.

On Christmas morning of 1969, I was shot down for the second time, taking nineteen hits in my aircraft during a supposed cease-fire"period negotiated in Paris, France. Half an hour later, we climbed into a replacement helicopter and flew back to the same lz again under intense enemy fire. On our third approach from different directions, we successfully evacuated nine wounded, allied, South Vietnamese soldiers who'd been attacked in their isolated outpost on Barrier Island, about twenty miles south of Da Nang alongside the South China Sea. This story has been published eight times in national magazines and was republished in a Nebraska newspaper for Christmas of 2008 and the Storm Lake, Iowa *Pilot Tribune* newspaper, the same city where it all started with fake shoves on that building's roof 62 years before, for Memorial Day of 2009.

While evacuating seven wounded American infantrymen from an enemy mine field in early January 1970, I unknowingly set our left skid on two mines, one of which was estimated to be a 250-pound, anti-tank mine...neither of which detonated. An infantry first lieutenant and his driver drove 40 miles over an often-mined road in an open jeep to relate this information to me about a week later, or I never would have known. He was the platoon leader that day who, when they finally discovered the mines, used C-4 plastic explosive to blow them in place. When they blew, "the top of the hill came off," this lieutenant informed me. This story has been published six times. There were similar situations too numerous to mention here, that have been written about and published about my Vietnam experiences.

Understanding fear is a natural part of life. It's an experience not to be denied but met with confidence and hope. Each time a traumatic experience occurred in combat, I forced myself to return to the cockpit and resume flying. I didn't want the fear of death or heights to cause me to lose my nerve. In each case, I found the strength to fulfill this commitment to soldiers and civilians on both sides of the action who had severe wounds, their own fears, and were hurting far more than myself.

There was an adage among chopper jockeys in 'Nam I often recall. "Helicopter pilots don't fly. They just beat the air into submission." I've reminded myself of this concept various times and have applied this philosophy to my writing career. Many people don't feel comfortable attempting what seems to be impossible. That's why there's so much room at the top in many professions and areas of life.

If you want success, it's essential to face your fears, doubts, and dare to be different. You can't be afraid to go out on a limb because that's where the fruit is. Think of what I'd have missed in life if my fear of heights had been allowed to overwhelm me.

As an English major at the University of Maryland in College Park, where I received my undergraduate degree at the grand old age of 33, I read volumes of Shakespeare's work and attended many performances of his plays. If you've experienced a presentation of *Hamlet,* you know that the stage is littered with dead bodies in the final scene. Yet some of the actors are still alive because, regardless of the catastrophes that may occur in our world to us or others, life still manages to go on. Even the tragic ending, in other words, sent some characters—and all of the audience—out into the challenges of "yet a little while," of one more or several more opportunities. The catharsis at the end of tragedy and difficult times in a stage setting may leave the protagonist dead, but it leaves the rest of us thankful to be alive and somehow challenged to continue living as best we can. Real life is like that, too.

We are all human Titanics chugging through iceberg-filled waters while attempting to survive in this often dangerous and confusing world. Life isn't supposed to be easy. If it were we wouldn't have to die to get out of it. Still it's important to understand that what we feel, fear, and experience has been felt, feared, and experienced before. Our challenges and anxieties aren't unique. They've all been faced and overcome by other people throughout history. When fears are allowed to overshadow dreams, life is experienced through smudged and clouded spectacles. Excuses for feeling these fears may appear legitimate... but they're still excuses. Control can be taken out of fear by doing, over and over, what is feared.

What has been discovered in my flying and writing careers is that these professions are hard work. If I'd wanted an easy life I could have taken up quantum physics, brain surgery, or tried to open a McDonald's on the moon.

In combat my helicopters and crews gave patients hope. Your writing and what you do with your life can accomplish the same. It's essential, though, to put in those sweat hours and years while collecting your share of rejection slips like the rest of us. I don't ever give up on a piece of writing even if the editor burns my manuscript and sends me the ashes in my SASE. That's only happened a couple of times, I believe. Remember that chopper pilot adage about..."beating the air into submission?" This same principle and philosophy works for ground-pounding writers, too.

When momentary depression and disappointment surround current writing projects and persistent rejections, I recall one of my articles about a Vietnamese baby girl born on my aircraft in May of 1970. It's been published 23 times since 1979... but has also been rejected over 40 times. It causes me to reflect on other combat experiences of long ago. I remember one urgent medevac excursion into a monsoon in the mountains at night when the turbulence and downpour were so violent it was impossible to read any dials or gauges on my instrument panel and the force of the wind would shoot us up 1,000 feet and then thrust us down 1,000 feet. Even on "high," our wipers couldn't clear the windshield and I had to open my side cockpit window in an effort to stay clear of the jungle. Pulling in power and lowering power didn't seem to have any effect, so all we could do was ride it out until we were clear of the mountains.

I also remember rats the size of small cats waking me at night as they bounded across my cot, mosquitoes the size of 747s...and feeling blessed. Blessed because my "grunt" comrades, who always do the hardest work under the worst conditions in war, were attempting to sleep in a treacherous jungle in the rain and mud. They were eye-to-eye with "Charlie" the enemy, playing "hide-and-seek" with poisonous snakes, blood-sucking leaches, enemy ambushes, and booby-traps, while humping 70 to 100-pound combat loads in the muck, rice paddies, and mountains.

Then there were those times when I evacuated patients with bubonic plague—a disease that killed millions during the Middle Ages—malaria, cholera, rabies, leprosy, gas gangrene, and constantly facing enemy fire in an unarmed aircraft. I can't forget those pools of blood covering our cargo deck on a daily basis, miscellaneous body parts tossed aboard with the dead and wounded, mutilated and burned patients, and the ominous awareness that our next flight could be the one that would claim my life. This heightened sense of reality and dedication to our mission are always with me. So I know, even when things aren't going well, that I'm capable of overcoming any roadblocks. I can do it because I've been tested and survived so many times before.

Through years of struggle I've learned that all of us are surrounded by both challenges and opportunities. If I had only helped save one life in those 987 combat missions, and hundreds of other medical evacuation missions in Europe from 1970-1974, it still would have been worth the effort. And if all of my articles and short stories do nothing more than make one person think or be inspired, they were still worth writing. Wars are not won with pep rallies and lapel buttons. And you don't become a published writer without making sacrifices of time and energy. It also helps to have a marathoner's endurance.

Perhaps more than anything else, brilliant military leaders and noteworthy writers wield with dash and flare that most supreme of weapons...imagination. They put aside their fears, take risks, spring the unsuspected, and dare to dare. For ten years, from 1193-1184 B.C., the Achaean Greeks laid siege to Troy. In all of that time they were unable to enter or conquer the city. Then Ulysses, one of the Greek heroes, had a brilliant idea: "Let's build a giant wooden horse." One can only imagine what the initial reaction must have been from his peers. "A giant wooden horse? Right. Get real!" The rest, as they say, is history.

To be truthful, my anxiety about heights, from that traumatic afternoon in Storm Lake, Iowa nearly seven decades ago, hasn't completely disappeared. Yet this original dread no longer controls me. The fear that frightened me most was the same one that proved exhilarating when I fought my way through it. What may seem to be the worst possible thing that can happen to a person can oftentimes turn out to be the best. Perhaps acrophobia has been more of a gift to me than anything else.

On June 2, 1995, Air Force Captain Scott O'Grady was shot out of the sky in his F-16C jet fighter in Bosnia by a Serbian ground-to-air missile. He escaped and evaded for six days before being rescued by a U.S. Marine helicopter crew. I was watching his later TV interview at home in Lincoln, Nebraska when he admitted, "I didn't want to punch-out because I'm afraid of heights." This admission made me smile. It was obvious I hadn't been the only aviator in the world who had to deal with this fear.

My lifelong journey on this spinning ball of clay has been one in which I've learned to make a variety of fears my companions; my friends. They have stretched my understanding of life. I've become more sympathetic to others and lost my impatience regarding those who have their own distinct anxieties to deal with, their own "little bag of rocks" to pack around. It's not helpful to become so entangled in fears of failure or calamity that I wind up immobilizing myself when confronted by reality.

My recommendation is to face your individual fears of not being published, of feeling unworthy, or of being rejected—whatever they may be as a person or as a writer—and be turf-tough. Use the talents you've been given, on loan from God, to impart information and bring enjoyment to others. Your experiences in life can be like exquisite jewels or fine paintings. They can inspire, bring joy, and provide hope and insight to fellow travelers. Encourage your readers to be risk-takers, too. Challenge them to find their own special literary niches in life.

At one point in "The Flamingo Kid" movie I recall the father tells his son, "There are two things you have to find in life: what you are good at and what you love. And if God is smiling at you, it'll be the same thing." That's what flying and writing have been for me. On a combat mission or in an article and short story, you never know whose life you will step into or who will step into yours. This makes life interesting and worthwhile. As President Franklin Delano Roosevelt was so eloquent in noting on March 4, 1933 in his first inaugural address, "The only thing we have to fear is fear itself."

The bottom line is that publication is achieved by trying, and trying, and trying some more. Memorable writing does not come from just the head. It comes from the gut and heart. If what you write is important to you, there's a chance it will be interesting and of value to others as well. If it's good enough, there will always be a market for it somewhere. It's like trying to hit the ground when your Lycoming jet turbine engine is shot out at 1,500 feet. You can't miss. And I should know.

In the final analysis, none of us may have been born or blessed with the talent of a Twain, Dostoevsky, or Steinbeck. But if you have drive, discipline, and display professionalism, you can write and be published over and over and over again. So press on with fulfilling your writing ambitions and dreams. Be doers, face and fight your fears, never give up, and success will be yours. I guarantee it.

❦

Robert B. Robeson has been published 880 times in 320 publications in 130 countries, in addition to 47 anthologies. He's a life member of the National Writers Association, VFW, Dustoff Association, and Distinguished Flying Cross Society. He commanded medical evacuation detachments in combat and in Europe. He's also been decorated eight times for valor by two governments. After retiring from the U.S. Army as a lieutenant colonel with 27+ years of military service on three continents, he served as a newspaper managing editor and columnist. He lives in Lincoln, Nebraska with his wife of 47 years.

Dogs are smart. They know when you are happy and love them, and they know when you are mad. They know when they are about to get a bath and they try to hide. They know words like "sit" and "stay", but why is it they still insist on getting on the sofa and leaving all that hair?

—Barbara Mott
92-year-old author

GROWING UP
IN LAREDO, 1933-1950

Edward Wright

A unique childhood.

Scanning some old pictures recently I came across photos of my experience as a soapbox racer in Laredo, my home town. Soon I found myself reminiscing about growing up in such a unique place in such an interesting time in history.

Ninety-five percent of the population spoke Spanish at home. Most of the younger generation spoke English, but Spanish or Tex-Mex was a common language. Society was segregated by the language spoken at home, regardless of ancestry. I would guess that is still common in Laredo.

Only a few of the streets downtown were paved until after World War II, although a steam-driven road grader regularly worked the gravel on Convent Avenue and a few of the more traveled roads. Streetcars rumbled on a few downtown streets.

Fruits and vegetables were purchased once a week from a horse-drawn wagon. The driver would park on the side of the road and call out "OOOOOOAAAAA," bringing maids and housewives pouring out of the houses to bargain for what they needed.

Meat came from Raymond's Butcher Shop and the corner grocer's two blocks away. A block of ice was delivered to our icebox three times a week. Bread and tortillas were available at a panaderia or the corner grocer. There were two movie theaters which showed both English and Spanish films depending on the day of the week. Besides radio, telephone and the *Laredo Times*, the local newspaper, there wasn't much outside influence on life in Laredo.

Laundry was done by hand. Once a week, Mom laid out three tubs outside on a bench. One held a washboard for scrubbing, another for rinse and a third for bluing. It was absolutely forbidden to walk under the clothesline which held wet and cooling sheets.

In 1933, most children were born at home. I was born in the front bedroom of my grandmother Ida Wright's home on Convent Avenue, eight blocks from the International Bridge. My grandmother acted as the midwife, although Dr. Powell was called and showed up at the last minute. Grannie had plenty of experience. She bore eleven children from 1888 to 1911; raising them alone from 1912 on after Grandfather Wright died.

They say that it takes a village to raise a child. That is true but, in my case, family has to be listed as the biggest influence. With ten aunts and uncles on one side and six on the other there was no lack of examples, encouragement, and education on how things were—or ought to be. By the time I came along, the Wrights were an eclectic group, living all over the country, but mostly in Laredo. They were loyal and supportive of their mother and of each other, I suppose because they all had to pitch in after my grandfather died.

They all influenced me at various stages when I was growing up. Wilbur contributed a love of music. Edna, George, and Clarence demonstrated entrepreneurship. Emma and Fred, a gentle disposition. Leo and Joe influenced my career choice, and Clara taught me conflict management. They showed me by example how a life should be led.

Of course, Edward, my father, was my guide and my goad. He was responsible for my priorities and my values, my ambitions and expectations. A devout Catholic, he was tolerant and accepting of everyone's circumstances or choices in life. My mother was more able to define people and their motives and call a spade a spade. I was the eldest child, so my parents both expected success in school, sports and career, but I never felt pressured. My father backed up my endeavors with his presence and support on the sidelines. He had hoboed in the 1920s, worked as a roughneck in the oil fields, as a carpenter for the H.B. Zachry Company, but I can only remember his career with the Government Services Administration starting in the boiler room of the post office until, at his death, superintendent of all federal buildings in Laredo.

Dad was a sports enthusiast and encouraged me to get involved. He was a baseball and football player, and was the first in his family to graduate high school. His older siblings had to go to work when their father died.

We lived across the street from my grandmother, who had a good ear. Frequently, when she heard crying, Mom got a phone call. No doubt, my siblings and I took advantage of that, but I have no memories of any conflict between the two women. Mom had nothing but respect for her mother-in-law.

My sister, Mary Paul, was four years younger; twins Pat and Mike, six years younger; so for several years I was an only child, and the separation in ages was enough that we each did our own thing growing up. I was in college when Mary Paul entered high school. We became closer as adults, and are certainly so as seniors.

Grannie's house was on one of two adjacent lots. The rest of the block was occupied by the clan of the Bonnie Leyendecker family who had matched the Wrights child for child over the years, and the kids were lifelong friends. Grannie's extra lot held a citrus orchard, garden, and barn. The Wrights first came to Laredo about 1888 when my Grandfather James took a contract to build railroads in Mexico. The family lived in a railroad car on the construction train and many of the children were born in Mexico. Deeds show that the family owned the Convent Avenue house by 1896. When the children reached school age they lived in Laredo with relatives and attended the convent school taught by Ursuline nuns.

Across the street from Grannie, our house had two bedrooms, one bath, and a wraparound front porch. The folks purchased the lot next door where my father built a garage. All the Wright men had been especially good carpenters for generations before that, and are to this day. Dad was more of a jack-of-all-trades. He could fix his car, wire a house and do plumbing. Unfortunately, he didn't pass the plumbing and automotive skills on to me or my brothers. He built us a terrific swing set, and designed and built slide sets which he sold over the years.

Our next door neighbors were the Claflins. The wife, Pauline, was part of the Leyendecker clan. Most of their children were older, but Dorothy and Marvin were close to our age. Dorothy was something of a baby sitter for us as she was three years older than me, and she kept us abreast of how things really were. When she was eight she was detailed to take me, five or six, and my sister, Mary Paul, three, to the movies on Saturdays. We walked the mile or so downtown to the theater every week.

People of Mexican descent occupied the rest of the neighborhood, and I had friends among them. Separation was more by language spoken at home than by ethnic background, although I felt prejudice from the earliest years. Once I was old enough to walk or ride my bike the two miles to school I found I had to bypass certain neighborhoods or expect to dodge rocks and verbal abuse. I learned what it meant to be a gringo.

My mother, Blanche Brown Wright, taught school until she was 71 years old, only taking time off when she had a child. When the twins were born, she took a full semester. She hired a lady named Eva to be my baby sitter while she was at school. I do not recall Eva's last name but one of my earliest memories is walking three blocks with her to get pan dulce at the Panaderia her brother owned. There is no doubt I was spoiled.

Grannie had a maid named Santos Aguilar. She had come from Mexico with the family as a teenager in 1911, and worked for my Grandmother until 1939. When my brothers Pat and Mike were born, she came to work for my mother. A second mother to us all,

Santos retired in 1955 after my father built a house for her near Holy Redeemer Church. She spoke no English, so we learned our Spanish from her. Unfortunately, she was not the most educated Spanish speaker, which I discovered when I worked in Mexico years later and used the words she taught.

When I was five, I was enrolled in pre-primer at St. Joseph's Academy, a new school taught by the Marist Brothers. These brothers were of various nationalities, many of whom had been evicted from Spain during their civil war. A teaching order of monks, they were all well-educated and dedicated teachers. I attended that school through high school and owe much of my philosophy of life to those men. I did not have to work too hard to keep up in school as many of my schoolmates were from Mexico and had a language barrier. Even so, the education I got was broad-based and effective as I cruised through my freshman year of college after graduation. I received the benefit of a small boy's school, and was able to participate in four sports, debate team, drama, choir, the school newspaper and annual. The only experience I missed was that of interacting with girls, something my wife points out frequently.

Another memory of that time I'm sure I share with many people my age is of two particular radio broadcasts, one in 1939 when I was six. My father listened late into the night about the German invasion of Poland. The second was when I was eight, telling of the attack on Pearl Harbor. I remember standing outside our house listening to news broadcasts through the open window and asking my father if we might be invaded. On into 1942 there was much speculation as to what the effect would be on our lives. As it turned out we were all affected for the rest of the century, and no one who was alive then will forget the anxiety of that time.

I recall vividly the scrap iron drives, paper drives (for which they let us out of school), war bond drives, rationing of gasoline, food shortages and unavailability of many commodities (chewing gum and sugar notably for children). Early in 1942 we worried about being bombed. Each city was divided into sections with block air raid wardens. My Uncle George, who was warden for our block, appointed me as his assistant. The one night they declared a blackout, we wore helmets and went around checking that curtains were closed.

Sugar was rationed in the US, but not in Mexico. As a ten or eleven-year-old I remember walking across the international bridge to the market in Nuevo Laredo to get five pounds of unrefined sugar so Mom could bake Christmas cookies. Not something someone that age would try today.

The younger men began to be called up or enlisted. Dad tried to enlist, but at 42 was told he was too old. He did enlist in the Home Guard, which I suppose was a last line of defense in case we were invaded by the Germans and Japanese. My Uncle Wilbur enlisted in the Air Corps as did my cousin, Phillip. I remember not being able to say goodbye to Wilbur as he was departing for overseas. I couldn't deal with the emotion. George, who had three children, volunteered for the navy a little later in the war. There never has been a total national effort like it. Every family was affected.

Probably the most important change in Laredo's landscape was the construction of the Army Air Base. Rushed to completion in 1942, it brought thousands of young men to learn how to fly. There was no infrastructure to support the soldiers and their families. Housing was non-existent, so residents rented rooms, apartments, whatever was available. My parents enclosed our front and side porch to fabricate an apartment which shared our one bathroom. Most everyone in town did something similar. The young sergeant and his wife who stayed there for the duration of the war became our fast friends.

The war even entered into our play time. For instance, fall leaves piled up at the edge of our lot were topped by a cardboard box decorated and labeled "Hitler's house." Then we burned it to ashes with a grim face.

My mother's brothers, Bernard, Paul and Les, either volunteered or were called up. Bernard and Paul suffered greatly, and we all held our breath as their stories unfolded.

When my twin brothers were born in 1939, my father purchased a Jersey cow and calf and began milking her every day. He tried to get me to do the job when I was a little older, but I never did a good job so he finally gave up on me. I still had to take the cow over to the empty lot in the next block, stake her out so she could graze in the morning, then retrieve her after school. Every Sunday afternoon for four years we piled into the 1939 Chevrolet and drove up the mines' road with machetes and pointed old broom handles. At the ranch of one of Dad's friends we would cut down prickly pear, toss it into the trunk and bring it back to the house. Dad rigged a gas pipe to an old stove burner, burnt off the spines, chopped the nopales (cactus leaf) up, and used it to supplement the alfalfa we fed the cow. The milk tasted a little strange, but we got used to it.

We had a fan in the master bedroom, but never had air conditioning until I moved away for college. Once I was old enough, and as soon as weather permitted in the spring, I slept on a cot under the umbrella of a large tangerine tree. (A breeze from the ocean 150 miles away comes to Laredo shortly after the sun goes down.) We covered up at night. Swamp cooler-type air conditioners became popular about 1950 after I'd gone off to A&M.

In that era "Spare the rod, spoil the child" was the theme. I suppose it had always been the way to train a child. In our family a misbehaving child was punished by having to wait till our father came home. At that point, we were sent to the salt cedar tree in our back yard. It had branches which made particularly good switches, which we were required to pick to be used on our bare legs. We were sent back if the switch was not up to standards. A serious negotiation ensued as to how many strokes the crime merited. The most agonizing part was the waiting till Dad came home. We turned out okay.

When I was about six, I spent a week at my Aunt Norma and Uncle Floyd's ranch near Bruni. By then I was an avid rider and (I thought) roper. I admired a small white toy Shetland pony in a pen and was told, "You can have it, if you can ride it. It's never been ridden." I remember they placed the pony in their circular breaking pen, put a saddle on it, and I got on. When they released her, the pony didn't buck;

111

she bolted straight to the fence, put on the brakes and rolled over with me. The saddle horn caught me in the stomach and knocked the wind out of me. I shed a few tears, but finally got back on. By the end of the week, I got to keep the pony, bridle, blanket and saddle.

We kept Honey in Laredo for four years before I outgrew her, and Floyd came back to get her. I added the pony to the cow in my daily stake-out in the empty lot. That was one clever horse. She could use her front hoof to scrape the bit out of her mouth, would scrape her rider against a gate as she passed through, and she would bite if she didn't want to be saddled. She didn't kick often, but you learned not to get behind her. You had to know her bad habits to be able to ride her.

During those years my friends and I had many adventures riding all over the town—two on the pony and others on bikes. One summer my friend, Artie Mullen, and I hitched Honey to a wagon and toured the barrios, peddling Mexican pottery and jars which my Aunt Edna bought at U.S. Customs auctions. My Spanish improved and we learned to negotiate. I think we either broke too many or sold several below her cost because she fired us. Those jars were still in her backyard years later.

My sister reminded me recently that Artie and I used a Tarzan yell to call each other from the house.

Uncle Floyd owned the rodeo arena and horse race track with assorted stables in the small town of Bruni, twenty miles from their ranch. I was fascinated to ride with him and listen to all the activities that went on there. Horse racing involved two quarter horses racing from a gate and running with a low rail between them for up to 550 yards. Betting was between individuals and there was much macho posturing and conversation, including a few fights. The rodeos were educational to a city boy. They were real cowboys matching home-grown skills. Years later, I played high school football in that arena. There was not a lot of grass.

One memory that still stands out is a fight between two Santa Gertrudis bulls. Floyd was one of the first to own that new breed (to me) of giant animals. I'd never seen anything like that fight, and I don't think Floyd had either.

In the 1920s they had discovered oil on the property and well pumps were powered by centrally located diesel engines driving a rotary turntable, which moved rods connected to pump jacks circling the area. Those diesels never stopped their chug-chug noise. Even though they were quite a way off, you had to tune the sound out. Of course, they are all electric powered now.

In the summer of 1941 at the age of eight, I got my first job. My Aunt Edna invited me to become a clerk in her small newsstand, across the street from Jarvis Plaza at the center of the town. I learned to work the cash register, make change, and inventory newspapers and magazines. Because of its location, the store was the center for any local news or gossip, and Edna was called the "Mayor of Jarvis."

Our yard with two lots became a center for kids in the neighborhood. We all looked forward to Saturday night. Dad was the best storyteller I ever knew. Each tale began with ten or more kids from age five to seventeen seated on our back porch and steps, with a single electric bulb illuminating the backyard. Making himself the hero of all sorts of adventures, he told tales about being a member of the Northwest Mounted Police, Texas Rangers, Customs Agents protecting the border from smugglers and rum-runners, fighting bandits in Mexico—even piloting planes to rescue lost persons in the Sierra Madre Mountains. Each week he told a different "chapter" as the stories came to be known. At first kids would ask him to tell a story when he came out of the house on Saturday evenings. As time went by they asked him to tell a chapter. *Chapter* replaced *story* in our minds as a continued adventure or story was told.

I can recall most of those stories today. They were so detailed that we couldn't really tell if they had actually happened. The older kids would question his veracity, but he always had an answer for them—details which would convince you they were true. From this perspective I believe many of them were based on real adventures he'd had or heard of. We were convinced at the time.

After a chapter, a can was placed under the hanging lightbulb; a ten-foot circle scribed in the ground (we had no grass in our yard—it was completely worn down), and everyone played Kick the Can which could get rather rough. Usually an older kid was the first one to be IT, although when younger kids became IT, two usually served together. It was a rough game. Frequently the races between the find-ee and the finder were negated by a third party kicking the can after bumping the IT person when he was on his way to base. A hiding place was best located with a clear path to the can.

Saturday nights were special at our house.

Our yard became an athletic field in February and March. The Border Olympics took place in Laredo at that time. It was the first national track and field event every year, and colleges and high schools all over the country participated. Every boy in town was enthused. We held track meets most afternoons during those months. You were either a dash man or a distance runner, weight man or a jumper. I decided I was a dash man and a pole vaulter. My dad dug a jumping pit in our yard, purchased an eight-foot-long wooden pole, and I taught myself the techniques of pole vaulting. We measured the distance around our house in yards, decided so many laps were a certain distance, and then held track meets. As many as a dozen boys were on each team.

I'm not sure if I was yet twelve years old, but an opportunity came up to earn some money. A man I recall by the name of Troutman hired me along with my friend, Artie, to help transplant onions and tomatoes at his farm south of the city. He took us out early in the morning and brought us back at night. It was backbreaking work and the pay was 25 cents an hour. Aside from the money there was the benefit of mingling with my fellow workers. They were part of the Bracero Program the U.S. government set up with Mexico. Living in barracks-type quarters, whole families worked the fields seven days a week. There were school teachers, business owners and students in the U.S. for six weeks. When they found out I spoke Spanish, we became good friends. The experience instilled in me a respect and affection for farm workers.

Aunts and uncles were the source of many jobs for me. Wilbur got me a job with the Dr. Pepper Bottling Company loading the bottle washer; and my older cousin, Phillip, employed me to sand floors and clean rugs when I got to high school. I worked every summer through college and usually got a job by soliciting "connected" relatives. The Wrights were connected in Laredo.

In 1947 one of Mom's old school mates was the source of a job at Southwest Engineers, a surveying company contracted to build electric transmission lines in south Texas. Prior to that time, only city residents were provided electricity. Rural customers either had wind-powered generators or used coal oil lamps for illumination. The Rural Electrification Administration (REA) was a life changer for farms and ranches in the mid 1940s. At first my job was to cut brush for the surveying crew. Later I progressed to tailing, then heading the measuring chain; by the age of sixteen I ran the transit. With the summer heat waves, I'm sure many a mile of power line in south Texas has wavy lines.

My Uncle Leo was the source of my next job. He was a pipeline superintendent at United Gas in Nacogdoches, Texas. After my freshman year at A&M, I took my first train ride to Palestine, Texas, and rented a bed in a rooming house—there being no rooms available. I slept in a cot at the head of the stairs. Each day that summer I packed a lunch in the kitchen, and got picked up and dropped off somewhere on one of the pipelines in our district. I walked all day looking for leaks which were found by seeing dead grass or bubbles at creek crossings. Finding leaks meant overtime pay. I was paid $1.00 per hour. I saved money by mailing my laundry home each week for my Mom to wash and return in a small, hard cardboard suitcase which had a metal-framed address pocket, and was secured with the attached military fabric belt. I used that cardboard suitcase through college and then on my first job, traveling with the gas company.

Joe, my uncle who lived in Shreveport, Louisiana, was an important accountant with United Gas. He and Leo saw to it that I would have an opportunity to work in their Corrosion Department if

I would switch majors to Electrical Engineering. I switched and my grades went from A's and B's to C's and D's in the remaining years.

❧

Edward Wright grew up in Laredo, Texas, graduated from high school and never went back except to visit. After earning a bachelor's degree in electrical engineering at Texas A&M, and two years' active duty as an officer in the Air Force, he spent 35 years in the electrical sales field. After retirement, he spent two years as a consultant in Mexico. In the years after that he and his wife published two historical novels (*Branches* and *Todos Santos*) based on the lives of ancestors.

In the Kitchen with...

Don Johnson

Most of us macho he-man types like to traipse around a lot in the Great Outdoors. If there's one thing I've learned in all my years of traipsing, it's this: if you traipse around in the Great Outdoors long enough, you're going to want to eat, and you're usually going to have to do it in the Great Outdoors, since that's where you're traipsing.

Anyhow, here's one of my favorite outdoor grub-fests, adapted from the original recipe of a genuine, Texas cattle-drive era chuck wagon cook, back in the days when men were men and women were glad of it.

❧

Son of a Bitch Stew
3-4 pounds raw, red meat, in big chunks
3 pounds spuds
4 large onions
1 bunch of carrots (if the horses haven't eaten them)
1/2 shovel salt
2/3 shovel cayenne pepper
4-5 double handfuls chili peppers
1/2-pound lard
12-15 cans beer (16 oz. size)
1 chainsaw
1/2 plug chewing tobacco

You're going to need a twelve-quart Dutch oven to cook this, and I mean a REAL cast iron Dutch oven, not one of those citified, limp-wristed frying pans with a lid. No self-respecting macho he-man would be caught dead with a cheap imitation, no more than he would sew doilies to his sleeping bag or put ruffles on his camouflage rain parka. No, a REAL Dutch oven sits on three legs, has a tight-fitting flanged lid to hold coals on top for the baking of cobblers and the scorching of biscuits, and has a sturdy bail handle for burning your fingers. In a twelve-quart size, it will weigh more than Greenland, and between trips you can store it by hanging it from the gun rack in the back window of your pickup.

First, you go out with your chainsaw and cut yourself a bunch of firewood, preferably hickory, oak or mesquite. I've found that the sawing seems to go faster if you have at least one tattoo. Then you arrange the wood in a compact pile in your fire pit, and light it by any method approved by the U.S. Forest Service. My own favorite method is gasoline.

If you sit close enough to the fire while you're igniting it using my preferred method, you won't need to worry about shaving for the next couple of days. You don't really NEED eyebrows in the Great Outdoors anyhow.

As long as you have your chainsaw warmed up, you might as well cut the meat into smaller pieces, preferably fist-sized or smaller. First, though, you might want to check your meat for freshness by poking it with the blade of your survival knife or the toe of your boot. If it makes a noise or tries to crawl away, it probably isn't quite dead enough. If, on the other hand, vultures begin to circle and alight within twenty feet of your food preparation area, it may be a bit TOO dead—either that or you should check up on your macho he-man camping companions. You'll develop a feel for this with experience.

Anyhow, toss the lard into the Dutch oven along with the meat, and set the oven into the fire long enough for the meat to brown. When you quit coughing from the smoke, it's browned enough. While you're waiting, you can cut up the vegetables. I suppose you can wash and peel them first, if you're a sissy.

Take the pot off the fire and toss in the vegetables, along with the chilies and the seasonings. By this time, your fire should have burned down to glowing coals. Dig yourself a hole next to the fire about two feet across and a foot and a half deep. Then scoop about one-third of your glowing coals into the hole. BE SURE AND USE YOUR SHOVEL!! You already have it in your hand from digging the hole.

Put the lid on the Dutch oven, place the oven in the hole, and shovel the remaining coals on top of the oven, with a final covering of about two inches of loose dirt.

The stew will take about two hours to simmer slowly underground. While you're waiting, drink the cans of beer. Chew the tobacco, and spit the juice into the fire. When the beer is all gone, the stew is ready.

Most experienced macho he-man cooks will remember to prop up the bail of the oven prior to burying it, so that it will be easier to lift out of the hole. You, of course, will have forgotten to do this, so you'll have to fish around in the coals with a stick. Then, because you've drunk enough beer to float a battleship, you'll grab the hot bail without a potholder. You can tell that your fingers are burned enough when you hear them start to sizzle. Hop around a lot. Yell and cuss to taste.

Once you've wrestled the Dutch oven out of its hole, you're ready for the reward for all your effort.

First, find a dirty spoon. Take a generous taste of the stew, spit it out hurriedly, yell "SONOFA_____!!!", dump out the stew, and eat the Dutch oven.

Serves four to six hungry macho he-men.

Don Johnson is 67 years old and a Dallas native, currently living in McKinney, Texas.

WHY?

Gordon Smith

I have hit the big 8-0. It has taken me a lifetime to realize how fortunate I was to ask why when I was a child.

I was born in 1935 in deepest Delta, Mississippi. The Delta is quite expansive. People who were born and raised along the borders of it had more opportunities to rub elbows and ideas with the outside world, thus getting a chance to be enlightened.

But Sumner, my hometown, was as deep as it gets.

The little town of 600 was about half and half black and white. I am white.

What I learned at my mother's knee and in my father's grocery store, in school and church, in the homes of friends, was the concept of place. No one taught me to ask why there was such a thing. But it was obvious. It was just as much a reality, just as much a fact of life, as death and taxes.

The cook came in the back door and left the same way.

The yard boy had his own drinking glass—most likely a fruit jar—and it was washed and stored separately from our dishes.

White children of any age were addressed by blacks as Mister or Miss, plus the first name. All white adults were Mister, Mrs., or Miss.

Black people, regardless of age, status, money, or professional title had only a first name or nickname. As a young boy, I could even have called the black high school principal "Joe" and no eyebrows would have been raised. It was expected on both sides of the spectrum. If my father had suddenly lost his mind and referred to the principal as "Mr. Joe Patterson" in public, if he had made it through the day in one piece, a "for sale" sign would probably have appeared in our store window within the month.

We all know about the separate water fountains and rest rooms (in those rare cases where these were provided for blacks), the segregated bus and train seating, and the stepping aside on the sidewalk, and all of the other degrading practices. Liberals will weep over these at the drop of a tear.

What I weep over—every time I think about it—is that I was never told that practices of forced segregation were good and right, but I learned that truth by example from every white in town.

And I learned that since the blacks never protested (at least the ones who were still alive, still able to function), it must have been all right with them to be treated as sub-humans.

They would not have been happy to worship in our churches. They had their own way—like the songs they sang, swinging and swaying and clapping their hands.

They could not have learned in our tax-supported schools—they were too dumb, and they would have held our kids back.

And they were not about to date our white boys and girls, or be in the same play groups or clubs. That always led to marriage, and we all knew the outcome of that.

And so it went.

I don't know exactly when or where the first moment—the beginning of my lifetime of growing realization—started. I don't think that I ever had a "Road to Damascus" experience. There were just little rays of sunshine that penetrated the darkness and gloom and lit up the word "why?" in my mind.

I know that no daylight ever permeated the classroom, or the church, or my home.

It is possible the first inkling that something was seriously wrong with the Southern version of apartheid came to me one night in our little store. I was about ten.

It was a Saturday night, the night when field hands and their wives came to town from the farms and plantations to spend their money—actually to charge against the fall "furnish."

The men headed for Beale Street, and the women sat along the wall on sacks of flour or grain, making one soft drink last about an hour as they talked. They had little cash to spend for such luxuries.

My father was going around from group to group, taking each woman's verbal grocery order and then collecting the requested items. There was a woman visiting from Chicago. My father came back to me, as I stood manning the cash register, ready to deposit any money that came from these people who were the almost sole support of our income, and he said, under his breath, "If she forgets to say 'Sir' to me one more time, I'm going to slap her!"

That word why jumped into my mind. And the word forgets was telling.

Why stayed there and was replicated, and it widened over time. There were many places where I could ask the question every day.

My father was a good man. Deacon in the church. Honest with all. Dependable. Trustworthy. Loving father. Generous provider. Not a child- or wife-beater.

He was doing what he had been brought up to do. He was a product of the society which nurtured, guided and sustained him. He had never asked why.

One day the house where her black cook lived in my aunt's backyard caught fire. My father and I rushed out to help extinguish it. The cook, distraught over the fact that her small child was in the burning house, ran screaming toward the fire. When she learned that the child had been rescued, she swooned into my father's arms. Almost immediately he said, "Somebody take her—she's faking anyway." First, to hold her was verboten. And she had no real feelings.

In my hometown's courthouse, the acquittal of the two respected white men who murdered Emmett Till made me weep, and my tears are even now near the surface of my consciousness and my conscience. The defense attorney was our lawyer, and a close family friend. Our friends and family made up a large part of the spectators. I knew the jury members. I understood perfectly what was going on. And I was just a boy.

Why? Why do some people believe honestly and sincerely that they are better than others, based solely on skin color, and that they have a duty to maintain status quo?

Oh, I am still prejudiced, to some degree. But I think—I think—that it is based on other factors. I despise those who molest children or mistreat women or steal the life savings of old people. I cannot accept or approve of everybody.

But I will never again be guilty of accepting or approving the mistreatment of another human being, or the embracing of evil as being all right. I hope.

But I am aware that my lifetime is not over. I have to be on guard. It is easy to play follow the leader when facing moral and ethical questions. It is hard to buck the crowd and ask why?

❦

Gordon Smith is a retired public school science teacher. Born in Mississippi, he now lives in Hot Springs, Arkansas, with his wife, Carol, a retired high school English and journalism teacher.

Memories are such a gift, and age is the only way
we can relive special events, from childhood
to the present time. Even the mistakes we made
no longer seem so important. Thank goodness
for cameras and photo albums to keep the record straight.

—**Barbara Mott**
92-year-old author

Short Stories

First Prize

SMOOTH SHEILA

John Garzone

Our fourteen-year-old daughter, Kelly, came bouncing down the stairs holding a dusty narrow leather case. She had her mother's dark hair and eyes.

"Look what I found hiding in the attic, buried under a bunch of boxes."

"What is it, Kelly?" asked my wife, her brown eyes as intense as the first time I saw them.

"It's just what I need, Mom," she said, opening the case and revealing a gray and black two-piece pool cue.

"What do you want with that?" I asked.

"Linda and I are going to the billiard parlor with some friends and play pool."

Before I had a chance to reply, her mother asked, "Who said you could go? I'm not sure I want you hanging around a pool hall."

"Come on, Mom, this isn't the old days. It's a family place." She stood with hands on hips wearing an astonished look on her angelic face.

"She's right," I said. "It's not like years ago, rundown and full of seedy people. Our office manager, Ted, takes his family there."

She squinted those dark eyes at me, a look that said, "Bill, you side with Kelly on everything."

Kelly looked at me and smiled her mother's smile.

"Whose is it, Mom? It has the initials 'SS' on it."

"Well, Kelly, I guess you can go and use the pool cue, but I want to talk to Linda's mother."

"OK, great. I'll call Linda and you can talk to her Mom. Thanks, guys."

The pitter-patter of raindrops against the kitchen window held my thoughts. I took a sip of my coffee and looked deeply into the cup. My mind easily slipped back in time.

Briskly, I strode down the drab, dreary hall leading to the pool-room. Obscene graffiti covered the plaster-cracked walls. I reached the entrance, gripped by tension and excitement. The stale smoke invaded my nostrils. The impact of colliding billiard balls predominated. Noisy side-burned teen-agers gathered around an active pinball machine.

I hustled over to table one. Got lucky. Spotted an open seat at the far end of the table. I eased my lanky frame onto the uncomfortable wooden chair. Excitement grasped me as I pushed a wisp of brown hair off my forehead.

Big game day! Last week, Fat Bernie challenged Smooth Sheila to a game of straight pool for a hundred dollars. I wasn't about to miss this. Smooth Sheila was "top stick." At twenty years of age, on the tall side with long black hair, her fervent dark eyes could freeze you in a heartbeat.

It wasn't common for a girl to be the best, but she'd proven herself many times.

Smooth as silk, cool under pressure, she feared no one. She'd earned the respect and admiration of the regulars, who hung out in the pool hall.

Fat Bernie was new to the room. Short and rotund, he easily carried over two hundred pounds. His blond hair swished back in a D.A.—chubby face dotted with acne. Arrogance and skillfulness heightened his reputation.

I'd watched Smooth Sheila shoot pool many times. Fat Bernie, never saw his game.

Four guys wearing expensive suits and impeccably shined wing tipped shoes sat in the preferred seats. I heard they'd bet a large wad on the newcomer. Myself, I had a cool twenty on the smooth one.

A hush fell over the room. Fat Bernie and Smooth Sheila met at the head of the table. The heavyweight's round paunchy face oozed with confidence. Smooth Sheila, calm as always, her fierce dark eyes riveted on Fat Bernie.

The houseman, Joe "the Coin," a burly redhead with an honest reputation, explained the rules.

I reached into my black pullover shirt for a cigarette, lit up and blew a stream of smoke at the light bulb hanging above the table. It disappeared into the giant haze engulfing the room. I snapped my Zippo shut. Game on. Fat Bernie would break.

He stroked his stick expertly. The cue ball nicked the fifteen ball, pushing it against the side of the table back into the shelter of the rack. He played a good safe.

Sheila studied the lay from all angles. She stopped twice to gaze at the six ball. I rubbernecked but couldn't see any separation of the six from the rack.

With lips that barely moved, she said, "six ball corner pocket." A low murmur buzzed through the crowd.

If she missed, the rack would be open for Bernie. She stroked her cue three times; the third time the stick met the ball with a loud smack. The cue ball smashed into the front of the rack, blistering the six ball into the corner pocket. Thumping of pool sticks on the hard floor acknowledged the gutsy shot.

Balls were strewn about the green felt. The Smooth One ran the first rack effortlessly. She ran 40 balls before missing a tough shot, leaving the four ball hanging on the side pocket. Her full lips parted, she mouthed a curse and sat in her chair.

Fat Bernie smiled sarcastically and lumbered over to the table. He began to shoot, and he shot well. The balls glided smoothly across the table, dropping into the designated pockets. He ran 75 balls. Across the table, the four overdressed Mafia types smiled and nodded their heads after each shot. Beads of sweat formed on "The Coin's" forehead. Word was, he'd bet a lot of money on Smooth Sheila.

The obese shooter ran another rack, ten balls to go. It looked like my money would be gone faster than a G.I.'s paycheck on a Friday night. I was ready to kiss my twenty goodbye.

Suddenly, a hissing noise emitted from the crowded onlookers. Elbows jabbed one another and people gawked at the table. Fat Bernie had trouble. He'd played bad position on the previous shot and the cue ball rested against the rail at the far corner of the table.

I watched him stroke his cue. His hands shook. His eye twitched. He tried to play safe. The ping of the stick against the ball announced his miscue. The cue ball squirted up the table, unintentionally nudging the thirteen ball free for an easy shot. Fat Bernie had got the "apple," he choked. The tallest of the four men across from me swore.

Smooth Sheila bounced to her feet. With a low, calm voice, she said, "Hang up your stick, fat man."

She ran ball after ball, rack after rack, her arm and cue stick working as a single entity.

One final ball to make, she chalked her cue. The smooth one nodded to Fat Bernie and sank the eleven ball in the side pocket. A thunderous roar bellowed from the crowd! Smooth Sheila was still "top stick."

"Bill! Are you there? "Come back from wherever you are."

Her voice pulled me back to the present. I looked across to her and said, "Just thinking about the pool halls of years ago."

"For a while I thought you'd completely regressed into the past." She smiled at me, her dark eyes glistening.

I returned the smile. "I particularly remember a special game I saw."

A happy teasing look graced her eyes. "It must have been an important game for you."

"Yes, very significant. Not only did I win twenty dollars, I met the love of my life." I stood. Holding her tight, I said, "You're still a smooth one, Sheila."

John M. Garzone, 74, has self-published five full-length detective novels. He is a member and moderator of a local writers' group.

Sitting and dreaming is sometimes considered a waste of time. But is it? Fretting never achieves new ideas, or produces renewed energy to face a challenge. But if anyone asks, tell them you are solving problems with your mind.

—**Barbara Mott**
92-year-old author

Second Prize

RICE PADDY

Stephen C. Porter

I stopped the jeep as Mr. Phi pondered the route most likely to lead us back to our district headquarters before the certain rain began. The black clouds boiling along the southern horizon signaled the beginning of the monsoon season.

Phi gazed out across the flat, patchwork quilt of rice paddies. The narrow road we were traveling snaked around the wet fields and past a distant hamlet in a time-consuming serpentine. The paved highway to Gia Dinh was an hour away if we stayed on the road.

"Think we could cut straight across on one of these wide paddy dikes?" I asked.

My head was throbbing and I could see us being caught in a downpour, with no top on my jeep.

When my interpreter didn't answer, I leaned forward, trying to see his face.

Squinting out from under the green camouflage helmet, Phi resembled a box turtle.

"Am I being inscrutable?" he asked solemnly.

"I wish I'd never taught you that word."

"Is it not a good word?"

"It's a very descriptive word. And sometimes you try a little too hard to match the description."

My stomach began cramping again as Phi refocused his attention on the terrain ahead of us. Finally, he said, "I think to proceed carefully would be correct."

"I'm not sure what the hell that means," I said, "but I'm going across the paddy."

We had spent the day in the neighboring province of Hau Nghia on a liaison visit to several villages near the Parrot's Beak area not far from Cambodia.

As an intelligence officer in the province that surrounded Saigon, part of my job was to obtain information on suspected Viet Cong infiltration routes.

Phi, a civilian, was visibly uneasy when we made these frequent journeys away from the Saigon area. I increased his discomfort by making him wear the steel helmet whenever we took the jeep outside Gia Dinh. The helmet swallowed his small head and looked out of place with his unvarying uniform—neatly pressed white cotton shirt, baggy gray pants, dusty leather sandals.

We had completed our circuit of outlying villages by early afternoon. I hoped to be back at the province HQ filing my report by 1700 hours and heading for happy hour at the Massachusetts BOQ; however, protocol required that we visit the remote compound commanded by a tough ARVN colonel named Tranh.

Tranh's battalion of local militia called Regional Forces/Popular Forces, known to the advisors as "Ruff/Puffs," was responsible for the protection of the district. Despite the civilian bureaucracy, Col. Tranh was the real power in the region.

He greeted me with his customary bravado. After watching the movie *Patton,* he had begun carrying a swagger stick and wearing a pearl-handled .45.

I presented him with a carton of Marlboros—part of the monthly PX ration.

"Ah, cowboy cigarettes," he said, pantomiming a quick draw. Tranh was a great fan of American TV shows on the Armed Forces Network.

He ignored Phi altogether. He had no use for civilians.

My hopes for a brief visit dissolved when the colonel announced that he had invited several officials from the surrounding villages to join us for a luncheon of roast duck.

After eight months in Viet Nam, my digestive system had developed an uneasy tolerance for most native dishes—even the foul-tasting fish sauce, *nuoc mam.* I had successfully avoided a case of the trots for several weeks and wasn't eager to put my bowels to the test again.

We sat down under a thatched pavilion and my stomach held up pretty well until the wizened old village chief from Vinh Loc produced a set of dirty shot glasses and a plastic milk carton filled with homemade rice whiskey called *ba xi de.*

Encouraged by Tranh, the old man asked, "you fini with me, eh co van?"

This began a favorite sport—insisting that the American advisor toss down a glass of the raw whiskey with each of the Vietnamese.

Accustomed to this ritual, Phi watched impassively from the far end of the table. Through bleary eyes, I looked for his signal—a slight nod—that told me I had consumed enough of the rotten booze to satisfy my counterparts.

After what my interpreter deemed a decent interval, I stood up unsteadily. Pointing to the dial of my Seiko, I had Phi convey my appreciation for the information and the fine meal. Phi was also accustomed to such lies.

Col. Tranh walked me to my jeep and summoned an aide who brought me a farewell gift of six bottles of bitter beer call Ba Muoi Ba.

"Six pack to go!" Tranh proclaimed. We exchanged salutes and I eased myself into the jeep, grasping the steering wheel for support.

Determined to maintain my military bearing, I drove out of the compound and down the narrow dirt road. Once we were out of sight, I leaned out the side of the jeep and threw up the whisky, the duck, and the *nuoc mam.* No heaving or spasms; it all came up in one efficient gush.

I wiped my mouth with an olive drab handkerchief, and then put on my steel helmet.

Phi sat in stoic and polite silence until the jeep started moving.

"That goddamn Tranh gives me a case of the ass. Putting me through that drinking game in the middle of the day."

"Case of the ass?"

Yeah. It's an expression. You know, like a case of the clap."

"The clap?" he asked, smacking his delicate hands together.

"Forget it, Mr. Phi. And put your steel pot on. We're in Indian Country."

And so in an effort to beat the monsoon, we bumped along the top of a paddy dike, my guts rumbling and my head pounding and Phi grasping the metal bars under his seat cushion, trying to hang on.

Distracted by the sight of a small boy herding a huge water buffalo, I never saw the break in the dike.

The nose of the jeep plunged down, jamming the front tires into the soft red mud, almost sending Phi through the windshield.

I threw the vehicle into reverse, trying to back out of the mire, but succeeded only in wedging the left rear wheel as well. I felt like I might throw up again.

"You okay, Mr. Phi?"

He tapped his steel pot.

"Good crash helmet."

Still queasy, I dismounted from the jeep and heard the sucking sound of my boots sinking into the mud.

The boy herding the water buffalo stopped next to the jeep and stood thigh-deep in the water, watching me with alert brown eyes as I made my slippery circuit of the disabled vehicle. The close proximity of the buffalo only added to my irritation. While it was fascinating to watch those massive, ill-tempered beasts being led and goaded by small children, it was a sight I preferred to observe from a safe distance. With a wary eye on the buffalo, I completed my inspection.

"Shit. We're stuck, Mr. Phi. This jeep's going nowhere."

Phi ignored my grasp of the obvious. He had taken off his helmet and was standing at the front of the jeep, first scanning the paddies that surrounded us, then surveying the hamlet whose grass houses were only a hundred yards away. The sour odor of garbage mixed with the smell of rain heavy in the air. Our eyes met briefly, and I saw the faintest hint of uncertainty pass over his smooth face like the low clouds now blowing across the sky. Then the slight and constant smile returned.

"Does this give you another—umm, case of the ass?"

Off to the south, a dull rumble of thunder accentuated the seriousness of our situation.

"Looks like we don't have a lot of options," I said. "Unless you have a brother-in-law living in that hamlet who owns a wrecker service, I think we'll have to hike out of here."

Phi looked back at the way we had come, then turned and studied the distant tree line marking the Gia Dinh highway.

"It is a very long walk back to Col. Tranh's compound," Phi said.

"But Tranh can send one of his trucks to pull the jeep out of the mud. I can't just leave it here."

Phi looked at the sky. The sun was being swallowed by a huge, brooding cloud.

"It will rain soon. A large rain, I think."

Two young boys walked out from the hamlet to the place where Phi and I stood pondering our predicament. They watched us shyly, afraid to come too close.

The buffalo herder was less cautious and began talking to them with great animation and many gestures. Ignoring Phi and me, he stomped around the jeep, taking exaggerated steps in his bare feet. Then, placing his hands on his hips, he shouted:

"Shit! Stuck!"

The other boys howled with laughter and even Phi started chuckling. The boy had been doing a great impersonation of the angry American officer.

Soon more children appeared from the hamlet. With each arrival, the buffalo boy repeated his pantomime, stomping around the jeep with a serious expression on his face.

"Shit! Stuck!" he would cry, and the whole audience would squeal with laughter.

I dug around behind the seat of the jeep and pulled out my M-16 and a web harness containing two grenades and an ammo pouch with two extra magazines. Along with a .45 pistol, this was my standard traveling armament. I had left a neatly rolled poncho on the bed back in my quarters at Tan Binh.

"Think we should go ask the hamlet chief to watch the jeep until we get back?"

Phi looked at the hamlet for a long minute. Finally, he said, "No, I do not think so. This hamlet chief is not known to me."

"Well, I'm sure that fine beer won't be here when we get back."

"Like you say, 'easy come, easy leave'."

He replaced the steel helmet on his head, and then said, "Before we go, I am needing to drain my lizard."

He had learned that expression from me and the other advisors. He stepped down behind the paddy dike and relieved himself while I buckled on the harness and slung the rifle on my shoulder.

When Phi climbed back up on the dike, the uncertainty had returned to his face.

Glancing around, I realized that the children had disappeared, as though they had silently submerged into the dirty waters of the rice fields. The buffalo stood alone, tossing its massive head restlessly.

I don't know which I saw first—the bullets splattering the mud or the puffs of smoke from the garbage heaps outside the hamlet. In a split second I knew we were under fire.

I dove into Phi like a fullback laying the perfect downfield block. I knocked the slender man into the muddy water as I heard the deadly, unmistakable clatter of AK-47s.

Phi gasped for his wind, but nodded that he was okay as we crawled up against the embankment. His brown eyes were wide with fear; I could only guess what he saw in mine. We were well-protected by the paddy dike, but the shooting continued, the rounds thudding into the other side of the dirt wall.

We had landed close to the jeep and the rifles seemed to be spraying bullets up and down the length of the dike.

"We'd better get away from this jeep. If they hit the gas tank, it'll blow all to hell."

Phi raised his head slightly, listening. I was still clutching my M-16, but had given little thought to returning fire.

"I don't think they will shoot this jeep. Maybe they would like to have this jeep."

Although the two AKs were firing into the dike on either side of the vehicle, the obvious target hadn't been hit.

I motioned to Phi; he and I rolled over several times until we came to rest directly under the place where the jeep was mired.

Pulling myself up to the top of the embankment, I could see through a space between the mud and the underside of the vehicle. The puffs of smoke from the hamlet indicated two shooters about twenty yards apart, concealed in the stinking refuse piles behind the line of huts. They were aiming carefully, avoiding both the jeep and the water buffalo, which was sloshing about in the paddy between my vantage point and the hamlet.

By wedging the barrel of my weapon underneath the jeep, I would have a field of fire.

But if I did start firing, would my enemies change their minds about saving the vehicle?

And could I really see anything to shoot at?

While I was pondering these matters with great indecision, the firing stopped. Simultaneously the first big drops of rain began pelting the camouflage cover of my helmet.

From across the paddy, a high, thin voice shouted something in Vietnamese.

"They would like your jeep, Trung uy," my interpreter said.

"I really hate it when you're right, Ong Phi."

"He says we can go. Leave jeep."

"Would they settle for a six-pack of warm beer?"

The rain was falling harder now, plastering Phi's black hair across his forehead. His steel pot was submerged somewhere in the rice paddy.

"I can't just abandon U.S. Government property to the enemy," I said, without much conviction.

Dammit, I thought. If the VC bastards hadn't opened fire, they could have had the jeep without a fight by waiting until Phi and I were out of sight—assuming they could haul it out of the mud before we returned with Tranh's Ruff/Puffs. Now I was putting my life on the line for a hunk of olive drab steel.

The voice from the hamlet shouted over the sound of the rain.

Phi said, "He asked again for the jeep."

"If John Wayne were here, he would tell the sons of bitches to come and take it."

Phi hesitated. "Maybe we should not make them angry with our reply."

"Then don't say anything. Let 'em guess what we're up to."

"What are we up to, Trung uy?"

"I wish the hell I knew."

The rain was blowing in sheets now, a billowing curtain of water. The poncho would have been nice.

"Listen, Mr. Phi," I yelled into his ear. "You're a civilian. You don't have to be here. Just slip off through that paddy behind us while this rain is falling. You can angle over to the highway and get back to Gia Dinh."

"I will go to Col Tranh's compound and get help," he said over the wind.

"No. Too far and too dangerous. There may be *beaucoup* VC in that hamlet."

He put his hand on my shoulder.

"You come, too."

"I can't. Here, take my pistol." I unsnapped the holster, but Phi shook his head violently.

"I am not a soldier. I will go to Col. Tranh."

He held out his small, wet hand and I squeezed it.

"You don't even like Col. Tranh."

"That will make disturbing him more pleasant."

With that, Phi slid down the side of the dike and started moving through the water in a low crouch. He turned back to me, a goofy smile on his face.

"See you later, alligator," he called.

"Yeah, yeah, after a while, crocodile. Now get the hell out of here."

I watched his slender form dissolve into the storm. He would be exposed when he climbed over the next crisscrossing dike, but with the driving rain and near darkness, he stood a chance of being unseen—especially if I created a diversion.

I rolled to my left, away from the jeep, checking the flash suppressor of my rifle for mud.

I rose up and fired a burst of six at the garbage piles, then ducked down behind the cover of the dike. At least the bastards would know I was still armed, if not dangerous.

The AK-47s opened up again, but through the downpour, they sounded far away. I strained to listen for any sound coming from the direction Phi traveled. I heard nothing and rolled back under the protection of the jeep.

The rain continued to fall steadily as darkness settled in. No more shots were fired from the hamlet. With only two extra magazines, I had to conserve my own ammunition. I considered trying to reach one of the VC with a grenade, but decided even Joe Namath couldn't throw that accurately.

The buffalo was getting agitated, and through the storm, I could make out its dark form clambering over a dike.

I wondered how long it would be before the Viet Cong tried to circle around on either side of me. My watch had stopped at 4:37. How long had Phi been gone—and would he come back?

Why should he come back? He had told me on several occasions that his life was in danger because he worked as a translator for the Americans.

This calm and gentle man was an enigma. Among the Vietnamese, he was an intellectual. An educated man who loved books and spoke both English and French. When he wasn't painstakingly re-copying intelligence reports, he could be found at his desk, reading well-worn volumes of world history and European classics like Les Miserables.

About his personal life, I knew little except that he was married and had five young children. I had never met his wife, but on R&R in

Hong Kong I bought her a silver bracelet, for which Phi thanked me profusely. My gift to him was more practical—a black alligator belt to hold up his baggy trousers.

At Christmas I had gone to the PX near MACV headquarters and bought an assortment of toys for his children. A few nights after Christmas, Mr. Phi came to my quarters for the only time. Four of his five offspring were perched precariously on his Suzuki motor scooter.

They had come a considerable distance to bow politely and thank me for their presents. It was an unnecessary and risky gesture, and I told him so. Phi said simply that it is important to show gratitude.

Thinking of that as I huddled under my jeep, I knew that Phi would go to Col. Tranh.

The rain finally stopped, but the wind continued, blowing the clouds and revealing occasional patches of clear night sky. My wet fatigues and jungle boots felt heavy, and I knew my feet must be as shriveled and wrinkled as my hands.

Lying with my back to the embankment, I could see in the distance the airplanes taking off from Tan Son Nhut Air Base. One set of blinking lights ascended at a 45-degree angle, then banked to the east and leveled off. A freedom bird, heading back to the world with a cabin full of happy GIs and a cargo bay loaded with body bags.

Looking in the other direction, toward Cambodia, I spotted a distant helicopter gunship flying low. Then a flash of light, as hundreds of red tracer rounds from a mini-gun drifted to the ground. I watched the helicopter spraying some far-off target, silently willing the chopper to fly in my direction with its big Xeon light mounted in the door. But soon the lights were lost beyond the black horizon.

Although adrenaline had cured the ache in my guts, fatigue was beginning to take its toll. Despite my perilous situation, I could feel my energy and my vigilance draining away.

My mind drifted off in long thoughts to other places and happier times. A piece of a song came back to me and I remembered sitting in a circle around the embers of a dying campfire at Inspiration Point on an unseasonably cool night during Bible camp, singing in low voices:

Someone's praying, Lord, Kum Ba Ya...

I must have dozed off. I'm not sure for how long. The water buffalo woke me, thrashing and grunting somewhere behind me. The clouds had moved in again and a light drizzle was falling.

A man's voice shouted in alarm. Someone trying to slip around behind me had stumbled into the buffalo.

I yanked one of the grenades from my harness and pulled the pin. Taking a deep breath, I flipped the handle off and lobbed the grenade in the direction of the noise coming from the next rice paddy.

I buried my face in the mud and waited what seemed like an eternity for the concussion. It came with a spray of paddy water, mingling with the rain.

The water buffalo let out a bellow that became a terrible, gurgling roar. But I was sure I also heard a human scream.

Hoping I couldn't be seen, I stood up and fired off the rest of my magazine into the sounds coming from the paddy. The buffalo's wail diminished to a low moan. I heard no human sounds, and as the rain began falling harder, it was impossible to see anything.

I loaded a new magazine, sure now that the other VC must be someplace close by, and wondering how many others might have joined in the attack.

In that moment, I was sure that I was about to die. My body was shaking, and I pressed against the muddy dike to steady myself. There was nothing to do but wait.

Then I heard a low rumble. Trucks. Several of them. Peering around the jeep, I could see their headlights probing the hamlet. Mr. Phi had brought the cavalry.

The rain stopped with the dawn; Phi and I went with Col. Tranh to inspect the jeep. In the rice paddy next to the vehicle, the dead water buffalo was half-submerged and already buzzing with flies in the morning heat. Several of the Ruff/Puff's tugged at the carcass, revealing gaping shrapnel wounds along one flank. A soldier digging in the mud and water under the beast shouted triumphantly as he pulled out a slime-covered AK-47. There was no sign of the owner, and rain had washed away any footprints or blood trail. The colonel smacked his thigh with his riding crop and said something that caused his men to laugh. Phi translated.

"Col. Tranh says you are a great hunter of buffalo."

Several men from the hamlet began butchering the animal where it lay.

"I guess I owe that buffalo a lot, Mr. Phi. He ran some pretty good interference for me."

"Interference?" he asked.

"Yeah, like in football."

He still looked puzzled.

I put my arm around his narrow shoulders and said, "Ong Phi, it's time you pulled your nose out of those books and learned about something really important—the Super Bowl."

One of Col. Tranh's trucks pulled the jeep out of the mud, and after some cleaning, we got it started and were back on our way by noon. Phi slept most of the way to province headquarters.

Weeks later, I learned that shortly after we left, Col. Tranh stood the hamlet chief and his deputy up against the tin wall of the meeting hall and personally executed both of them with his pearl-handled .45—as a warning to the VC sympathizers in the area.

Tricky Dick Nixon ordered a reduction in force that allowed me to leave Viet Nam a month before my tour was scheduled to be over.

Mr. Phi foresaw the end before I left. He knew that once the Americans pulled out, South Viet Nam could not stand.

"What will you do?" I asked him on the afternoon I cleaned my things out of the small desk we shared in the district compound at Tan Binh.

"My brother is a farmer in the central highlands. I will take my family there. I will become a farmer, too."

I studied his smooth face for a moment to determine if this was one of his jokes.

"Excuse me, Ong Phi, but it's a little hard to imagine you as a farmer. When I was a kid growing up in Lubbock, I used to visit my grandfather's farm in the summer. He had rough, callused hands and his face was creased like an old boot. I remember the day he had his first heart attack and drove his combine off into a ditch. That's when I decided that being a farmer sucks. You may come to the same conclusion."

Phi said, "I cannot stay here. The Viet Cong will know that I worked for the U.S. My family will not be safe, and I will be killed. So I will go to the highlands and learn to be a farmer—to save our lives."

"Some Vietnamese are leaving–going to America," I suggested.

"Only the rich, and the politicians, Trung uy."

I gave him my 35mm camera and a new Seiko watch. It didn't seem to be nearly enough.

We promised each other we would keep in touch, but I received only one letter. It arrived eight months after I got home, while I was studying for my first set of law school exams. The letter was in an airmail envelope bearing the return address of some sergeant in II Corps—the usual way the Vietnamese were able to send out letters to the U.S.

Dear Lieutenant:
I and my family are well. We are now living in the high-lands. You were right. Farming is very sucking.

My brother is a good farmer. He will teach me how to do the work. And my children can learn better.

I brought my books and have some time to read. All of the Americans are going back to the USA now. When they leave, I think the NVA will come here soon.

A Vietnamese poet wrote a poem that says:

"I see you in the green of the long grass and in the rising of the golden sun, and I recall the days we spent together."

My memories of you are very green. You showed me great kindness, and I will never forget your friendship.

I hope that you and your family are having good fortune. Have you been buffalo hunting lately?

Yours truly,
Vu Hong Phi

I sent back a letter in care of the sergeant, but never received a reply. I suspect that the NCO's tour of duty had ended prematurely with the big pullout after the Paris peace talks.

When Vietnamese refugees started arriving in the U.S., many of whom were neither rich, nor politicians; I hoped that Phi would be among them. But I never heard from him again.

His education and his former assistance to the American advisors may have cost him his life. But I prefer to think that by day he walks the rice paddy fields he helped clear out of the jungle, his rumpled pants still held up by a worn alligator belt.

He stands and stares off into the distance, watching and waiting. And at night, he takes down his precious books to read to his children and perhaps his grandchildren. And yes, Mr. Phi, my memories of you are also very green.

Stephen C. Porter is an attorney, Viet Nam veteran, and aspiring writer. His previous writing credits include short stories published in *The Texas Review, RiverSedge, descant,* and *The Stable Companion.* His non-fiction has appeared in *True West* and he has reviewed books for *The Dallas Morning News* and written for legal publications.

Third Prize

CHUPUNZA: IF IT HAS FOUR LEGS, IT CAN RACE

Valerie Gardner

The annual Chapunza horse races in South Africa were a highlight of our rural African farm year. The first Saturday and Sunday in September were set aside for this grand event. The entire district came for the fun and excitement of seeing their friends make fools of themselves, including the Chupunza Hospital staff where I was a nurse.

Chupunza's older folks initially disapproved of the wild, high spirits, but they soon joined in the carnival atmosphere. Our whole population divided into fiercely partisan camps. This wasn't merely a local horse gallop, but the apex of our social entertainment year.

The entire community, rich and poor, Africans and Europeans, staked their bets with enthusiasm. This rampant betting outraged our new, highly unpopular minister, Reverend Bandan. Lines of both African and white farm children, with greasy rags and soapy water buckets, ferociously cleaned cars on Main Street to earn betting money. The Reverend moaned at this corruption of the dear little children. Those "dear little children" were tough hardened punters.

In our Chapunza prison, 'bandits' and guards carefully pooled their combined income and seriously studied the racing form. Local farmers and ranchers—the would-be jockeys—were eyed anxiously.

Was he getting a bit flabby, putting on weight? "Ha! That's a new ranch horse? Any good? Can he run fast?"

At the Farmer's Co-op, Robin Moore was paying his bill when he happened to look out the window. Three African urchins and six elderly white people were all peering anxiously into the open mouth of Robin's stallion, Mpika, assessing his teeth. Convulsed with laughter, Robin said, "if it isn't bad enough my being poked in my fat belly by locals to test my fitness as a jockey, it's to see old Mpika having his teeth and hocks checked by every amateur punter in town!" Mpika rolled his eyes nervously and bunny hopped, scattering both children and adults. This was taken as a good sign and beaming smiles indicated a bet on Mpika-to-win. To both town and country, it was a riotous game, Rio Carnival and Kentucky Derby all rolled up in one dusty small village in Africa—the most exciting and glorious event of the year.

At Chapunza Hospital, our ward staff jockeys were pampered with special food. Volunteers took additional shifts to allow aspiring jockeys extra rest. Our African staff had the best jockeys. In past years, the hospital had covered itself with glory and race ribbons. Selection of jockeys was keen. I fell off regularly when riding anything on four legs, a source of great mirth to nurses watching my ungainly, spectacular falls. Our Catholic Irish nurse, Janet, included this racing event of the year in her "bliddy local heathens" category. Rumor had it that she had secretively placed four bets on the Rufaro Ranch stallions.

This year's grand race was divided into creative sections, from thoroughbreds (ribald laughter from farmers who suspected hints of mule ancestry in both rider and steed), mule madness, cow and bull dashes, donkey derby (the best event in my opinion as all kids from the remote villages and farms entered with breathless anticipation). Then the Grand Finale: a new category.

Entries poured in from farmers, ranchers, town, hospital—we were all there. Chooks, our popular veterinarian, was organizing this new event. Handicapping would be severe. Anything with four hooves, two ears (this ruled out ostriches) and a tail could race. Goats were disallowed as they'd butt anything on sight when all fired up—the horizontal pupils of their eyes shining with demoniacal fervor. Sheep riding events were run earlier for very small kids. One rotund African lady and a tall, skinny farm wife did a gleeful rural jitterbug when their two boys tied for first in the sheep derby. Small kids grimly clutched greasy wool as sheep were prodded into top speed down the track, little faces changing with moments of stark terror to bravado. A vast children's first prize was shared: two orange, iced popsicles and a giant pink candy floss.

In the Grand Finale, slow plodding oxen would be handicapped to start first, according to size, followed by a huge donkey entry, then mules, stray zebras ("must be well tamed and all zebras must wear muzzles.") There were seldom any zebras. Last to start were horses of varied ancestry. "Rider and Steed Must Finish the Race TOGETHER." Running beside one's steed was definitely not an approved way to cross the finish line.

Handicapping was finally finished. Excitement grew as the racing lineup formed. At the rear came the horse quadruped section which included a large collection of jittery stallions. They were handicapped heavily, and wild young farm assistants were their jockeys. They rode these horses each day on the ranches and lovingly labeled them "stallions," giving them confident assurance that they'd win by an easy margin. Meanwhile, the sixteen to 25-year-old jockeys were more intent on showing off their macho bodies and muscles to a gaggle of young ladies. They pulled in their stomachs under the jockey outfit (open sandals, khaki shorts and shirts gently frayed to softness, stained with wear of farm life). The girls relished this avid male interest, flirting shamelessly. The air was hot with seething testosterone. Much alcohol had already been imbibed and frequent falling off of horses was a consequence. Most stallions were facing the wrong way, a fact the inebriated riders failed to notice. They ogled the young ladies and didn't bother to face the start line.

Mules in front of this group were of sterner stuff, chewing their long, mottled, mulish lips and refusing any command whatsoever in true mulish fashion. Their heavy black hooves were ready to send unwary spectators into the rails with a thud.

Ahead of the Stallions Section, behind the oxen, was the Donkey Section. There were donkeys everywhere—black, brown, grey, grizzled, aged and young. We nurses and staff were lined up, cheering wildly as this was our hospital's main entry. Dozens of staff and orderlies, cleaners, lab assistants, anyone brave enough to mount, were perched on donkeys and wore red and white hospital colors. We called ourselves the "Blood'n Gore" entry, in line with an imagery of our Chapunza Hospital emergency room. Samele and I wore red scarves as did all nurses, happily yelling out names of all our hospital's jockeys. They beamed at this encouragement and waved, to the fury and panic of assorted donkeys. Irascible, kicking, bucking donkeys were creating braying mayhem as officials flapped newspapers to keep the donkeys and riders reasonably intact (that is, rider on top of donkey and not the other way around). This fired the donkeys up to more asinine chaos and cacophony with screeching, braying and baring of teeth.

Peter, our beloved orderly, was on a tough, dirty brown little donkey with greasy, wooly curls, named Mustafa. Unknown to other participants, we had been feeding Mustafa for a month on extra maize and molasses to strengthen him up. Peter was bone thin, and six feet of him was a lot for the small donkey. Peter's long, stork-like legs were pulled up into the stirrups, so his knees nearly touched his chin. This gave him the hilarious appearance of an elongated brown tarantula spider perched on the saddle which further freaked out the opposition donkeys.

Peter's face was grim and focused; he felt the success of his beloved hospital hung heavily on his thin shoulders. We cheered him wildly. His little Mustafa gave sideways rabbit jumps of nervousness.

Final category at the front was Farm Oxen, massive animals with fine, red-spotted hides. They were used for ploughing when the ancient tractors broke down. They pulled heavy old farm wagons that were still utilized in wet weather to heave loads through glutinous red mud. The driver sat in high and mighty disdain, flicking his long whip made of hippo hide. This show was for the open-mouthed audiences as he called lovingly to his beasts, urging them on.

Marula Ranch had entered two huge animals. A rich brown color, dusted gold with the local sand, they stood grimly, dourly disapproving of the cheerful pandemonium. The veterinarian had ordered large chunks of cork to be hammered onto the tips of all oxen horns for the safety of the general public. This gave the two oxen the ridiculous demeanor of ancient spinsters with hair curlers. Their two young African riders from Marula Ranch, ignoring all ribald remarks, hung onto a belly strap and rope reins assembled for the race. They had the ebony carved faces of Roman soldiers before battle. Behind each ox stood an African teen-age ranch boy holding a finely sharpened stick. We couldn't fathom the reason for these sticks but weren't worried. Oxen were phlegmatic. They plodded slowly, no competition for our heroic hospital jockeys on speedy, irate donkeys.

Ten minutes to go, all bets had been placed. Tensions grew. Real money was at stake here. Spectators clutched their tickets in nervous sweaty fists. Our fat clergyman had been singled out to fire the starting gun which had a real bullet. People thought it would be kind to include the minister in a position of importance. His stout wife was overdressed in a tight chiffon dress, high heels and a flowered hat that the donkeys eyed as edible. She stood talking loudly in an over-refined accent, waving her fat arms which jangled with gilt bracelets, and emanating an attitude of high society and pseudo importance.

Never having fired a gun, even in the air as required on this occasion, Reverent Bandan was anxious and hot. Raising his arm to mop his red, dripping fat brow, he accidentally caught the trigger on his bifocal glasses.

BANG—the pistol fired.

"Rupert, you. f…fool" screamed his wife, refined accent lapsed to an undignified Cockney scream "You nearly killed me you nasty little….."

Fortunately, her words were lost. At the bang, the whole race took off in various directions at full speed.

Pandemonium!

No jockeys were ready, but they hung on in contorted postures. It

150

was a hysterical rout of epic proportions. Stallions, facing the wrong way, mowed down the young females as the hysterical female horses galloped off in totally opposite direction from the finish line in unstoppable mayhem ejecting their inebriated young jockeys. Mules, who were facing forward, thundered up the track tangling with legions of braying, eyeball-rolling donkeys now fleeing the scene anywhere they could find an opening. It was an apocalypse. Hysterically happy and convulsed audiences were holding each other up as they wept with gales of laughter. The Best! The Best ever!

Peter, still grimly focused, took off galloping straight toward the finish line. His small donkey, scared of the melee, was trying to bolt. Peter somehow put his boots on the ground, clamped his small donkey between his legs and all six feet of him careened drunkenly towards the finish with six legs trotting together. Huge roars of encouragement came from all of our hospital crew with Nelson yelling, "Peter, Peter, mount up, mount up or you'll be disqualified!" His voice was lost in a surging, roaring wave of noise and air pounding fists.

The nefarious plan of the Marula Ranch hands came into play. The teenagers standing at the rear of the two oxen each grabbed an ox tail, bent it and bit it simultaneously giving a wicked poke with a pointed stick at their oxen's rear and tender genital undercarriage. The outraged oxen, facing the finish line, took off at a ferocious speed, snorting, moaning and bellowing their wrath. Their teenage riders, grey with terror, hung on for dear life. All the judges and the veterinarian waiting at the finish line jumped swiftly for tall trees and safety. They hung there like ungainly, large ornamental fruit, bowing the branches.

The oxen swept through in first place and kept on running, great clouds of dust and screams from the jockeys marking their path as the oxen headed straight back home to their cherished Marula Ranch.

Peter tore across the finish line a close second, still with his small donkey under him being virtually pulled along, protesting loudly in anguished, trumpeting brays. Peter was beaming from ear to ear as we all converged on him, hugging and thumping him on his back.

151

Doc descended with difficulty from a tall tree he had climbed when the maddened tide of animals swept past him. He was puffed up like a turkey cock, elated with pride at his hospital's victory. He hugged our redoubtable orderly and pushed a wad of money into his pocket. Peter and his little donkey were declared second-place winners in spite of the illegal, six-legged tandem run. The hospital staff went wild. We were weeping with laughter, hugging each other and doing an African war dance for our hero, Peter the Great. Peter had won a prize.

Truly a race to remember.

<hr />

Valerie Gardner's blessing was to be born and live in the Rhodesian bush on a gold mine and farm. Nursing was the escape key for jobs in rural hospitals. Rhodesian bush hospitals were her sunlight years.

True stories from her years at four African hospitals are woven together to form the stories of the single hospital she has called *Chapunza*. Valerie was a guest speaker on Africa across the American West, mainly to women's groups. Stories of Africans, farms, animals, bush hospitals, the laughter. Disney invited her to Disney World as a guest artist.

She sold glorious Zulu, Botswana and Zimbabwean baskets, helping support countless basket weavers. Here she also told tales of Africa, safaris, the splendor of the wildlife, the people. Audiences identified with the stories; would ask, tell again the story of axe in head, the horse race, Mbudzi the Hospital goat. The people, animals and hospitals that Valerie loved live on with laughter and tears.

Honorable Mention

I MET MY WIFE AT THE "KID SHOW"

Hyce Shaw III

I grew up in the late 1950s on the "M" streets of East Dallas. Back then, it was a 96-acre tract of two-bedroom Tudor style cottages on tree lined streets, whose names all began with the letter "M." Developed in the late 1920s, the neighborhood is only five miles from downtown Dallas but it truly served as the edge of "city living" at the time. Obviously, Dallas has changed significantly since then and now the area is a real estate gold mine as developers have begun demolishing many of the older homes and replacing them with similar looking two-story cottages. Greenville Avenue, a noteworthy transportation artery, is the Western boundary of the "M" streets and runs north and south.

In 1946, the year before I was born, the Granada Theater was built on Greenville among neighborhood service shops and retail stores. The interior of the Granada was a smaller version of the downtown theaters with lots of murals, back-lit plaster figures, and a stage with red curtain valences fronting the screen. Seating was limited to around 500. The exterior still has the brightly lit art deco style which seemed to be the industry standard for that time. Geographically, it was situated on the boundary line between two elementary schools: Stonewall Jackson on the north and my school, Robert E. Lee, on the south. It was a convenient location for young students who walked or rode their bikes throughout the neighborhood. Every Saturday, the Granada offered approximately four hours of escapism and fun for young kids while fortuitously providing an opportunity for parents to get weekend shopping errands done without them. At age nine, I became a regular Saturday movie goer along with hundreds of other neighborhood kids.

The "Kid Show," as it was known, opened its doors at 11:30. After sliding your quarter under the glass to the attendant in the booth outside, you'd get half a ticket in return, which you always kept with you. Walking a few steps behind the booth, you entered through one of the heavy red vinyl covered doors, with brass tack trim, and entered a lobby that fully challenged the senses. On those hot, Texas summer days, you were immediately embraced by the coolness of the air conditioning as your eyes were drawn to the dramatic lighting which showcased the murals on the ceiling. Thick carpeting covered the lobby, with its blend of rich and lush colors. You were overwhelmed by the smells of fresh popcorn, hotdogs, mustard, and sweet candy, all emanating from the snack bar, which was centrally located with its under counter lighting. It was absolute nirvana for kids of all ages.

Every Saturday, the snack bar was supervised by one cheerful little woman much older than our mothers. She miraculously maintained order with the hordes of kids queued up to place their orders, some barely tall enough to see over the counter. We never knew her name, but since she was always there, we always imagined she lived in a small room behind the snack bar. It was some years later, while riding the bus one morning to junior high, that I saw her coming out of her little house to pick up the morning newspaper, which dispelled that long-held notion.

The large silver-plated machine that popped the corn constantly worked to keep up with demand. I never understood how that thing worked, but I always liked watching the attendant salt the popcorn, and then grab the black handle, and pour out hot fresh popcorn into the glass collection box of the machine. Popcorn was scooped up with a small shovel and put into red and white cardboard boxes the attendant had squared and folded. The sides of the boxes read "popcorn," lest there be any confusion as to its contents, and cost 10 cents a box. More on the boxes to follow.

The brightly lit case of the snack bar was all glass. The thick glass countertop showed a web of scratches, caused by years of sliding nickels, dimes and quarters across it. The glass shelving under the counter had neat rows of brightly packaged edible treasures. Just about every Mars and Hershey confection was on the shelves. Tootsie Rolls were my favorite because they were large and very chewy, took a long time to finish, and only cost a nickel. I lost a couple of baby teeth in those Tootsie Rolls.

Off to one side of the front counter was the fountain dispenser with choices of Coca Cola, Dr. Pepper and Pepsi labeled on three levers, all dispensed through a single spout. As I learned early on, by observing the older boys, it was a clear exhibition of reckless abandon when you asked for a "suicide." The little woman would get a Sweetheart brand waxed paper cup, (no styrofoam back then), scoop up crushed ice from below the dispenser, set the cup under the single spout and pull all three levers at the same time, thereby creating an unrecognizable, carbonated concoction that cost a dime. For 50 cents, you're now ready for an exciting afternoon of entertainment. Looping around two sides of the snack bar were deep carpeted inclined hallways leading to the main seating area. The main lower floor had three seating sections divided by two carpeted aisles. It was backed up by a low wall and then another aisle which separated the lower floor from the balcony seating. The Granada's balcony was not much more than an elevated seating section eight steps or so above the main floor. You had to be at least twelve years old to sit up there.

There was a 30-minute window from 11:30 until 12:00 and you could either get your snacks, locate your friends, or find your seat before the show started. Most of us learned to exercise a little restraint regarding snacks, opting to make seat selections first while the lights were still on to find seats that didn't have old chewing gum in the fabric, or broken seats and badly worn armrests. The painted concrete below the seats was always sticky from previous or current drink spills. With few exceptions in those days, kids played fair and if you and your friends had seats when the show started, that was your seat throughout the day. You could go to the snack bar without worry. If you came in after the lights were out and the show had begun, it was tricky to find a seat among the hundreds of kids already seated. There was no usher with a flashlight waiting to assist, so you had to rely on the flickering light reflecting from the screen. Often, if you happened to spot the silhouette of an empty seat, it was usually occupied by some kid whose head didn't rise above the back of the seat. After a frustrating trip down the aisle, you would find yourself down front in the auditorium looking back at bluish gray faces in the reflected light, trying to find your friends or even just an empty seat. There was always a contingent of small kids who would sit on the very first row because it allowed for an unobstructed view of the screen, regardless of the crazy angle that ultimately distorted the view of the picture.

Occasionally, mothers would accompany a group of kids celebrating a birthday and would usually be challenged to find group seating. Additionally, they weren't aware of the constant up and down movement in the seats and in the aisles, or the continuous noise from the movie goers. We kids were never quiet for very long, and sometimes the movie dialogue could be near impossible to hear especially during romantic scenes, as young kids preferred action. The one large usher everybody referred to as "Gut," was constantly up and down the aisle, always on the prowl for the older seventh graders from both schools who sat on the outer extremities of the auditorium getting better acquainted with each other. You'd often see his flashlight highlight a boy and girl kissing, which was usually followed by laughter and cat calls from the rest of us. Embarrassing? No. They just waited for the light to go out and they'd reconvene. I remember the day I was sitting behind a mother attending to her young party group as she flagged down Gut.

"Can't you do something about the noise in here?," she asked. "We can't hear the movie."

"Lady, this is the 'Kid Show'," and off he went with his flashlight in search of more teenage miscreants.

The format for the "Kid Show" was always the same. It started to loud cheers from the audience as the lights went out and the first Warner Brothers cartoon started. After three cartoons, the weekly series began. These were "short reelers," usually in black and white and lasting around fifteen minutes. Each series had weekly chapters. The central theme was usually the battle of good versus evil, or right against wrong, always with cliffhangers in which the protagonists were in perilous circumstances at the end of each reel. You had to come back next week to see if Dick Tracy jumped out of the burning car before it went over the cliff, or parachuted out of a plane before it crashed. Great suspense.

Following the series, the black and white *Movietone* newsreel would play. This was a montage of several narrated film news shorts highlighting big events that had happened in the last months around the world. Like a Neilson Survey, you could immediately tell which of the news reports captured the young audience interest. Showing the running of a horse race or some royal family visit was a real killer and talking levels in the auditorium got a little louder, as did movement in the seats and in the aisles. If it showed a huge building fire in New York City or the aftermath of some blimp crash, or massive flood, movement and talking dramatically decreased, indicating great interest.

After the newsreels, three more cartoons ran and then the kid show would begin. These were one-time showings, each Saturday, designed to capture the attention of young audiences. I recall watching, for the most part with my hands over my eyes, the old scary movies like *Creature from the Black Lagoon, The Wolfman,* and a number of movies about giant insects taking over the earth. We also watched a lot of Abbott and Costello: ... *Meet Frankenstein,* ... *Meet the Mummy,* ... *Meet the Invisible Man.* We watched a lot of westerns and full length cartoon movies like *Bambi* and *Snow White.*

As if the movies were live performances, the young audience always responded in kind: spontaneous screams for scary movies, laughter for Abbott and Costello, or complete silence and sniffling when Bambi loses her mother. Explosive cheers and applause erupted when the cavalry arrived or when the United States Air Force dropped its new atomic bomb designed to kill the marauding giant grasshoppers or ants, which had ironically been created as a result of some earlier atomic mishap. The intermittent outbursts funneled to the lobby, always getting the attention of the stragglers hanging out around the snack bar, who would then start running toward the auditorium to see if the ceiling had fallen in or some other calamity.

The kid show audience had an active participating role. The popcorn box I'd mentioned earlier had an afterlife. It was great fun, when you finished eating the contents, to unfold it, press it flat and throw it up toward the ceiling. Of course everybody in the audience watched the shadow of the box arcing across the big screen, and perhaps Dracula's face in the movie. There was the usual audience approval for someone's effort from the dark. Where it came down, nobody really cared. Gut had long since given up trying to police that type of behavior.

At the end of the kid showing, the lights would come on in the auditorium and everybody was out of their seats, in the aisles and crowding the small stage in front of the screen. Walking down the crowded aisle toward the stage would come Gut, on point, creating a path for the short theater manager who followed closely behind walking the gauntlet of young souls with their hands out, always asking for free movie passes. This was the time when you reached for the half ticket you'd been saving in your pocket or purse.

While Gut took a position at the stairs, the manager would climb the five steps onto the stage and attempt to quiet the crowd. He would select one of the older teenagers to accompany him on the stage to draw five or six half-tickets out of a box. The manager then called out a three-digit number on the half ticket and waited for someone in the audience to respond who had the other matching numbered half. At the bottom of the stairs, Gut would check the stub to make sure it was correct and allow the young person passage to the stage where the manager would present him with a prize, and then the winner left the stage for the next called winner to come up. Waves of chortles were exchanged back and forth to young colleagues left behind in the audience. I was a lucky winner one Saturday and received a parakeet in a cardboard box as my prize. I sat in my seat during the movie trying to catch a glimpse of the bird through the punched air holes in the box, listening to its clawed feet making scratching noises. My friends held the box to get a look. When the show let out, I couldn't wait to get home to show my mother my prize. I ran into the house and opened the box. A green flash of feathers flew out of the box, as the bird made one quick circle of the living room and flew directly out the same back door my little brother had opened as he was coming in from outside. "Aw man!"

After the prizes were handed out, the two-and-a-half-hour "Kid" part of the show was over, and some of the younger kids would depart for home. Most of the older ones would stay for the showing of the main movie features. I watched a lot of Rodgers and Hammerstein musicals which were very prevalent in those days.

I turned twelve in 1959 and started the seventh grade. Life began to change for me in subtle ways, accompanied by a new sense of awareness and self-identity. The rock-and-roll era had taken hold of young people, introducing us to Elvis, Buddy Holly, Chuck Berry and many other singers. Hollywood was quick to catch on to this new trend and started producing low budget movies like *Rock Around the Clock* and *Jailhouse Rock*. The audience matched the action in these movies as girls started screaming and boys would start yelling when the music started. It was like, "this is our thing and we're going to be part of it."

Rock-and-roll fostered a growing rebelliousness in young people. Movies like *Rebel Without a Cause,* with James Dean, and *The Wild One,* starring Marlon Brando, were very popular and introduced us to a new lifestyle. The old rules of conduct seemed to give way to a need to test conventionality. It affected our self-image and demeanor, the way we dressed and our hairstyles. I noticed subtle changes in my classmates. For the girls, the "poodle skirt" was long gone, being replaced by "pedal pusher" slacks, pony tails, and look-a-like black leather purses. The black motorcycle jacket with zippers and "duck tail" haircuts were de rigueur for some of the boys. It was performance art paying homage to the movies.

There were a few older teenagers who fully endorsed this image.

159

One particular young man the kids called Snake, probably because that's what he wanted to be called, lived in a big two-story house in the neighborhood. Rumor was that his dad was a lawyer who represented big time criminals. Snake, while diminutive in size, wore the jacket, had the duck tail and rode a Triumph motorcycle. He had the reputation of being part of a gang, engaging in fights with knives and chains, and although no one was actually a witness to any of this, it created a certain juvenile delinquent panache for him. You could hear his motorcycle on the streets before you saw him, no doubt on his way to meet up with other gang members for some malevolent event. Most kids were afraid to make eye contact with him.

This anti-establishment style had little draw for me, as I identified more with the Beach Boys and the *Beach Blanket* movies that came a couple of years later with lots of music and lots of girls in bikinis. All of my friends were awakening to a new sense of feelings and realization regarding the difference between boys and girls. Those movies helped us make the transition, much to the consternation of our Sunday School teachers. Girls not only stirred some primeval interest, they smelled good, and boys started stealing shots of aftershave from their dads. We began engaging girls in conversation with our unqualified worldly wisdom and wit. Many times it worked, but even when it didn't, we ventured forward.

In class at Robert E. Lee Elementary, my friends and I would ask girls if they might be going to the kid show that Saturday, in hopes of sitting together. The seventh graders at Stonewall Jackson Elementary were apparently going through the same selection and interviewing process. Lee's contingent always sat on the right side of the theater, Stonewall on the left, with the demilitarized zone being the central seating area on the main floor. Each school year provided Gut with new targets of opportunity for his flashlight. I kissed my first girl at the Granada while watching *Hound Dog Man*, starring Fabian. Having watched my friends make that big leap in the dark, I finally worked up the courage to try it. I was driven not so much by desire, but curiosity. She was a willing participant, and I considered this as some rite of passage. We went to a lot of parties in the seventh grade, playing a lot of 45rpm records and dancing with a lot of girls.

As I got older, life's obligations made trips to the kid show infrequent, especially in the summer. I mowed neighbors' yards to make a little money in addition to my paper route. As I entered junior high, our seventh grade class get-togethers at the kid show were inherited by the classes that came behind us. During the winter months, I'd go occasionally out of boredom, since there wasn't much to do.

By then, I was old enough to climb the eight steps to the balcony of the Granada. At thirteen, most of the older kids moved to this upper location, mainly to avoid Gut and the chaos on the main floor, but also to be alone with our selected girl of the moment. In the dark you could see shadows of couples of various ages getting acquainted with each other, and the uninitiated, like myself, covertly watching them in an instructional sort of way.

War movies were always popular, and I went to the kid show one day where the main feature was *Heaven Knows Mr. Allison,* starring Robert Mitchum and Deborah Kerr. It's an interesting story of survival between an isolated nun and a marine on a Pacific island surrounded by the Japanese Army. Someone at the local marine recruiting station thought this might be a great opportunity to introduce young kids to the Marine Corps. I walked into the lobby of the Granada and saw a Marine in dress blues. He had inflated a yellow life raft and there were about ten kids playing in the raft, bouncing off the sides, working the paddles and pretending to row it across the lobby, with another ten or so kids waiting for an opportunity to share that experience. I felt sorry for the harried Marine standing there, probably wondering about the wisdom of this idea. I was a little too old to participate, so I just hung around the snack bar watching the lines of kids coming in the front door. Always with a watchful eye for someone new and interesting.

On New Year's Eve Day 1962, an interesting person caught my full attention as she walked through the doors of the Granada, accompanied by her girlfriend. I was fifteen years old. Tall and thin with a pretty smile and high cheek bones, and a carriage of mysterious self-confidence, she moved across the lobby with her friend. I stared at her, in the crowd of kids in the lobby, without her noticing. Her understated sexual presence registered loud and clear as my antenna was turned to maximum reception, and I knew immediately she's unlike any of the other girls I know. Yielding to some metaphysical interaction, I'm sure I'm in love before I even know her name. Not sure if my thirteen-year-old younger brother has noticed her or not, but he's noticed her girlfriend. So, like two sharks, we begin circling together, attempting to get closer, and thus, noticed.

How do you meet girls you've never met before? I don't remember the specifics, but I do remember meeting a person who exhibited a wisdom beyond her stated twelve years of age. We start the usual childhood interrogation and trading of information: name, grade, school, simple stuff. My brother and I are going out of our way to impress them with our humor and wit. They seemed to be buying our stuff, and finally we ask if they would join us in the balcony, as if it's some exclusive seating area. They said yes.

The main feature is already playing as the four of us climb the seven or eight steps to the balcony in the dark. We find four seats together about midway in the balcony. My brother and his new friend step into the seat row, and then my new friend and I move in. You could smoke in the balcony in those days, and as I look back up into the darkness, I see a couple of red dots of lit cigarettes, along with shadows of a few older people and the smell of alcohol. We get settled in and I wonder what grown person would be sitting in the balcony at the tail end of a kid show in the middle of a Saturday afternoon. I then remind myself this is New Year's Eve Day, and those people in the back have started their holiday a little early. The main floor below the balcony is in the throes of its normal kid show chaos, sailing popcorn boxes and lots of noise, so we're able to talk with our new friends without worrying about disturbing anybody. The more we talk, the more smitten I'm becoming with the person beside me. I find out she lives on an "M" street about two blocks from the Granada, along with lots of other interesting stuff.

Pillow Talk, with Rock Hudson and Doris Day, is the featured movie for that day, and Rock, posing as a wealthy Texas rancher named Rex Stetson, is trying to rope in Doris. In one scene, Doris asks Rock about Texas and he responds, "Well, Texas is a great state."

Behind us, in the dark, comes a thunderous outburst from one of the adult patrons, slurring as he yells,

"WELL HELL YES TEXAS IS A GREAT STATE, AND WHOEVER DON'T THINK TEXAS IS A GREAT STATE CAN KISS MY ASS!"

As the words echo off the walls, the theater immediately goes quiet, as if the audience is making a value judgement of what they think they've just heard. Hearing no opposition, the noise and chaos starts up again. Of course everyone in the balcony stops making out and is looking around trying to determine the source of this comment. Lots of going up and down stairs with friends, conferring with other groups and laughing. Lots of young curiosity.

"There's some drunks in the back of the balcony," says one kid.

"Yeah, and I heard there's gonna' be a gang fight in the parking lot after the show," says another.

Suddenly, word passes among the teenaged cognoscenti and the kid show atmosphere becomes electric, in anticipation of some real life scene right out of the *Wild One.*

"Is Snake and his gang going to show up?"

"Who's the other gang?"

"Are the drunks in the back of the balcony part of this?"

"Are cops going to be called."

"Can I have the rest of your popcorn?"

Of course my brother and I, being noncombatants in gang warfare, are going to stick around with our new friends and other kids to watch the show after the show. At the conclusion of the main feature, hundreds of kids run out of the darkened theater straight into a blast of bright afternoon sunshine. Scrambling and running into each other with squinty eyes, we make our way to the gravel parking lot behind the Granada. Everybody is just hanging around waiting for something to happen. A couple of older kids have joined the crowd sporting their black motorcycle jackets with zippers, and duck tail haircuts, but they're observers like the rest of us. The minutes are passing and attention deficit is challenging some of the younger kids as they start making their way home.

Suddenly, the sound of a Triumph motorcycle can be heard in the distance. Into the back parking lot speeds Snake toward the young crowd, sliding to a stop, kicking up gravel and dust. The crowd steps back a little, in awe. As the dust settles, Snake dismounts, extending to his full five-and-a-half foot height, he reaches into a satchel on his motorcycle and retrieves a twelve inch length of chain, which I notice looks brand new. He starts walking through the crowd trying to find out what's going on. Nobody seems to know, and nothing happens. No gang, no drunks, no cops. It's after 4 p.m. New Year's Eve day and the young crowd breaks up and leaves for home, without a chain being flung. My brother and I walk our new friends home. Spending that unusually exciting day at the kid show with my new friend becomes a defining moment in my life. We agree to see each other again. And so, years of long conversations and interesting times together begin. We were married on February 8, 1969, and have tread through life's setbacks and successes. We have two children and two granddaughters, and are enjoying retirement and a full life together.

Long before the iPhone or the computer, the kid show transported us from our familiar neighborhood to a larger world every Saturday. It was a social event, emblematic of a period in time when life seemed to be simpler and more coherent. As my wife and I approach our forty-eighth anniversary, we will always consider the kid show on New Year's Eve Day 1962 as our beginning.

Hyce Shaw III is 69 years old and has enjoyed a life full of comical experiences. He has told this story of how he and his wife met to many friends through the years. This is his first opportunity to write for publication.

Honorable Mention

Zugzwang

Don Shook

A light snow was falling as Charlie Reardon left the diner and made his way down Madison Street. Laurel had recently moved into an apartment three blocks away and he wanted to be there when she arrived. Tightening the navy blue scarf around his neck, he fastened his top coat while admiring the wet flakes brushing his cheeks. His eleven D's left footprints in the quickly accumulating sidewalk powder as he determined his stride would put him there in five to ten minutes. Across the street, squinting against the glare, a man crossed and fell in step behind, keeping enough separation not to be noticed, but not too much to lose contact.

Less than a mile in the opposite direction, Laurel Stanton ended her work day. She hated punching out but went through the motions and, slamming the heavy glass-paneled door behind, carefully hurried down the school's steep steps. Snow had begun to swirl and she noticed the concrete was glazing over. "God, where did this come from?" she muttered, bracing against a suddenly stiff arctic wind. Shivering slightly, she buttoned her light jacket, took a deep breath and girded mind and body for the struggle she anticipated walking home. Still, the exercise would do her good, perhaps even clear her mind.

Neither Laurel nor Charlie Reardon had slept the night before, each carrying the evening's argument to bed and rekindling it with every restless recall. Love tracks a jagged course and, after months of smooth, effortless sailing, they had hit heavy waves. A few restaurant patrons glanced over as their conversation roiled.

"That's ridiculous!" Charlie bellowed, totally frustrated.

"Says you," Laurel replied.

"Says anyone who thinks."

"You think I'm stupid."

"I think you're a bit chauvinistic."

"I'm no feminist, Charlie."

"Chauvinism has little to do with feminists. It refers to blind loyalty. And you're loyal to him without considering the ramifications."

Laurel swallowed a retort, biting her lip as she tapped an index finger on the tabletop. His ability to verbalize coherent sentences had always impressed her, but tonight made her furious. Charlie was on the edge of continuing when a smartly-attired waiter suddenly appeared.

"Dessert, sir? We have…"

"No sweets tonight," Laurel interrupted, glistening hazel eyes firmly fixed on Charlie.

"Check please," Charlie intoned, motioning with one hand.

Laurel moved to snatch the check. Charlie was quicker. "I've got it," he insisted.

"Fine."

There was a moment's silence as he examined the bill and flipped a debit card to the waiter who took it and left. Laurel sat quietly, random thoughts assaulting her consciousness. Unsure of his next move, she was mentally exploring alternatives. Unlike Charlie, she seldom acted without thinking things through. What he proposed had shaken her, sending a wave of emotion over her usual steady tide of logic.

"Well?" Charlie finally asked, looking almost defiantly into her eyes.

"Well what?"

"What do you say to my proposition?"

"I don't even believe I heard it."

"Why?"

"Well," she answered, her anger rising, "you're either the most audacious person I've ever met or you have absolutely no respect for my feelings."

"Explain."

"Explain? Explain what? You explain why you think I'd ever consider being someone's sex toy!"

"I never said that."

"Well pardon me, but that's what I understood. If you didn't say that, then exactly what did you say?"

"I said that if our relationship is as strong as I think it is, it would only become stronger."

"And that we should treat sex like chess, experimenting with different moves."

"That's right."

"That's sick."

"What's sick about combining fun with physical pleasure? Or perhaps you consider them mutually exclusive."

"What's that supposed to mean?"

"Laurel, our verbal rapport's a game, why not sex?"

"Oh sure, I could be your pawn you crown after we mate."

"You're mixing metaphors."

"What?"

"You crown in checkers, not chess."

"Whatever!"

"I hate that."

"What?"

"Using 'whatever' as a surrogate for 'whatever' it is you mean."

"Why don't you learn to talk like everyone else so I can understand you?"

"Why don't you learn to understand me so I don't have to talk like everyone else?"

"Oh screw you!"

"Best idea you've had all night."

"Sometimes I just hate you!"

"And sometimes you love me..."

"I...I know." A smile nipped the corner of her mouth. "Sometimes I do love you."

Charlie smiled back. "Then why don't you just forget him and be with me?"

"Exclusively?"

"Exclusively." He sat back and waited.

Laurel started to speak, then stopped, cueing a long silence which seemed to fill the gulf that had opened between them. She stared deeply into his pale blue eyes. Finally, Charlie broke the silence.

"Well?"

"I don't know," she answered, absently looking away.

"Don't know?"

"Mark and I have been together so long. It's not easy to just..."

"I thought you were going to tell him..."

"I'm trying, but..."

Suddenly he erupted. "What the hell's the matter with you?"

"Huh?" Laurel responded, shocked and taken completely off guard.

"For two months now you've been breaking up with the guy."

"I know...but we've talked about this."

"Too long."

"I've told you, I owe him."

"And me?"

"I want you."

"But you still need him?"

Laurel started to speak, paused, then responded with an emphatic, "Yes! And I'm not sure how he'll react...what he'll do."

Charlie sighed and stood up as the waiter returned his card.

Two minutes and twenty steps later, they hurried into the night, the restaurant's marquee lights bouncing off indurate expressions, a falling barometer failing to cool simmering temperaments.

"Thanks for dinner," she spat sarcastically.

"My pleasure," he responded, opening the car door. No further conversation ensued on a silent ride to her apartment and a stout clunk of his car door as she headed inside and he roared away.

But that was last night. Both had thought it over during their sleepless hours and, with the weather, tempers chilled.

Charlie walked faster as the light snow thickened. He was anxious to make amends, to apologize for trying to force her hand. It had resulted in a bad scene in a public place...never a good idea. Why hadn't he waited? He knew about Mark Johnston when he'd begun seeing her. She was gradually pulling away. She'd even told Johnston about him. Why hadn't he waited?

Only moments earlier, while sipping coffee at Webb's Diner, Charlie had examined the gift he purchased. Surely, the pearl necklace would make an impressive peace offering. Laurel, like most women, loved ornaments, and this one was lovely. Like her, he thought, delicate yet solid and steadfast. Second guessing was instinctive for Charlie so, naturally, self-excoriation drowned rational thought and a gift was the answer. It said: "I'm sorry. I was wrong. Forgive me and let's forget it." He should never have made such a radical suggestion at dinner the night before. But, also instinctive, was his proclivity for following through on occasional bad ideas. He held the necklace at arm's length and smiled.

Across Madison Street, masked in the shadow of an office building and focused on the diner's picture window, the man watched Charlie lower the necklace and put it back in the box. His eyes continued to follow as Charlie rose, walked to the counter to pay for his coffee, then shuffled out into the sudden storm. It was then he crossed the narrow street and fell in step.

Meanwhile, still some distance away, Laurel fought the wind's sharp bite, her light jacket offering scant protection. *I should have called a cab,* she thought, hurrying while assessing her current crop of bad decisions. Juggling Mark and Charlie had only diminishing returns. She should never have told either about the other. She couldn't have them both.

For months now she'd clung to the past while grasping for the future. She knew you couldn't square a triangle, but each man filled the other's gaps. Charlie was new, kind, considerate and, until last night in the restaurant, predictable. On the other hand, she had been with Mark forever, but she simply couldn't attach her future to him. In the beginning, his propensity for the unexpected had been stimulating. She never knew what was coming next. But two years of surprises had become tedious. If stability was an island, Mark was a tsunami, whose surge had swept away any hope of domestic bliss.

The wind howled through the canyon of buildings bordering either side of Madison, a dropping thermometer prompting a brief pause in Laurel's trudge homeward. Leaning against one of the many small frontage shops, she caught her breath, wondering if she should venture inside and warm up before continuing, maybe even call that cab. Already exhausted, she still had three or four blocks to go.

Charlie Reardon sensed he was being followed. As he snapped his head around, a quick glance through the downdrift revealed a figure looking his way perhaps 50 yards down the deserted street. A white cloak coated the parked cars and, as Charlie grabbed another look, the figure moved a hand inside his coat, apparently fishing for keys in his pants pocket. Charlie sighed and resumed his walk toward Laurel's, haunted by an eerie uneasiness.

Having taken shelter in the small boutique, Laurel glanced at the various knick-knacks gorging the narrow bins. Generally speaking, the store was ram shackled clutter, reeking of jasmine, honey-suckle and an array of other aromatic clusters...yielding a pleasant, intoxicating aroma. In the back corners, incense burners yielded thin veils of spiraling smoke, a noisome intrusion to the room's aromatic warmth.

She contemplated staying there until the storm weakened. Another bad idea. If anything, the snowstorm was becoming a blizzard, wind whipping thick flakes horizontally, lashing the few brave, struggling souls Laurel saw pass by outside. No, she'd better sit tight for a while longer. Surely, the storm would let up soon.

Mark Johnston wasn't sure if he'd been detected or not. He had reacted instinctively, unlocking his car door. His rival had stopped briefly, looked back, but then turned and kept walking. Mark realized they were approaching the apartment building where Laurel lived and had thought to proceed on foot. Trailing Charlie from the diner in his car was exasperatingly slow, but when he parked and got out, he was seen almost immediately. So now he amended that option.

Earlier in the day, Laurel's unexpected call had surprised and angered him. Several hours of fuming, a quart of eighty-eight proof, and a subsequent rage had spurred a series of actions, the first of which was locating his adversary. The next, and the one in which he was now engaged, involved his dealing with the source of his angst. He was calmer now, under control, and had mentally designed an insidious plan for dealing with Charlie Reardon. Absently, he patted the .38 Special inside his coat pocket.

A light snow had been falling when Charlie Reardon left the diner and headed down Madison Street. Mark was close behind almost as quickly as the snowfall had begun to increase. In less than a minute, the full force of the norther hit. However, the cold air blast and increasing snow failed to deter Mark from his resolve. Deducing the obvious, that Charlie was headed to Laurel's apartment, he had already decided what had to be done. Now it was a matter of execution. Bad weather wasn't going to change that.

Laurel's relationship with Mark had been exciting in the beginning. He courted her constantly with expensive gifts and excursions to exotic places. A dozen times he had popped the question. Each time she had hesitated and delayed, somehow sensing that Mark was not what gifts implied. There was some underlying, almost sinister, proclivity that frightened even as it stimulated. A year after it had begun, she knew it was over but had done nothing about it until Charlie came along.

Meeting at a poetry society gathering, she and Charlie had instant rapport…emotional fireworks leapt between them and ignited both libidos, leaving Laurel wondering what had happened. When he called her the next day she was thrilled, broke a planned evening with Mark, and she and Charlie began a whirlwind romance. It took six weeks before his frustration with romance minus sex became a problem. Then he discovered that she was still involved with Mark. He pressed her to make a complete break. Her response was not what he wanted.

"What's the problem?"

"I'm just not ready."

"You certainly seem ready up until the magic moment…"

"I know, but I'm just not ready."

"But the way we kiss, the way we touch, everything tells me you are ready. And I certainly am."

"Charlie, it's going to happen…soon. I promise. But first…"

"I know. First you have to get over him."

Laurel turned away.

"Right?" he persisted.

She looked at him, eyes unwavering. "Yes, when I'm over him."

"Well, don't you think it's about time?"

"Not yet."

"Then when?" Charlie pleaded.

Today, Laurel thought, casually handling a jar of colorful potpourri, inadvertently lost in the multicolored mixture. Something about the brilliant contents, or perhaps the intoxicating aroma of the room, seemed to soothe and focus her jumbled thoughts. It suddenly became obvious what she had to do. Today's the day I end it with Mark. I love Charlie and he deserves my all. No more scenes like last night. Today. Looking up and out the storefront window, she saw no letup in the snow storm; but she did see a couple outside struggling successfully and decided she could do the same. Placing the jar back in place, she walked toward the front door. Her head was spinning.

Charlie paused at the bottom of the red-stone stoop leading up to the door of Laurel's apartment building. Though the snow was swirling around him and the wind howling incessantly, he reached inside his coat pocket and withdrew the box holding the pearl necklace. He had to confirm its presence, the reassurance that one final look at his peace offering would provide. He would be waiting just inside the apartment house entrance and when she opened the door he would dazzle her. Waving thick, wet flakes aside, and using his back as a shield against the wind, he pulled the lid off the box.

Suddenly a strong gust tore around the corner of the stoop. It ripped the box lid from his hand, whipping it up into the air. Startled, and automatically shoving the box into his coat pocket, Charlie lunged and then scurried after the wayward lid as it careened down the street, seeming alive...bouncing off one obstacle then another.

Fifty feet away, obscured by what had become blinding snow, a dark figure in a heavy, black coat and pull-over cap lumbered toward Charlie. Earlier, he had watched through the diner window as Charlie examined the necklace. He had trailed Charlie through the building storm, careful not to be seen. But now, unexpectedly, he saw his chance...there was an opening he had not expected.

Simultaneously, a silver Lexus slid to a halt at the far-side curb. Forcing the door open, Mark Johnston fought his way out and onto the street. Charlie Reardon was about to get the fright of his life. But what the hell was he after in the snow? And who was the large dark figure that ran after him? No matter. He had made up his mind. Struggling to stay upright against a fierce crosswind, he moved forward.

Shivering with each quick stride, Laurel had only a block to go. The warmth she'd absorbed in the curio shop vanished the moment she stepped out the door and into the arctic cold sweeping down Madison Street. She had to move faster. She had to get home...home and inside. Her new apartment would be warm, inviting, out of the wind and the dreadful snowstorm. She had to walk faster. She would call Charlie, ask him over, and make love to him. Yes, yes, yes warm and soothing love with Charlie. She had to walk faster.

The lid was gone. Charlie stopped and watched its erratic trip down the street, whipping past cars, garbage cans, and other stone stoops. Then, taking flight between the canyon walls...it was gone. Charlie cursed, caught his breath and turned back toward Laurel's apartment building. As he approached the stoop, the impact knocked him off his feet.

Mark was in the middle of the street when the huge figure crashed into Charlie. He started to yell; but no warning would have prepared Charlie for the collision. Suddenly he was on his back, seized by his scarf and having his head beat against the snow-covered concrete. Dazed, he felt a hand fumbling through his coat pocket. Instinctively he flailed away but could tell his strikes were impotent. The necklace was yanked out of his pocket. The assailant released the scarf, jumped back, and turned to run. Charlie twisted up and grabbed a leg. "Stop!" he yelled, only to be answered by blows raining down on his face. Still, he held on. "Stop, damnit, stop!" A desperate, violet kick cracked Charlie's rib. A gunshot rang through the storm.

Clutching his ribcage, Charlie rolled into a fetal ball. The huge man pulled away and trudged up Madison Street. Mark Johnston held the .38 Special at waist level, its barrel the only warmth on the street. He quickly stuffed it back in his coat, got in the silver Lexus and drove away.

Laurel Stanton had heard the gunshot, but wasn't sure what it was. Now, as she approached her apartment building, she was rudely bumped by a huge figure scurrying past. Too cold to respond, she watched him fade up the street, disappearing into the storm. When she turned back she saw what looked to be a man on the walk below her stoop. Cautiously she approached the groaning figure, confused by the dark crimson blotches staining the white mantle between them.

Two blocks away, Mark Johnston sat behind the wheel. He was sober now, his mind clear. My God, what had he done? Negotiating the silver Lexus away from Madison Street, he drove very slowly, very carefully...no time to be stopped. He had only meant to frighten Charlie, not to...My God, what have I done? He had no permit, had a record, and so had to disappear. Surely, some airline would be departing...even in the storm.

David Ray Carter, ex-pro wrestler, used the alley wall to brace himself, in fact, to stay on his feet. Looking down at the brilliant pearl necklace in his hand, he figured it would buy lots of Jack Daniels. David Ray looked skyward, seeing only a distant grey separating dark silhouettes of old city buildings. The flakes now drifting down between the buildings were getting smaller, the storm was letting up. The snow felt good on his face…cold and soothing. Despite his tattered, dark coat and sock-cap, which were warm enough, he was feeling cold all over…not just on his face. Yes, he was beginning to shiver, cold everywhere but just below the ribcage on his left side. There was heat there. It was hot and moist, and the source of the sticky liquid running down his pants leg…beginning to pool in the snow at his feet.

It had taken 20 minutes to help Charlie up the steps and into Laurel's apartment. Getting his clothes off had taken almost as long. Cleaning his facial wounds and wrapping his ribcage took her even longer. But now, two hours later, he was securely resting in her bed, propped up on Styrofoam pillows, watching television while sipping a cup of hot tea.

It was warm inside and like most upscale, new apartments, Laurel's smelled freshly scrubbed. The storm was tapering off, the fierce wind subsiding, bequeathing only tree limbs scraping against the bedroom window. The police had been called and the report made. It would be several hours before the corpse of David Ray Daniels would be found lodged between two garbage bins in the alley a block away; and another 10 days before Laurel would hear from Mark, hiding in Panama.

In the meantime, there was a game to play:

"Sorry," Charlie said, "it's hard to make that move."

"Bull. You're just using the ribs as a diversion," Laurel replied, snuggling closer to him in the bed.

"I told you it would be like chess," he chuckled.

"One more word and I really will crown you."

"There you go again."

"I know…mixing metaphors."

"Yes, I…"

"Charlie…shut up."

She laid her head on his shoulder and promptly fell asleep. Charlie smiled, turned and looked out the window. A light snow was falling as he mentally left the diner and made his way down Madison Street.

※

Don Shook, past president of the Fort Worth Poetry Society, was also founder and head of The Actors Company, one of the nation's leading theater companies. He is a writer, actor, director and producer who has worked with such stars as Dick Clark, Cybil Shepherd, Debbie Reynolds and Betty Buckley. Formerly with NBC in New York, he has performed in theatre, film and television across the country including an opera performance at Carnegie Hall, New York City and five years as a resident performer at Casa Manana Musicals in Fort Worth. He is the author of a recently published novel *Bluehole,* and two poetry books, and was selected as 2009 Senior Poet Laureate of Texas. Current head of Don Shook Productions, he offers entertainment productions ranging from full-scale murder mysteries to one-man dramatic presentations.

Honorable Mention

JUST A PETTY THIEF

Donald McElfresh

Bennie Raskin was just a petty thief. Short and thin, he had a pinch-nosed look to him. When he looked at you his eyes seemed to follow along the length of his nose, as if it was a rifle barrel and he was zeroing in on a target. Bennie never felt that being short was a problem. In fact, in his profession it was often an advantage. The only time being short had worked against him was when he was drafted in '68 and went to Vietnam. Because he was short, they put him in the tunnels chasing the Viet Cong. He did his best to forget, but sometimes the memories came back and reminded him that there were worse things than bad tempered cops.

Bennie did not like the dark of night. However, in the dark he could fade into the shadows and become one with the dumpsters and garbage stacked in the alleys. As long as he could see where he was going, Bennie could handle the dark. It was when he got into tight areas where he couldn't move around that it bothered him. That fear was deep within him. So deep, he couldn't get over it, no matter how hard he tried.

Bennie's window air conditioner wasn't working and the bedroom was hot and sticky. He was having a hard time sleeping and as he drifted off his old nightmare began again.

It was 1968 in a Viet Cong tunnel in Chu Lai Province, South

Vietnam. Private Bennie Raskin and Corporal "Rabbit" Dietrick were crawling through a narrow dirt tunnel, pistols and flashlights in their hands. Rabbit crawled in front of Bennie. Rabbit was the lead "tunnel rat" for the team. Hard packed clay, with tree roots hacked off, but still projecting, formed the walls of the tunnel. It was a communication tunnel and somewhere ahead of them were the tunnel rooms for supplies and hospital. The tunnel took a hard turn and there in front of Rabbit was a wall at the end of the tunnel. Turning his flashlight upward, Rabbit spotted a trap door carved out of the ceiling. As he looked toward the trap door, it quickly opened and a hand dropped a grenade into the tunnel. Immediately, the trap door closed.

Bennie yelled, "Rabbit…grenade," and twisted around toward the entrance of the tunnel. As he looked over his shoulder he saw Rabbit also turn away from the grenade, when an explosion rocked the tunnel. Bennie didn't get hurt. Bennie saw Rabbit reach for him when another grenade went off and the tunnel collapsed.

There was a rapid knock on the door to the apartment, accompanied by a loud female voice that brought Bennie out of his sleep, and his nightmare.

"Mr. Raskin. Mr. Raskin. You okay in there?" It was Mrs. Grabowski, from Apartment 2-G, across the hall. The knocking on the door became louder and more insistent, "Mr. Raskin." Bennie rolled over and rose up.

"Yeh, Mrs. G., I'm okay, just a nightmare."

"You sure? I could hear you yell all the way to my apartment."

"Yeh, I'm sure."

"Goodnight Mr. Raskin. Try to get some sleep."

Bennie turned on the light next to his bed and looked at the tangle of wet and twisted sheets. His hand shook as he reached onto the nightstand for a cigarette. As he lit it, and lay there propped up against the headboard, he thought and took deep drags on the cigarette. His fear lay there with him.

Bennie liked children; maybe because they were short like him and never questioned who he was and what he did. Mrs. Grabowski's two kids, Alicia and Fedor, wanted to go to the zoo today, and he had nothing else to do. Besides, he liked Mrs. G., and knew she looked out for him. So, the three of them left the apartment building and went to the corner where they took first one bus, then another, and got to the zoo by ten o'clock. There was plenty of time to see all the animals and birds and snakes and reptiles.

They were standing in front of a large glass case full of snakes when Alicia tugged at him and pointed to a large snake in the case and said, "Uncle Bennie, what's that?"

"That's a jungle snake, they live in the rocks and jungle vines. You gotta look out for them. They'll crawl into where you sleep." The damn snake reminded him of Nam! "You don't gotta worry sweetie, you'll never be where they are."

"Were you ever in the jungles, Uncle Bennie?"

"Long time ago." *But never again,* he thought.

"What was it like?" asked Alicia.

"Hot, wet and dirty," answered Bennie, looking at another case full of snakes.

"Why did you go there?"

"Didn't wanna go, but the Army sent me anyhow."

Bennie had lost sight of Fedor while talking to Alicia, and began looking around the display area to find where Fedor had gone.

"Alicia," said Bennie, "you see Fedor anywhere?"

"Maybe he's behind that case over there," said Alicia, pointing to a large, floor-to-ceiling case full of snakes. Three of the sides were glass and one side was a painted wall forest scene with dangling vines and tree limbs.

Bennie took Alicia by the hand and walked toward the large case. The room was dark with low level lights spaced infrequently along the walls. The air was wet with humidity, leaving a light sheen of moisture on the marble floor surface. Even though his eyes had adjusted to the low level of the lights, he couldn't help but bump into the wall in the hallway behind the large case. Alicia tugged at his hand and pulled him forward into the gloomy passageway. Bennie pulled back and her hand slipped out of his. He turned to look for her in the darkness.

"Alicia? Fedor? Where you guys?" There was no answer. Bennie turned, and then turned again; he became disoriented and confused. The narrow hallway seemed to fill with a dark, heavy fog. Fog so warm and thick that he couldn't find where he had entered or where he could leave. He began to sweat and his breathing quickened. He smelled the mold and stagnant air within the fog. His shoulder muscles tightened and it felt as if a band had encircled his chest making it even harder to breathe. Bennie shrank within himself. A name slipped out of his lips, "Rabbit." Fear and panic overcame him. A child's hand touched his and as quickly as it had filled the hallway, the fog drifted away until he could see through the gloom.

"Uncle Bennie, I found Fedor." It was Alicia. Her small, round face, and large, dark eyes were illuminated. "Uncle Bennie," she repeated, looking into his face. He looked down at her. The band gradually slipped away from his chest, his breathing slowed, and finally barely able to speak he said, "Where'd you go?"

"Fedor had to go pee pee and I found him. He should a told us, shouldn't he, Uncle Bennie?"

"Yeh, sweetie, you're right," said Bennie. Holding tight to her hand, Bennie and Alicia walked back into the display room where Fedor stood next to a case, tapping on the glass to get the attention of a large snake. Fedor didn't look up as they approached and kept tapping on the case.

Bennie and Squirrel Kagan, one of Bennie's buddies from the old neighborhood, were seated in a booth in a near empty "Long Gone Joe's" bar on 83rd Street.

"I tell you Bennie, we oughta try the house I told you about. It's gotta be easy pickings. Them people are gone most of the evenings. I think they both work nights. The streets and houses got lots of trees and bushes. You could march an army of whores off State Street through there at 9 o'clock at night, and no one would even notice. Them people sit and watch their TV's and then off to bed."

Lazy Harry was tending the bar. Lazy was putting the make on an over fifties lady, who wore too much makeup, carried too much weight, and drank too many shooters. Watching Lazy with the lady, Bennie said, "They sure are made for each other," and chuckled.

"Bennie, forget Lazy and listen to me. I tell you it's a cinch. You could jimmy a door or window in no time. The house is an old house and easy. I've seen in through the windows. They keep a big jewelry box on top a dresser in a bedroom on the side of the house. I saw a big diamond ring on the dresser, next to the box. I bet you she don't wear that one when she's at work. You could be in and out, as quick as greased lighting. I'll stay outside and keep a look out. We'll be gone before anyone knows."

"I don't like it Squirrel, I'm not a house man," said Bennie, "and I like to work by myself."

"Yeah, I know, but this is special. It's an easy one."

"How we get there? I ain't got no car and yours ain't exactly a get-away car."

"I got 'at covered. I can borrow my brother-in-law's for a night, just as long as I get it back before he goes to work in a morning. He don't care."

Bennie threw down his shot, sipped his beer, and then moved the cardboard coaster under his glass, back and forth, back and forth. He didn't say anything.

"Well, what about it, you wanna do it?" said Squirrel.

"Let me think on it," said Bennie.

"While you're thinking, I'm gonna get us another round. Hey Lazy, bring us another round, will you?"

Lazy Harry, looking up, nodded, "Just a sec!"

Bennie frowned at Kagan. He didn't like doing a house; people in houses are too personal. Not like people in apartments. Those in apartments are like those in the subway, strictly transients. He let go of the glass, lit a cigarette and took a deep drag. He said, "Okay

181

Squirrel, we do it next Tuesday night. We meet here at nine. You can get the car?"

"No sweat," said Squirrel.

"But, it's gotta be easy."

"No sweat."

Bennie got out of the Chevy, and looked down at Squirrel where he sat in the car with the driver's window rolled down. "You stay here, and if you have to, slump down in the seat so no one can see you if they drive by. I'll be back in about fifteen minutes. Don't get antsy, leave here and go look for me if I'm more than fifteen minutes. Just stay put. You know?"

Squirrel, dimly seen in the light from the street, nodded. In a dry, squeaky voice, Squirrel said, "I'll wait here, but you make it quick."

Bennie cleared his throat, spat and started down the alley. The light from the cloud shaded moon and the little light spilling out of the few lit windows on the sides of the alley helped Bennie see where to walk. The alley was nothing more than hard packed dirt, cut into rivulets by the thick tires of the garbage trucks. Every so often he would brush up against a large, soft sack of stinking trash. Trash that smelled like something dead; something decomposing from the heat. He climbed over the low, wood framed fence into the backyard of the house.

The fence couldn't have been more than three feet high. He wondered, who they think they gonna keep out with this? He walked with care as he made his way through the yard. To walk on the hard, dry clay, with little or no grass or weeds as cover, was as if he was walking on broken pieces of concrete. In the dark the wall of the house appeared quicker than he had expected. Bennie touched the wall with his fingertips. He could feel the rough faces of the brick and the sandy feel of the mortar in the masonry joints. He moved along the wall toward the front of the house where deep, black shadows blocked out the light from the street. Soon he was able to find the narrow wood stairs to the front porch, where he crouched and with short, careful steps made his way onto the covered porch. Bennie crossed the porch to the screen door at the entrance. There were no lights on inside.

Guess Squirrel was right, they're gone, he thought.

Bennie opened the screen door and sheltering the door with his body, turned on his flashlight. The front door was an old wood door whose finish had peeled off a long time ago. The lock was a simple keyed lock. Bennie reached into his windbreaker and pulled out his wrapped tool kit. Removing the thin strap from the tool kit, he opened it and selected a set of keys from the side pocket. The third key unlocked and opened the door. He moved inside, straightened up and gently closed the screen door and the heavy wood door to the porch that he relocked with care. Afraid that someone might see his light from the outside, Bennie kept his flashlight covered as he moved through the room looking for the bedroom with the diamond ring.

Squirrel better be right, Bennie said to himself.

Off the living room was a narrow hallway with four open doors along the length of it, with two on each side. As he walked along the hallway he would stop at an open door and flash his light inside. The first three doors were to two small bedrooms and a bathroom. The fourth door was the master bedroom, complete with an oversized bed, two side tables and two dressers. At the foot of the bed lay several plastic bag enclosed garments; probably just returned from the cleaners. The big jewelry box was on the largest of the two dressers. Bennie went to the box, opened it, and flashed his light inside; nothing but costume jewelry. No diamond ring; nothing worth taking. Bennie moved his flashlight around the room. The dressers and tables had nothing on them but mounted photos and books. He opened drawer after drawer, and found clothes and cuff links, but again nothing worth taking.

I knowed I should'a stayed with apartments, thought Bennie, *I should'a never let Squirrel talk me into this.* Bennie went to the corner of the bedroom and opened the door to the large, walk-in closet. The closet had hanging clothing and boxes in it. There were boxes on the floor, boxes under the clothing and even upper shelves that were stacked with shoe boxes. The house ceiling wasn't low like in an apartment, but high like the old timey houses. So high that there was a ladder in the closet that leaned against a wall. It was almost hidden by hanging suits and other garments. After he closed the closet door Bennie turned on the closet light above him by pulling the light chain. He looked through the boxes as quick as he could; sometimes people put valuables in shoe boxes. There was nothing there.

He used the ladder to climb up and look in the boxes on the shelves near the ceiling. After he climbed down, he returned the ladder to its hidden position. He kneeled down and looked in the boxes on the floor under the hanging garments. No luck there, either. On the floor of the closet he found a square panel. *Maybe they hid their stuff under the house,* he thought. *They can do that in a house, where they can't in an apartment.* Using the blade of his pocket knife he found the joint between the panel and the floor. He pried up the edge of the panel. It was difficult due to the limited space in the closet; but he didn't want to open the closet door, to turn off the closet light, and use only his flashlight. He placed the panel on the floor next to the opening. Below the opening, Bennie could see dirt under the house and about a foot and a half below him, the crawl space. Bennie stepped down into the opening and as he crouched with his flashlight, he looked around under the floor in all directions. There was nothing. Only a musty smell, old pieces of pipe, lumber and empty beer bottles. No boxes or anything that looked valuable.

The silence was broken by the sound of the front door being shut. It was like a loud scream had pierced through the house and into the closet. Fear sent blood charging through his veins. For several seconds Bennie crouched frozen; unable to move. He heard footsteps in the hallway coming toward the bedroom. Bennie finally broke loose and pulled on the chain, turning off the closet light. He slipped down into the crawl space and as he lay on his back he pulled the panel into place above him. Shaking and breathing heavily, Bennie gulped and held his breath as he tried to be quiet. His heart beat so loud that he felt sure that whoever was in the house could hear it. The closet door opened and someone pulled the ladder from where it lay against the wall. After a few minutes the person left the closet, walked out of the bedroom, and soon shut the front door to the house. Bennie, still on the ground beneath the floor, began to breathe again. Exhausted, he raised himself upward and reached for the floor panel.

Outside the house, at the curb, a car sat idling, its lights off with a man seated in it behind the steering wheel. The man looked up as the door to the house closed and a woman's figure came down the steps and opened the door to the car.

"Are you set now?" he asked of the woman as she closed the car door.

"Oh yes," she replied, "I'm sorry we had to come back, but I needed to pick up a couple things from the cleaners and my dress shoes that were in boxes in the top of the closet. I told you it would only take a few minutes."

"Did you lock the door?"

"Of course, I did. But, there's nothing there for anyone to steal. I've put my valuable jewelry in our lock box at the bank, and have only my wedding band with me. I can pick up the rest when we get back in two weeks."

He switched on the car lights and they drove away for their first real vacation in years.

Bennie held his flashlight in one hand and pushed at the bottom of the floor panel with his free hand. The panel wouldn't move.

"It's stuck," he said out loud. He began to panic, and then pushed harder. Above him in the closet, the ladder the woman had used was still in place above the panel, with the top of it wedged between the wall and the shelf. Bennie pushed still harder. The heat and humidity in the crawl space grew in intensity. He lay there for a minute. His mind raced, with the twin shadows of fear and panic engulfing him – his two, always available, unwelcome visitors. Bennie lay on his back with his legs bent. He was able to push with his feet on the panel above. He exerted all the strength he could muster in pushing against the panel. It barely moved. It was as if it was nailed in place. Bennie felt bands around his chest increase in intensity. He rolled onto his side and slowed his breathing, to regain control. He reached into his pocket and pulled out his pocket knife. He rolled back under the panel, and opened his knife. With his flashlight he was able to find the joint between the panel and the rest of the floor. Bennie pulled at a sharp piece of broken wood in the corner of the panel; he could feel it give a little, and then snap back into place. He reached upward with his knife until he found the corner again. He inserted the knife blade into the joint and tried to cut into the wood.

"If I can cut a piece out of the wood maybe I can get my fingers into the joint and work loose whatever has stopped the panel," Bennie said out loud.

The light from the flashlight dimmed, and the panel joints got harder to see. Sweat from his forehead trickled into his eyes. The salt from the sweat stung so bad he had trouble seeing the panel. With his right hand he quickly carved slivers of wood off the edge of the panel. Again, the flashlight began to dim. Bennie tore at the wood in the corner of the panel with his knife when the flashlight went out and the knife blade snapped. The crawl space became pitch black. The bands around his chest tightened, and his mouth got dry. Bennie's screams started from deep within him and grew until the space under the floor reverberated with his screams. Memories of Rabbit and the tunnel returned as he clawed at the panel with bleeding fingers. Bennie's screams became lower and quieter until all that was left was the darkness and the harshness of Bennie's screams as they turned into choking sobs.

❦

Donald McElfresh is 84 years old, from Chicago's south side, was a destroyer sailor during the Korean War, spent 50 years in the building industry, and has been happily married for 32 years to a former Delta flight attendant from Oklahoma. He writes about real people and real life. Worthy of note: it took him 4-1/2 years to graduate from high school because he failed an English class.

FACING THE PAST

Carol Kuczek

The doorbell rang. Pam glanced up at the wall clock as she stopped washing her breakfast dishes. "Who's bugging me at 8:15 on a Saturday morning?" she muttered. She grabbed the kitchen towel off the counter, stepped around the oscillating fan, and marched down the hall, drying her hands along the way.

The stained glass panel in the door hazed the figure on the other side, though she could tell it was a man who stood on her front porch. Pam flipped the damp towel over her shoulder, turned the dead bolt, twisted the brass knob, and pulled open the door.

"Good morning," he said. "I have an overnight delivery that needs your signature."

Pam signed the driver's digital pad. "Thank you," she said, and took the envelope.

"Have a nice day." He turned and headed to his truck.

Still annoyed, Pam made her way back to the kitchen. She had to deal with interruptions at work all the time. She didn't need them on her day off.

At the table she examined the mailer addressed to her: Pamela Morgan of Madison, Wisconsin. She pulled the tab across the cardboard wrapper, fished out the contents, and started to read.

The further she read the medical report, the more Pam shook her head in disbelief. There isn't any way I'm going along with this.

While mulling over the urgent news, Pam pitched the letter onto the kitchen table, but before it landed the breeze from the oscillating fan floated the paper to the floor. When she reached to pick it up, she noticed the sheet had flipped over. A handwritten message, in bold strokes, covered the page.

He begged her to come, pleaded with her to help him. Couldn't she find it in her heart to do what he asked?

Pam had left him a long time ago. She never thought of it as abandonment, just the right path to take for a girl so young.

She felt now like she did back then…wanting to run and hide, to become a faceless person in the crowd. After all these years, my past came back to dredge up the horrible memories I kept buried. How did he find me? The records weren't made public. That was confidential information. Right?

She continued to read at a faster pace. Anger and resentment rose inside. Someone uncovered her well-kept secret.

After pressuring herself into going, Pam arrived in Rochester, Minnesota later that day. She checked into the Marriot Hotel. When she called earlier, only suites were available. She wanted to be close to the hospital so she booked the room.

Once she pulled her wheeled, overnight bag through the French doors of the bedroom, she collapsed crossways on the mattress. The day had taken its toll. Pam questioned what she was doing here. She kept vacillating between what she felt she wanted to do and what she thought was expected of her.

While she laid there with her arms draped over her head, she stared at the ceiling hoping her mind would shut down and stop rehashing what had happened over the course of her life. She closed her eyes and started to drift off when the phone rang.

"This is the front desk," the woman said. "Jason Hollister is here to see you."

"Put him on the phone."

There was a pause. Soon a male voice came on the line. "I thought we should talk."

"Your letter said if I decided to do this, we'd meet tomorrow. To-day is out of the question." She switched the phone to her other hand. "Hey, how did you know where I was staying? Did you hire someone to follow me?" Her words sounded harsh.

"I'll tell you later. Plus, I have some questions that really can't wait until tomorrow."

"Are you sure?"

"Yeah, besides, I'm already here."

"I guess I have no choice," she said.

"I'll be there in..." She disconnected before his last words reached her ear.

Pam opened a complimentary bottle of water from the fridge, took several drinks, and wiped her hands off on her pants. She wiped them again. At first she thought it was condensation from the bottle, but nervous perspiration dampened her palms.

There came a knock on the door. When she opened it she could not believe what she saw. The similarities in their looks were aston-ishing: same thick brown hair, same deep-set green eyes. The ears hugged closed to his head. The only dissimilarity she noted before asking him in were his dimples.

He stood in the doorway not moving.

"You were in such a big hurry to talk. Come in," she demanded. "Let's get started."

Pam figured Jason would follow her as she walked from the kitch-en to the sitting area. When she turned around, he stood a few feet from the closed door, just waiting, seemingly deep in thought.

"You know you can sit down." She pointed to the couch.

"Just because you chose to be absent from my life, I never stopped thinking about you," he said, shoving his hands deeper into his pock-ets. "I dreamt about this day since I was nine. That's when my mom told me I was adopted. Can I give you a hug?"

Immediately, Pam put her hands up like stop signs. "I'm sure you have a wonderful mother that gives you all the love you need. I'm not a demonstrative person."

"I must have gotten my affectionate side from my father," he said, sounding irritated.

Pam remained silent, keeping her emotions in check.

Jason moved to the sofa and plopped himself down. "I want to know why you didn't keep me."

Inside her feelings pounded against her like a tidal wave, making it difficult for her to breathe, but she remained silent.

The level of his voice heightened. "I'll ask again. Why didn't you keep me?"

"Be thankful I didn't have an abortion." No sooner had the words slipped from her mouth when she knew he felt rebuffed.

"Why are you so angry?" His face flushed. "You've been snapping my head off ever since I walked in here?"

"You really want to know?" she asked.

Jason nodded. "Yes."

"Your father raped me outside the student union my freshman year. It was dark out when he grabbed me around the throat, pushing a knife blade against my skin. I never saw his face. He put a blindfold over my eyes. But I'll never forget the sound of his voice, or what he did to me after he dragged me into the woods." The back of her neck felt hot as she stood rigid next to the club chair, holding on to the back of it to steady her trembling body. "My life spun out of control. I had to leave college, face the ridicule of family and friends, and realize my dreams would never happen." Her chest heaved. "It destroyed my life."

"I had nothing to do with that. I'm the innocent one here." Jason lowered his head. "I spent so much time wondering why a woman would put her baby up for adoption." He rubbed his fingertips through his moist eyes. "You're my mother and you left me. Can you imagine the scars I have?"

"You have to understand neither of us had control over what happened based on your father's actions. Be mad at him, not at me."

"I still don't get it," Jason said.

"Without going in to it all, let me say, I didn't have a lot of choices."

"The choice you made sucked."

"I'll tell you what sucks. You've been out of my life for 19 years. Then I get an overnight letter telling me you want me to give you one of my kidneys. Your adopted parents aren't candidates. Without a donor you will die. How do you think this news hit me?"

"I'm sure it came as a shock."

"A shock? That's an understatement. I'm pissed that you were able to track me down. I thought adoption records were confidential."

"You need to know that in nearly all states, adoption records are sealed and withheld from public inspection. But there have been instituted procedures where identifying information can be obtained. Due to my circumstances, I was able to cut through a lot of red tape and find out who you were. With the Internet, you can find most people. It's harder to track women because they get married, but you still have your maiden name."

"I see." Pam looked at the floor for a second then asked, "How did you find out where I was staying?"

"I started calling the hotels nearest the hospital." Jason rolled his eyes as if to say it was a no-brainer.

"Have I answered all the questions you wanted to go over?"

Jason shifted his weight to get comfortable. "My doctor told me if a suitable donor is found I can have surgery right away. He said the sooner the better in my case. So...I'm thinking the surgery could happen in a few days. Will that time frame work for you?"

Pam turned to the window and looked out. With her mind full of thoughts, she gave little notice to the people milling around on the street below. She did catch a glimpse of her reflection: ridged, unmoving, and lifeless. Moments passed before she turned around to face Jason. "When I came here I hadn't convinced myself I wanted to go through with the surgery. Let alone the recovery time needed or the risks involved." She swallowed hard. "I don't love you enough to do this."

Jason shot up from the couch. "You know someone in this room needs surgery more than I do," he said, with his voice cracking. "You need a heart transplant, 'cause you don't have one. Damn it, you were my last hope." He rushed out of the room. The sound of the slammed door reverberated in her head.

191

When Pam walked into Mayo Clinic to start her series of tests, she didn't know if Jason would even show up. After she upset him, and he rushed out of her hotel room, he probably figured she'd go back to Madison. Over the course of the evening, Pam did a lot of soul searching. She remembered going to the hospital to be tested after being sexually assaulted. It was three hours of being probed, prodded, and swabbed. Pam felt humiliated. The report stated she had intercourse. There were signs of physical force, yet her parents never believed she was raped. Her mother said the sex probably was consensual until he got rough, explaining her bruises and lacerations. Her father told her she got what she deserved teasing a young man like that and then pushing him off her. No wonder he hit her. It was bad enough to be going through this trauma, but without the support of her parents, her thoughts turned suicidal. She never could forgive them for not being there for her. It cut her deep. This was the same kind of pain she inflicted on Jason yesterday. Shouldn't we learn from past mistakes? The answer to that question made her change her mind.

Pam finished having blood work, an EKG, and a CT scan, among other tests. She now sat comfortably in the lounge area waiting to find out the results.

Jason burst into the room out of breath. "The doctor caught me on his way here. I ran ahead to tell you. We're a match!" Jason stared at her through wet eyes. "I didn't think you'd show up today. What made you change your mind?"

"Yesterday...I met my son." Pam smiled at him. "Can I give you a hug?"

Jason smiled back. "You bet."

Carol Kuczek has had several short stories published in periodicals, helped start a writing organization in her local community, and belonged to a writer's group for many years.

PADDY'S NEW GIRLFRIEND

Joseph Vadalma

Blarney's Bar and Grill was a favorite hangout frequented by people of mostly Irish descent. On Friday and Saturday nights, when a local band played, the place was mobbed. The smoke was so thick you could cut it with a knife, and the volume of noise made conversation a shouting match. On such a Friday evening Patrick O'Brien, a divorced man in his thirties, swaggered in and sat at the bar.

"What'll it be, Paddy?" asked O'Shaunnessy, the six-foot-five hulk of a bartender.

"The usual, fire and brimstone." Fire and brimstone was Paddy's name for a shot of whiskey and a pint of Guinness.

O'Shaunnessy poured out a shot of rye, drew a pint of Guinness and set them in front of Paddy. Paddy picked up the whiskey, held it up, cried, "Satan get behind me," and downed it in one swallow.

"Speak o' the devil," said O'Shaunnessy. "If it ain't Miss Anysbryd. Ain't seen you in a month of Sundays."

When Paddy glanced over his shoulder to see who O'Shaunnessy was addressing, his mouth dropped open. Standing behind him, preparing to take the empty stool next to his was the most knockout gorgeous woman he'd ever seen. Her low cut cocktail dress revealed cleavage so deep it was like staring into the bottomless pit. Her waist was narrow; her hip flaring. Her ivory sculptured face was capped by flaming hair. Her full lips were a devilish carmine, and the mascara on her green catlike eyes made them glow mysteriously.

"Oh O'Shaunnessy, don't be so formal. I thought we were old friends. Call me Scarlet."

The bartender grinned and said, "So, what'll be tonight, Scarlet?"

"A brandy, I think."

Paddy, his heart thumping wildly at having such a lovely woman take a seat next to him, asked, "May I pay for that, Scarlet?"

Scarlet stared into his eyes with a Mona Lisa smile on her lips. He gazed back, mesmerized. Her smile widened. "I never refuse a drink from a gentleman." She turned back to O'Shaunnessy. "Please introduce me to this fine man."

O'Shaunnessy winked and introduced Paddy. Scarlet held out her hand. As Paddy brought it to his lips, he noticed that her fiery red fingernails were long and as pointed as daggers. "It's always a pleasure to meet a lovely woman such as I find you to be, Scarlet."

"Charmed."

They clinked glasses and made small talk. "How is it that I haven't seen you in here before?" asked Paddy. "O'Shaunnessy seems to know you well enough."

"I've been away. Far away."

The Irish band began a waltz, and several couples moved onto the dance floor.

"How about a bit of terpsichore?"

"I thought you'd never ask."

Paddy led Scarlet to the dance floor, grasped her firmly and whirled her around in three-quarter time. When the music slowed as the band played a plaintiff love song, Scarlet laid her head against his chest. Paddy was in heaven. Even his dancing improved, and they moved as one. After that they danced almost every set, stopping only to refresh themselves with O'Shaunnessy's fine whisky and beer. Paddy was adept at all the different figures. He even did an Irish jig for Scarlet's admiring eyes. Although the band played many Irish tunes, it also had a repertoire that included rock-and-roll, tangos, salsa, rumba, polkas and fox trots.

Paddy was delighted that this beauty enjoyed his company. Since he divorced Mary, he had not been having much luck with the ladies. And her name, Scarlet, was unique in this neighborhood of Marys, Bridgets, Colleens and Kathleens. In Paddy's eyes this enhanced her image as an exotic, mysterious sort of woman.

At the end of the evening, sweating, exhausted and a bit tipsy, Paddy offered to take Scarlet home.

"It's aways," she replied as they exited Blarney's arm in arm.

"I'll call a cab."

"It's easier to reach by subway."

"Sure. Why not?" Paddy was agreeable, figuring he'd saved himself the cost of a taxi.

They rode the subway downtown.

"We can enter my hotel from the subway station," Scarlet said, taking Paddy's hand to show him the way.

Strangely enough, instead of riding an escalator up to the station entrance, they rode down. This confused Paddy, but he'd had enough whiskey in his system for him not to worry. At the bottom of the escalator was a doorway with a sign above it that said, "Welcome to Hotel Hades. Lowest rates in the city. Always a vacancy."

The lobby was dark except for the light of a roaring fireplace and a few well-placed stanchions with scented oil burning in cups on their tops. The place reminded Paddy of pictures in National Geographic of the inside of Egyptian pyramids. However, his nose wrinkled at the odor of rotten eggs. Paddy shuddered. Something evil about the place gave him a strong desire to leave. But Scarlet's soft body next to his, as her arm encircled his waist, drove such thoughts from his mind. Nonetheless, Paddy was glad to enter the elevator to escape the ominous suffocating atmosphere of the lobby.

"What floor, Darlin'?"

"Thirteen."

But when Paddy gazed at the controls, all the buttons were marked "Thirteen." He pressed one at random and was surprised when the elevator descended, very fast and a long way. He scratched his head. Paddy, you may be drunk, he thought, but something ain't right here.

First the escalator goes down from the station and now this elevator is going down. I've never heard of no hotel what's mostly underground.

Nonetheless, when it stopped, Scarlet led him to her room. They stopped in front of her door, and Paddy stole a kiss. It was returned quite ardently, so he moved his hand over parts of her body. Her breathing became heavy, and her tongue, which was sort of strange, since it was forked, entered his mouth. Another thing Paddy noticed as his hands tangled in her hair, she had a pointed knob on each side, like tiny horns. When they came up for air after heavy petting, she asked, "Would you like to come in for a nightcap, Paddy?"

"Love to."

After they entered, Paddy was a bit taken back by the decor. Everything was in shades of red and black and very plush. Since the hotel was billed as cheap, he figured that the rooms would be tiny and stark. He gazed around at the paintings on the wall, which were of nudes being chased by satyrs.

Scarlet went to the bar and mixed a purple concoction that steamed and boiled. Paddy sipped his slowly. It was bitter and strongly intoxicating. The room began to spin. It also had the same effect on a part of his anatomy as Viagra. Scarlet pushed him onto the sofa and said, "Be right back, Sweetie. I want to change into something more comfortable."

After a few moments, she returned, stark naked. Although Paddy was well pleased by her gorgeous figure, he was a bit surprised to notice that she had a short tail with a barb at the end that wagged as she sashayed toward him. Moments later, she swept him up in her arms and carried him to her bedroom. On red velvet sheets, they had hellishly wild sex. So wild sometimes that at times they seemed to be floating around the room. Something happened that Paddy had never experienced before, multiple orgasms. He had always thought that such a thing was impossible for men. The entire experience made him fall head over heels in love with Scarlet.

When they were both exhausted, Paddy fell asleep. Sometime during the night, he awoke to the sound of chanting outside his door. He tiptoed to the door and glanced out. A dozen or so monks in ankle-length robes and cowls that hid their faces slowly paraded down the hall, holding candles and chanting in Latin. The word diablo was prevalent in their chant. A faint stench of musty decay came from them that reminded Paddy of ancient corpses. Paddy shuddered and wondered, what kind of damned hotel is this, anyway?

He slipped back under the sheets and put his arm around Scarlet for comfort. Still exhausted from his earlier exercise with her, he fell back to sleep quickly. A few minutes later, however, he was awakened by a great thumping and growling in the room next door. He shook Scarlet awake. "What's that?"

Scarlet patted him on the cheek and said sleepily, "It's nothing. Just The Beast. Its keepers will calm it down soon. They'll feed it a sacrifice."

The Beast? Paddy thought and felt like running out that room and keep on running, but he was too frightened to move. Scarlet kissed him and soothed him until he finally returned to slumber land.

About noon Paddy awoke with a horrible hangover. He opened one eye to realize that he was back in his own bedroom. He ran to the bathroom and vomited. After he emptied his stomach, he took Alka-Seltzer and four aspirin. He sat on the edge of his bed and went over his mind the events of the night. Some things that happened were too weird to have been real. He wondered whether that lovely woman, Scarlet, had slipped him a mickey, perhaps a hallucinogenic drug. But why did she bring him back to his own room, he wondered. In fact, how did she know where he lived. His head still hurt. Nothing made sense about the entire evening.

He checked his wallet. Most of the money he'd started the evening out was still there, and none of his credit cards were missing. He concluded that Scarlet was not a thieving prostitute.

He showered, shaved and slipped into his old jeans and a tee shirt. By that time, his hangover abated, and he went down to the diner, where he had a breakfast of pancakes and eggs. After a second cup of coffee, he actually felt good. His thoughts turned to Scarlet, and the night that they'd had together. But what was real and what was dream, he wondered?

He wandered over to Blarney's. The bar was empty except for the usual morning sots. O'Shaunnessy was leaning against the bar, waiting for the day man to count the register so that he could leave. "Say O'Shaunnessy, me memory's a bit hazy about last night. Can you fill me in on what I was up to?"

The bartender chuckled. "You did have a few, especially after you picked up that woman, Scarlet Anysbryd. You two sure danced up a storm. I didn't know you had it in you. You left with her about two in the mornin'" He winked. "Can't say what you did after that. Maybe you want to tell me all about it."

Paddy winked back. "A gentleman doesn't kiss and tell. But O'Shaunnessy, old pal, you and the lady seemed to be old friends. What can you tell me about her?"

"We ain't friends or anything else if that's what you're thinkin'. A couple of years ago, she was a regular. She flirted with a lots of guys. I think she went home with any that struck her fancy. I take her for a man eater."

"Man eater? What do you mean?"

"Y'know. The kind of woman what takes up with a gent for a while and drops him like a hot potato when she tires of him. If I were you, I'd forget her. She'll tear your heart out." He dropped his voice to a conspiratorial whisper. "To tell the truth, I'm not sure she's human. There's something about her that makes me think she's a witch or something,' the way she bewitches men."

Paddy nodded. But he knew it was too late; she'd already cast her spell on him. He couldn't get her out his mind.

As Paddy strolled home, he wondered whether to come back to the bar that evening to see whether Scarlet would show up. When he went to the night stand to fetch his cigarettes, he noticed a business card. In blood colored script was Scarlet's name and phone number. Scribbled below it were the words, "I'd like to see you again, Paddy Dear."

Paddy's heart leaped for joy. He almost picked up the phone immediately, but thought the better of it. After the night they'd had, she might still be sleeping. Jumpy as a cat, he wandered about the apartment, watched TV for a few minutes, went to kitchen and made a sandwich, paced back and forth and so forth, unable to settle on any one thing to keep busy. When the kitchen clock said one, he felt that was late enough. He dialed her number, six-six-six thirteen-thirteen.

"Hello," she answered in a husky contralto that sent shivers up Paddy's spine.

"Hi. It's me. Paddy."

She sounded genuinely pleased, which gave Paddy a warm glow. "Oh, I'm so glad you called, you little imp. I had a wonderful time last night."

"Me too. I was wondering whether I could take you out to dinner."

"I'd love to go out with you. What time can you pick me up?"

Paddy hesitated. The thought of returning to that weird hotel was daunting. "Perhaps we could meet somewhere."

"Better yet. Let me pick you up. I've got a car."

"Okay. Let me give you the address of my building."

"No need. I know where it is."

Of course. She's brought me home and left that card. Again, he wondered whether there wasn't something supernatural about the whole business. Maybe she was a witch like O'Shaunnessy had said. Or worse.

When he didn't reply immediately, she said, "Sevenish?"

"Yeah. Great. Ring the bell under my mailbox."

The next several hours were agony for Paddy. His desire to be with Scarlet again was like an unscratchable itch. By six, he was dressed in his best suit, tie tight against his Adam's apple, pants pressed to a perfect crease. He even cleaned the apartment and bought an expensive bottle of wine.

The ringing of the bell made him leap out of his seat like a man whose pants were on fire. He buzzed her in and waited by the open hall door. When she appeared, she was more luscious than he'd remembered. They kissed, sending him into a tailspin.

"Would you like a glass of wine before we head out to the restaurant?" he asked.

"Sure." While he poured two glasses, she plopped down on his worn sofa and crossed her legs. They toasted each other and made small talk.

After a few minutes, he said, "I made reservations at the Amor for eight. We'd better leave now." A friend had told Paddy that The Amor was an extremely fancy French restaurant.

When they went down to where she had parked her car, Paddy was taken aback. Her fire engine red Porsche convertible was sleek with white leather seats. By golly, the lady's rich as well as beautiful, he thought.

As soon as he clicked the seat belt, Scarlet put the pedal to the medal. They screeched away from her parking spot, leaving a cloud of smoke and debris flying out behind them. The speed limit on the city streets was 25. She had the machine up to 70 in minutes. They careened like crazy, in and out of traffic, going through stop signs and red lights like they didn't exist. At one point, Paddy swore that they were flying. Before he could catch his breath to tell her to slow down a little, the sirens and flashing of a police car were behind them.

Scarlet turned to Paddy and winked. "Should we have some fun. This machine can easily outrun that cop. I've had it up to 175."

"No!! Please. Just pull over."

She curled her lip into a pout, but pulled over to the curb. The cop stuck his head in the window. "Hey lady. Not only were you doing 50 miles over the speed limit, but you completely ignored every traffic signal. Are you nuts or what?"

She smiled at him sweetly. "Oh dear, did I do something wrong?" She stared into the cop's eyes for a few moments. Slowly, as though he were in a trance, he put away his book, tipped his hat, said, "Try to be a little more careful next time," and walked back to his patrol car.

Paddy watched in wonder. He said, "Uh, no need to rush. We're almost at the restaurant."

She drove the rest of the way at a reasonable rate of speed, obeying all traffic rules.

They had a pleasant evening at the Amor, stretching out the meal for a couple of hours. The place was expensive, taking most of a week's pay for Paddy. The food wasn't terribly good nor were the portions large, but the waiter had the proper amount of haughtiness, and the atmosphere was dark and romantic. Paddy didn't care. It was enough that he was with Scarlet. He enjoyed simply staring at her lovely face and bare shoulders as she talked.

After dinner and coffee, Scarlet asked, "Should we go back to my place?" She arched her eyebrows enticingly.

Recalling the previous night, Paddy said, "How about if we go to my apartment tonight? We could finish that bottle of wine we started."

"If you like."

Scarlet drove like a maniac through the almost empty streets and had them home in ten minutes. They began to neck and pet in the hallway. Shortly afterwards, they had torn each other's clothes off. They didn't bother with the bed, but did it right on the living room carpet.

Afterwards, Paddy stared into her eyes and said, "Y'know Scarlet, sometimes you scare me. Some very odd things happen when you're around. O'Shaunnessy said that he thought you were a witch. And the way that cop left you off without giving you a ticket was strange. Tell me the truth. Are you human?"

She looked down. "I may as well tell you the truth. I'm not."

"What are you?"

"An angel. Do you want to see my wings?"

This wasn't what Paddy expected her to say. An angel? Really?

"Yes. Show them to me."

She stood up, and two enormous bat-like wings unfolded from her back.

"I thought angel's wings were white and feathery."

"They used to be like that. But I'm a dark angel; one of the rebels. When we were thrown out of heaven into the void, they turned black and leathery. I guess it was part of our punishment."

"You're a demon then, one of Satan's minions."

She looked downcast. "Yes. But some of us are not as bad as you've been told. Oh Paddy, I really like you an awful lot. But, I suppose a good Catholic like you couldn't have a girl friend who's damned."

Paddy's heart thumped in his chest. She wants to be my girl friend. He felt like he'd found a four-leaf-clover, kissed the Blarney Stone and met a leprechaun all in the same day. "Well, I ain't exactly a saint, meself. I even missed Easter mass this year. And a demoness ain't so bad. It ain't like you were a Protestant."

They kissed and did the other thing. Paddy asked her to move in with him. She agreed. "I never did like that hellhole of a hotel anyway."

So Scarlet moved into Paddy's bachelor pad. He found that having a demon for a girl friend had advantages. For one thing, their sex life was unimaginable. In addition, she was a great cook, although most of what she made was on the spicy side. Best of all, she could do magic. She'd snap her fingers, and the apartment was clean. She entertained their friends by performing what the friends thought were sleight-of-hand, but was real magic. She was always giving Paddy expensive presents that she produced out of thin air.

The couple were deeply in love. Their life was idyllic...until the day his mother called. "Patrick, you're breaking your poor mother's heart. You haven't called or visited in months. And now I hear that you're living in sin with some floozy."

Paddy flushed with the awful guilt that only a Catholic boy who'd neglected his mother could feel. "I'm sorry, Mom. But I'm very busy lately. And Scarlet is no floozy. I'd like you to meet her."

"Scarlet? What kind of name is that? She's not one of those Hungarians, is she? Why can't you meet another Irish girl? You know you've sinned by divorcing that nice Mary O'Dary."

Mary nice? She was as much a big mouthed shrewish woman as I'd ever met. Nonetheless, he kept this thought to himself. "Scarlet is Irish," he said weakly.

"Oh. Very well, bring her to dinner tomorrow night. We're having your favorite, corned beef and cabbage." Paddy hated corned beef and cabbage.

After he hung up, he said to Scarlet, "Uh...I'm bringing you to meet my parents tomorrow evening. We're invited for dinner."

"How lovely. We're like a real human couple now."

Paddy dreaded the encounter, but didn't see any way out of it. His family would need to meet Scarlet sooner or later. "Uh Scarlet. I...uh...told them that you were Irish."

"That's okay. I've always felt Gaelic. Back in the old days, the druids worshiped me."

Paddy smiled weakly. He didn't want to think of all the centuries that she'd been in existence. It made him feel like a teenager with a crush on an older woman.

As Paddy rang the doorbell that fateful evening, he had awful premonitions of absolute disaster. His fifteen-year-old brother, Michael, answered the door. Mike took one look at Scarlet, cried, "Wow. What a hotty!" and licked his chops like a dog who'd just been given a sirloin. Paddy ruffled his hair and said, "And she's all my mine, Mikey."

Scarlet followed his lead and ruffled Mikey's hair too, which made the teenager grin from ear to ear. "Hi Mikey. You're as handsome as your big brother."

Paddy's father had been sitting in an easy chair, reading the newspaper. He peered over the edge, got a silly grin on his face and stood up.

"Pop, I'd like you to meet my friend, Scarlet Anysbyrd."

His father took Scarlet's hand. "It's a great pleasure to meet such a fair lass. I never in my born days would've thought Paddy would've hooked such a beauty."

"Thank you, Mister O'Brien. Now I know where Paddy gets his blarney."

His mother came from the kitchen, wiping her hands on a dish towel. "Mom, this is Scarlet, Scarlet Anysbyrd."

His mother's eyes went wide. She cried, "Anysbyrd is it." She crossed herself. "Jesus, Joseph and Mary, Heaven save us."

"What's the matter, Mom?"

"Don't you know that Anysbyrd means evil spirit in Gaelic? How did you come by such an awful name?"

Paddy and Scarlet looked at each other guiltily for several seconds. Finally, Scarlet spoke up. "I was orphaned at an early age. The nuns at the orphanage called me that. I suppose because I was a mischievous child."

"Oh you poor dear." Paddy's mother came over and hugged Scarlet.

During dinner, things went well. Among Scarlet's many assets was that she was a good conversationalist. She knew several jokes about priests, the devil, the saints, the Catholic faith in general and the Irish, which the family enjoyed enormously. Afterwards, Paddy's mother took him to the side and said, "She's seem like a very nice Irish girl. You must make an honest woman of her."

"I'll ask her soon."

"Why not tonight?"

"I need to buy a ring."

True to his word, the very next day Paddy bought a diamond ring. A week later he got up the courage to ask Scarlet for her hand. After a candle lit dinner, he got down on one knee and proposed.

"You want to marry me, a demon, a succubus? Oh darling,..." She began to weep.

"What you are doesn't matter to me. I love you." His eyes filled too. He was afraid that she was going to turn him down.

"I love you too. I know such beings as I am aren't supposed to be able to feel love. But you've been so good to me, I couldn't help myself." She paused for several moments. "Yes Paddy, my darling. I'll marry you."

They both started bawling and crying and hugging. Paddy was delirious with happiness.

Of course, Paddy's mom insisted that the couple have a grandiose church wedding. She met with Scarlet many times to plan the wedding. She picked out her wedding gown, her bridesmaids and their gowns, rented the hall for the reception, hired a band, ordered flowers, made out invitations and did everything else that needed to be done to make the wedding perfect. Scarlet merely had to nod her agreement with Paddy's mother's choices. Paddy rented a tux and hired a limousine. His best man planned a bachelor party at a strip club.

Two nights before the wedding, Scarlet came to Paddy with a

worried expression. "Y'know Paddy, I've never been in a church in all of my long existence, unless you want to call Stonehenge a church. I don't know whether I'll know how to act."

Paddy placed an arm around her. "Don't worry. Simply walk slowly up the aisle. When you come up to the priest, just follow my lead. Do what I do or what the priest tells you. There's nothing to worry about."

Finally, the great day came. First Paddy and the best man arrived and took their places by the altar. Next the church filled with Paddy's relatives, friends and neighbors. The bride and her entourage arrived. As the great organ played The Wedding March, the flower girl sprinkled petals as she made her up the aisle. Next came the ring bearer, followed by the bridesmaids. In pure white gown, her coiffured hair partially covered by her veil, Scarlet solemnly paraded up the aisle.

But something happened as she passed the last pew at the back of the church. A rumbling came from below, like the start of an earthquake. Next Scarlet's pure white dress turned black. Smoke curled out of Scarlet's ears. Before she reached the center of the church, she burst into flames and disappeared in a horrendous cloud of sulfurous smoke. A thunderous evil voice said, "She's one of mine. Thou shalt not have her."

Everyone in the church started screaming and running about. The scene turned to chaos.

Nobody was more stunned than poor Paddy. His lady love had gone all to Hell. And they hadn't even gotten married.

❧

Joseph Vadalma is 83 and the author of over 50 published works, mostly as e-books, but a few paperbacks included, available at most online book sellers. His novels and short stories are in the fantasy and SF genres for the most part. He did not start writing seriously until he retired at the age of 59. He also wrote a history of his family that included most of the 20th century and part of the 21st.

MISS DONATELLI

Frank Burd

My senior year in high school I had a teacher named Miss Donatelli. I don't often feel superior to anyone, but as for Miss Donatelli, I thought that I was smarter than my English teacher.

We had to write a book report every two weeks. I hated it. I was a notoriously slow reader even when reading things I liked. And 99% of what I read, I didn't like. I didn't dislike those books, and it wasn't because they were bad. They were books by Eliot, Dostoyevsky, Twain, Hawthorne, and Zola. I didn't like them because I didn't like to read at all. It was so much work for so little reward as far as I was concerned.

I bought the *New York Times* every day, faithfully, for eight years starting in the fifth grade. I bought it, not for the news, but for the sports section, then tossed it out or brought it home for my parents. If John Drebinger, Louis Koppet or Arthur Daley, *Times* sportswriters, wrote something, then I read it. I read every word as Mickey Mantle won baseball's Triple Crown in 1956. I followed Maris' race after Babe Ruth's home run record in 1961. I could answer any question about baseball from anyone. I wrote away to *The $64,000 Question*, a TV quiz show I'd hoped to be on. I never got an answer. If I did, my mother threw it out. But let me get back to why I knew Miss Donatelli was not as smart as me.

As was often the case, it was the night before a book report was due and I had no book in mind. I went to my friend Ed's house. His parents were teachers and they were fun, too. I asked them for a short book. They suggested *The Pearl* by John Steinbeck. They suggested *Animal Farm* by George Orwell. I looked them over but wasn't interested. Even short books were too long.

Books were used for different purposes in my house. They were used to sit on during Thanksgiving dinners so you could reach the table. They were used to put dry leaves in so they would be pressed just right. They were spread out across the floor to make a highway for my cars and trucks when I was a kid. I could even build bridges with them. Books were fun if I didn't have to read them.

My father had another purpose for books. Whenever he went to the toilet, he'd first go running around the house, searching frantically for the latest *Reader's Digest.* He would then retreat to the inner sanctum of the bathroom. Having read a chapter, he moved his bowels and came out. That's what he called it, moving his bowels. When we were little, he called it making a duty. We were creating even when we were on the can. It led to a lot of giggling when *Howdy Doody* was popular on TV. At any rate, I rarely wanted to hold, let alone read that issue of *Reader's Digest* after he came out. As for *Reader's Digest,* I just assumed that it must have been a scholarly book since my father was a lawyer.

I can only remember my mother reading for a few months. She told me that she read lots of books when she was young. She told me that she used to read from the light of the street lamp outside her window. She told me that was the reason she needed glasses by the time she was 14.

The reading I remember of hers was during the months of her nervous breakdown. I didn't know then it was a nervous breakdown. I just knew that she stopped cooking and cleaning and she started watching TV and reading. I remember the books she had around. She read *Peyton Place, Lady Chatterley's Lover,* and something by Henry Miller that she hid in her top right drawer when she finished.

I saw her sitting in a chair reading because I was sleeping on the sofa. It was too hard to get me up and down the steps with my huge cast, covering my newly broken leg. I was supposed to be sleeping but

I'd wake up when otherwise I'd have just turned over. The cast was too heavy to lift.

When she finished *Peyton Place,* she put it on our only bookshelf. She knew that neither my older brother nor I ever got books from there, so it was safe from our prurient interests.

I remember that shelf so well. It was in the basement and it was built by my brother in a wood shop class several years before. On it were six volumes of *Reader's Digest Condensed Books.* There was a Bible and a very fat, two volume, yellow and red dictionary. It had the worst definitions. A word was defined by using the word itself in the meaning. The best part of the book was the textured design on the cover. I got a good grade in art when I made a rubbing of it. But the dictionaries were in the basement because they were rarely used. Although I grew up on them, my parents switched to telephone books for the dinner table when my younger brother was little. He fell off his seat many more times than I did. They thought he was clumsy. But I knew that he was always falling because the paper covers of the phone books slid more readily than the hard cover dictionaries.

Also on the shelf were about ten cookbooks. I remember an Italian one, a Jewish one, and a Chinese one. My mother never cooked anything besides hamburgers, steak, and chicken. And I knew she never even opened the Chinese cookbook so I used that one to straighten out the bent baseball cards I'd won while flipping.

There was *Exodus,* something by Howard Fast, my brother's scout books and some old *National Geographics.* I never saw anyone look at the *Geographics.* They just appeared one day. And it was in some of those magazines that I saw my first pictures of naked ladies (that was long before I started using the word women). The ladies were either Asian or African so they didn't look like real people to me. Real people were people who lived on your block or who were on TV.

When I finally learned to get around with my cast, I made it down the steps to the basement and discovered *Peyton Place* on the shelf. I picked it from its place. I thought it was entitled Park Place and was something about the game Monopoly. In reading that book of about 500 pages, I was reading a book almost three times as long as any book I'd read previously. It was very sexy. I didn't know everything that was happening but I knew I liked it. Perhaps if I'd been given books like *Peyton Place,* I might have enjoyed reading more.

In Miss Donatelli's class, we were reading *Arrowsmith* by Sinclair Lewis. There is nothing worse than reading a chapter a day except reading it and listening to Miss Donatelli explain it. I used to write silly poems and give them to Tracy, the girl who sat next to me. She laughed a lot and it made me feel good. But every now and then, Miss Donatelli would call on me. As I wasn't listening, I often didn't hear the question.

"That's a good question," I said. "And it ties into Arrowsmith's doctoring and his desire to help people." I often believed that Miss Donatelli didn't read some of the books she taught. Her questions were so hollow. I thought she copied the questions from a teacher's manual. She went on, "Yes, that's true. But what abou...." (She'd repeat the question). I'd make up with an answer which she accepted as correct. I don't know if I knew the answers or if she just didn't want to bother. She'd move on to another question and I'd turn back to Tracy.

Tracy was my age and she was beautiful. I sat next to her for two months making her laugh. I wanted to ask her out but I was too shy and fearful of a rejection. Then one day we were talking about a movie we both wanted to see. It seemed like she was hinting to me. Finally, I blurted out of nowhere, "Why don't we go and see it this weekend?"

"Are you asking me out on a date?" she asked. She seemed surprised.

"Sure," I said with my confidence fading fast. "Would you like to go?"

"Oh, that's sweet," she said. I sensed I wasn't going to be going out on a date with Tracy. She turned then to Renee, her friend who sat in front of her. "Renee, Michael just asked me to go out with him this weekend."

I wondered what was going on as Renee turned to another friend and whispered. I didn't want to hear anymore. I tried to tune in to Miss Donatelli. If only she could be attractive. "Miss Donatelli, I wonder if you would like to accompany me this weekend to listen to a distinguished American scholar summarize chapters of *Huckleberry Finn*."

She was busy. "Why," she asked, "did Arrowsmith choose pure research rather than the more practical side of medicine?" Because he didn't want to deal with people, I thought. Someone in the front row said something about research being the purest form of science. Was my interest in Tracy just pure? When I turned back to Tracy, it seemed as though there were a half dozen girls looking at me. They seemed to be saying tsk, tsk as they shook their heads.

Finally Renee said, "Didn't you know that Tracy was engaged? He drives up from the base and they go away most weekends. He's a marine."

"Jesus," I muttered under my breath.

The bell rang and everyone got up to leave. I was spared further stares.

That night I tried so hard to feel what Martin Arrowsmith was feeling. Our assignment was to write a summary of each chapter. After ten minutes, I opened my *Cliff's Notes* and rewrote their summary.

I don't know how the generations before me got through school without *Cliff's Notes* and *Monarch Review Books*. Not only were they concise, in many cases they were better than the books they summarized. *Silas Marner* was such a dull book but the *Monarch* 15-minute version almost made it readable. And when Miss Donatelli taught us *Silas Marner*, every one of her questions came from that review book. Needless to say, I knew all the answers. They were listed right after the questions. But that wasn't the reason I got an "A" in the course. It came from that night at Ed's house.

Ed's parents tried hard to find a book for me. Nothing seemed interesting and I rejected everything they offered me. I'd read the first page. If the book's first page wasn't good, I reasoned, then the book couldn't be any good. After all, if I wanted to sell a book, I'd try to write a sizzling opening paragraph.

"Giselle lay naked at the bottom of the cliff. She was dizzy from the sun but her bound hands were tied firmly to the tree."

"He cried when he heard the news. His bride-to-be had awakened when she had heard the noise in the kitchen. She'd come down the steps to investigate and probably never felt any pain. The bullet ripped right through her head."

"I hated my sisters. Why did it have to be me who was one of quintuplets? Or at least, why couldn't two of us be boys instead of just me? My relationship with women was doomed from the date of my birth. I hated them all."

Instead, books start with a boring description of a place and a character. The author always goes to great length to carefully describe the characters. I didn't need that. For me, the characters I read about looked however I wanted them to look. I would recreate their characters and settings to suit myself. It made no difference to me if the author described a short plump woman. If I wanted her to be tall and sleek, I made her so in my mind.

Only if there were pictures would my imagination have to fight hard. But as I got older, there were fewer and fewer pictures anyway. Actually, I was glad to see the pictures disappear. They resembled no one I'd ever known or cared to know. If only the illustrators of the *Classic Comics* did illustrations for books, I thought. Then, I might like the pictures. But for years, I had to deal with Alice and Jerry. They were the kids in my first readers.

Alice and Jerry were perfect little children. They washed their faces and brushed their hair and never picked their noses. I don't think they ever went to the toilet. The only place they might have gone was to the country to visit their grandparents. Did you ever see their grandparents? They looked like grandparents. And they were always smiling. In *Engine Whistles, Through the Green Gate,* and *Singing Wheels,* nothing ever happened worse than Alice staining her calico dress while picking berries or Jerry losing his fishing pole while fishing with his cousin Carl.

211

And then there was their dog, Jip. Jip was always smiling.

In one of the stories, they brought back venison. I remember venison because it was a vocabulary word. So was calico. Anyway, two men were carrying a dead deer upside down on some poles. There were no bullet holes in the deer. But I can still recall that deer. Dead, it was still smiling.

I hated those readers. But my biggest dread was the workbooks. We had to answer 43 zillion questions every time Alice or Jerry or Jip ate another pancake. Certainly my parents don't deserve the total blame for my hatred of books. The school system deserves its share of the credit.

As the evening grew later, I started to worry that I was going to get a zero. Although I wasn't motivated by books, I was motivated by good grades. My older brother was a very average student with very average grades. Every now and then, he'd fail a course. I, on the other hand, got good grades. The result was that they were always on his back. This interfered with his free time. Meanwhile, I avoided lots of potentially difficult times by bringing home good report cards. My parents beamed when they saw how well I was doing. But I knew how much I'd faked it. The IQ tests, the College Boards, the National Merit tests, et al, were accurate reflections of my ability. And my scores were very average. I'd so impressed my parents with good grades, they figured that the tests were not good measures of my ability. My parents were wrong. The tests were accurate.

Finally, exasperated by my reluctance to read any of the books they offered, Ed's mother said sarcastically, "Why don't you write your own?"

That was the answer. I'd write my own. I hated writing as much as reading. In the fifth grade, I failed the only course I'd ever failed, Written Expression. Of the five assignments due in the first report period, Mrs. Brownstein received none from me. My mother didn't like that one bit. Reluctantly, I wrote, and I discovered that I could write. During the National Fire Prevention week, I handed in an essay that won some sort of ribbon. In it, I was the fire.

At 10:30, Sunday night, the day before the book review was due,

I sat down to write. In fifteen minutes, I was finished. I wrote a book review. It was called *Lefty*. It was written by Simon Harper and published in Boston in 1946.

※

Tom Rooker grew up in the streets of Philadelphia during the Depression. After school, he delivered papers and two evenings he assisted Old Sam Harding in the Rexall Drug Store. His job was to restock the shelves, sell penny candy, and sweep up at the end of the day. He was like many teenage boys and girls helping their families during those hard times.

But Tom lived for only one thing, baseball. He loved the game with a passion. He played in every spare moment. There was always a game somewhere in Fairmount Park. And everyone knew Tom. At fourteen, he was one of the best players in the city. But fate threw Tom a curve that autumn.

He was delivering his papers one afternoon near his home when he saw one of the little Beattie kids dart out after a ball into the street. A trolley was bearing down on the boy when Tom leaped from his bicycle and pushed the boy out of the trolley's path. He rolled over to get out of the way but the braking trolley's wheels ran over his right arm, his pitching arm.

But this is not the story of a shattered dream. In fact, it is a special story whose outcome all baseball fans know. Tom "Lefty" Rooker pitched for fourteen years in the major leagues. A special plaque in the Baseball Hall of Fame honors Tom.

Simon Harper traces those painful years as Tom turned his life from despair to hope, from failure to victory as he became one of the finest pitchers in the game. It is a beautifully written book and should be enjoyed by sports fans as well as non-sports since it is more than the story of a baseball player. *Lefty,* as told by Simon Harper, is the story of the resilience of one man in overcoming overwhelming odds and succeeding.

When I was finished, I looked over the review. My only disappointment was that I would never read the book unless I wrote it myself. I certainly couldn't do that because there was no such person as Tom Rooker. Now, the question—would Miss Donatelli catch me? I couldn't wait to get to English.

I came in and sat down. Tracy was talking to Renee. I ignored them and opened my loose leaf to my review. I'd drawn a picture for a cover. In the picture were a ball, a bat, a trolley, and a boy with one short arm. Tracy turned to me.

"Did you finish your review?" she asked.

I nodded.

"Look, I'm sorry about the other day," she said. "I guess I thought everyone knew about Hank. We've gone together since I was fourteen. We'll be getting married this June."

"It's O.K. I'm happy for you," I said as I smiled. Actually, I'd almost forgotten the incident since I'd been so involved with the review.

"Friends?" she asked.

"Friends," I said.

"Well, then as my friend, would you look over my review? It was so hard to write."

Her book was *Dear Abby Talks to Teens.* Did I really consider going out with her? It was terribly written, full of misspellings and grammatical mistakes. What could I tell her? Once again, I was saved by the bell, this time the late bell, and Miss Donatelli came in and collected the papers.

The class droned along. I answered one of Miss Donatelli's questions about Arrowsmith's wife and knew I could safely tune out. I watched her mouth move as she read excerpts and asked questions of the class.

Agnes Donatelli (I saw her first name on a notebook of hers earlier in the term) was a plain woman. She had no special characteristics. She was about 5'3", about 35 years old, and she had dull brown hair.

She was a little on the heavy side but not fat. Her face looked vacuous. She reminded me of a librarian; no, that's unfair to librarians. She looked boring before I ever heard her speak. I was not surprised when I discovered that she was boring. I never hated her. She was just there. Her only noticeable characteristic was her glasses. The frames were large and curled upward near the temple. They were very ugly. I started to think how I'd never seen her without her glasses. Then I started to look more carefully at her. I tried to picture her lounging at home. I couldn't. I was sure that no one ever saw her outside that classroom. Thinking about her now, I can only picture her in gray colors.

It wasn't until Thursday that she returned the papers. I thought I caught her glance at me from the corner of her eye. I was nervous. She had discovered me.

Finally, she got to my paper. She handed it to me and said, "Very nice, Michael." I looked at the paper in front of me. A+ was written very small in the upper corner. I turned the pages to see if she'd made any comments. There was nothing. That was it, A+. She liked it. She loved it.

Tracy got a C-. Renee got a B-. In general, most people got B's and C's. After she finished handing out the papers, Miss Donatelli said, "There is one paper that was especially well written. Michael, would you please read your review to the class?"

Now I was scared. I looked around the room to see if any baseball fans were in the class who might know that there was no Lefty Rooker. I read it slowly. As I finished and sat down, two students applauded. I saw tears on one girl's face. Was it that good, I wondered?

"That was beautiful, Michael," said Miss Donatelli. "That is the way I'd like all of you to write."

Brian, a short kid in the front of the room called out, "That was good. Did you get the book in the school library?"

I told him and the class that it was my brother's book and that he had taken it back to college with him. I told him I'd ask him for it when he came back. I suddenly realized the power I had and I loved it. I also learned from it. Every two weeks, until the end of the term,

I created book reviews on topics ranging from westerns and mysteries to stories of love and hate. I didn't want to risk discovery so I made deliberate errors in some to be assured some B's. But I kept my average high enough to get the A.

Tracy broke up with Hank in May. She told me about it. This time, she did hint for a date. She was attractive and I still enjoyed making her laugh but I knew she wasn't right for me.

As for Miss Donatelli, who I never saw laugh, she continued to teach for many years after I graduated. She's still probably reading a chapter a day in *Arrowsmith* or whatever book she is teaching.

I eventually found a new use for books. I built huge book shelves and placed them against big white walls. On them, I put Nietzsche, Freud, Einstein, Bronte, Fielding, Tolstoy, Williams and thousands more. I bought them by the pound at auctions and tossed away the "trash." The book gave my various dwellings an intellectual look. They also provided an extra layer of insulation against the walls of my apartments, on cold wintry nights. And every now and then, I'd read one of them.

✿

Frank Burd was a secondary school teacher of math for 25 years. He also directed over 40 plays—community theater, school productions, and professionally. He is a serious photographer and has shown his work in several galleries in the Philadelphia area. Though he wrote lots of poetry in his twenties, he didn't arrive at the fiction genre until his forties. In the last five years, he's written two plays, a screenplay, and a novel.

No Thanks for the Memory

Shirley K. Wright

Blankets of bluebonnets thinned as the trim blue Corolla wound smoothly out of the Texas Hill Country. Ann took the back roads from Dallas knowing that early April was prime wildflower time.

When Aunt Grace passed away and left her $200,000, she resigned her job as a technical writer and resolved to devote one year to work on the novel she had abandoned soon after moving to Dallas.

She gathered her research material into plastic crates, stocked up on comfort clothes and a starter supply of groceries, and headed for the vacant family ranch southwest of San Antonio.

The colorful landscape gradually flattened out into brush country—spring green mesquite alternated with blooming guajilla.

The coming-home feeling never failed to settle in when she turned onto the highway that ran past the ranch. The familiar landmark cedar tree stood 40-feet tall in front of the big, white, wooden house, dwarfing the crooked TV antenna on the roof and the windmill to the south.

At 7:30, she drove across the rusty cattle guard and followed the white caliche road to the back gate.

She climbed the porch steps and unlocked the padlock on the screen door. She couldn't help smiling. In Dallas a padlock on a screened porch wouldn't be much of a deterrent, but this was the country.

As she began to unload the trunk, the cattle guard rattled again.

She grinned broadly when she saw Uncle Wes and Aunt Sue pull up beside her.

"We were sittin' on our porch, watchin' for you, and saw you go by," Wes grinned. "Bout to send out a posse."

"We ate about 5:00, but I brought you a picnic supper," Sue said, hugging Ann. "Honey, I know you want to stay here, but I wish you'd stay with us. I hate to think of you down here in this big house alone."

"Thanks, Aunt Sue, but I need to dig in and get to work on my novel," Ann said. "If Grandma Barnes could live here alone for her last ten years, I can do it for one month. Bill and Doris still live on the place in their trailer, don't they?"

"Yes," Wes answered. "But they're both away right now. Bill's still the only crop duster in three counties, and he's on a two-day job near Crystal City."

"At least let us give you a shotgun," Sue pleaded.

"O, Lord," Ann laughed. "If somebody broke in I'd probably get so rattled, I'd shoot my foot off. Quit worrying. I'll be fine."

"All right. Let's unload your car."

When they had finished, Wes said, "If there's anything you need, just give us a call. The phone's in the bottom desk drawer in Mom and Pop's room. We're going' into San Antone in the mornin' for our checkups. Think you can sleep through the country noises?"

"I always sleep like a baby the first night here," Ann answered. "Thanks for all your help."

Ann stood on the porch breathing the fresh country air and surveying the ranch to the west.

South of the garage, Bill's horse grazed in a small pen. Behind this lay the cattle pens. Along the north side of these was a crowding pen for guiding the animals into a chute where they were inoculated or doctored. Next came a squeeze chute—a device with two solid sides which squeezed together to immobilize the cow for branding or dehorning. Lastly was a now empty dipping vat twelve feet deep, where the cattle were forced to swim through a medicated solution to rid them of ticks or other parasites.

Ann noticed that mesquite trees were beginning to encroach on the chutes. Grandpa would never have allowed that.

On to the south was Bill's trailer.

Before he and his wife moved on to the place, thieves had broken into the house. Uncle Wes had struck a bargain with Bill. For $1 a month rent and use of the pen for his horse, Bill looked after the place, and his presence discouraged looters.

Ann turned and entered the house.

She stored her food and paused to look over the kitchen. Throughout the house, walls and twelve foot ceilings were of wainscoting salvaged by Grandpa Barnes from the demolished courthouse in town. All wood surfaces in the kitchen were painted what Grandma called apple green. The long table in the center of the room seated twelve at meals and served as a worktable for the ancient rust-marked sink and the porcelain range.

Ann decided not to indulge in the nostalgia that engulfed her. She turned out the kitchen light and went down the wide hall. She had chosen to sleep in Aunt Erin's room close to the kitchen and bathroom. She collected her pajamas and headed back down the hall.

The unused pipes delivered rust-colored cold water into the claw-footed bathtub but, by the time the hot water had traveled the long route from the water heater, it began to clear.

Soon Ann snuggled into the double bed feeling content and a little smug. The night breeze blowing in the window was cool enough to enjoy the faded wedding ring quilt that covered her. The windmill hummed as the vanes whirled, and the rod creaked up and down. Ann always expected it to keep her awake—more often than not, it lulled her to sleep.

In the distance a coyote howled, Mexico-bound traffic sped down the highway...crickets sang...an owl hooted...the old house creaked...the wind rustled through the brush...and Ann breathed regularly and deeply, sound asleep.

With no sense of how long she had slept, Ann awakened to the noise of a mouse scavenging in the closet. She sat up to tug the covers well clear of the floor. She was wakeful now as she listened to the night sounds.

Footsteps?

Suddenly, below the half-drawn shades at the open window, a man's upper legs appeared. Goosebumps rose on her neck. The legs passed on toward the sleeping porch door.

He must be trying to get in. Dear God, what am I going to do?

After what seemed an eternity, the legs came back and turned toward the open window. She closed her eyes and tried to control her breathing. As she silently cursed the bright moonlight, another eternity passed and the sound of stealthy footsteps forced her to half-open her eyes. The figure went off the porch and toward the back of the house.

I know I locked both the front and back screens...get to the phone and call Uncle Wes. The phone...I forgot to plug in the phone. Okay, Ann...you're the one who was going to be just fine here all alone.

She rolled off the bed, hoping the mouse would not run across her bare feet. She slipped on her terry cloth robe and slippers and felt her way down the hall to the back bedroom. With painful slowness, she turned the knob and opened the door.

Scratching?...he's cutting the screen!

Goose bumps raised on her back and spread down her arms.

Why didn't I take the gun?

Forcing herself to keep moving, she crept noiselessly across the room to the porch door. The cutting continued.

In slow motion, she turned the knob and pushed until moonlight showed through a crack. She tensed as her mind confirmed what her eyes saw—a knife, a hand, a widening hole in the screen, and the shadowy figure of a man, faceless with his back to the moonlight, but intent in his posture.

Her breath halted.

O, dear God, don't let me panic. Close the door...slow...easy.

She backed slowly away and turned to the other door.

Where, she thought? Lots of nooks and crannies—which one? Out the front door? What if he has an accomplice?

Instinctively, she moved slowly toward the stairs that led to the rooms above. Praying the creaking of the stairs would blend with the sounds of the country, she crept slowly upwards. At the top of the stairs, she stopped.

He saw the car—he probably saw me. Will he search for me, or just steal something and leave? Maybe he's just a harmless, hungry wetback. Maybe I should go back down and confront him. No...no way.

She had little time, but she knew the intruder would have to cut the screen again to get at the upper lock installed to keep toddlers in. Or, he'd have to cut an opening big enough to crawl through. Whatever...it would slow him down. He apparently wanted to avoid discovery as much as she did.

Where to hide? The girls' room...the ghost hole. It runs a long way on the side of the house.

Quickly, she tiptoed into the girl's room, closing the door behind her. Feeling her way to the bed on the left, she crawled over it and felt along the wall. Her hand traced the frame of the two-foot square trap door to the ghost hole until it reached the catch. She pulled and the door came toward her. She lowered the door to the bed and peered into the blackness. Gradually her eyes adjusted. In the faint moonlight, she could make out the underside of the tin roof and the rafters that held it in place.

Reaching through, she felt the rough flooring of the storage space. Dust and dirt under her hand made her grateful that she couldn't see more clearly—she might not have the courage to go in.

She put her head and shoulders through the hole and crawled in. Turning, she rose to her knees to close the door. As she straightened, her head brushed the sloping roof and dust drifted down on her shoulders. Something brushed her face. She raised her hand to her cheek...sticky cobweb clung to her fingers.

She could hear movement below. Her palms were sweating. She was beginning to panic. Carefully she pulled the door up and toward her. It thudded into place. The sound was obliterated by a clattering from below.

Instantly, Ann realized the intruder's foot had caught the leg of one of several metal folding chairs stored between the refrigerator and the wall, just inside the kitchen door. She'd nearly tripped on one herself earlier.

She exhaled in relief. The intruder cursed lowly. Ann knelt in the dark by the trap door. After a moment she could distinguish soft, careful footsteps. A door opened, and she heard shuffling noises. He's checking the rooms... knows someone's here, and only a dead person could have slept through the clamor when the chairs fell. Now, it's hide and seek.

A door creaked open below her. Sound carried well in the old house. Ann recalled, as a child, lying in bed at night listening to the muffled chatter and laughter of the grownups playing poker in the dining room—the boys giggling in their room as they told ghost stories.

A flash of light through a crack in the floor of her hideout startled her. Then she remembered how light from adjoining rooms would creep through cracks between the ceiling and the walls. The house was tight and snug at one time, but the arid climate had dried the wood and loosened it over the years.

The light disappeared quickly.

He has a flashlight. I can't move while he's right below... if I can hear him, he can hear me.

She listened for him to pass down the hall, straining to track his movements. She heard him grumble, cursing again.

For some moments, she heard nothing, then another door creaking. Grandma's room? Then, only faint movements. He's crossed through the front entry hall... going down the other side of the house. He hasn't found what he wants. If I'm going to move, it has to be now.

On hands and knees, she crawled toward the front of the house... over rough planks... through cobweb curtains.

Suddenly the makeshift floor ended. She slid her hand down the crossbeam under the last plank and felt wainscoting nailed to the underside of the beam, a ceiling for the room below. Would it support her weight? Pushing on it as hard as she could, she tested. It seemed solid.

She eased into the space between the crossbeams. The wainscoting creaked, but did not give way.

Lying perfectly flat and still, she listened. For a long moment there was only the sound of the windmill. Then she heard squeaking. Not a door... mice, here, in the ghosthole?

Just as her imagination began to run wild, she recognized the squeak of the swinging door between the dining room and kitchen. In her mind, she timed his movements in the kitchen.

He's checking the food pantry... walking along in front of the stove, checking the pan pantry... crossing over to the utility pantry... walking past the old kitchen safe... the refrigerator in the corner. Now, he'll either leave... or come upstairs.

She held her breath and her whole body listened. Every step on the ancient stairway creaked. The knot in her stomach pulled tighter... her breath came faster.

Oh, God, please, she begged, please.

The creaking stopped. Footsteps... another door... this room... the closet door... he'll shine his light on the trap door. Footsteps. The door is shutting... could I be so lucky?

She held her breath and listened again. She could track him down the hall beside the stairwell to Aunt Anna's room... the closet.... He'll probably check under the bed... the boys' room... the closet...

And down, she willed. Oh, please, go down... go away. If all he wants is the car, why doesn't he just take the keys and go? He had to find them. I left them on the dresser... no... in the pocket of my jeans... in the bathroom hamper!

She heard the door to the girls' room open again. The bed springs creaked. She took a deep breath and held it as the ghosthole door fell away. The beam of the flashlight swept the underside of the sloping roof above the door. The bed springs squeaked loudly, and she guessed he was leaning into the hole. The light began a methodic sweep. Ann pressed herself against the crossbeam. The light traveled down the planks until it reached the end and started back across the roof. As it passed the rafter three feet away from Ann, there was a chilling screech, and a large barn owl swooped toward the light.

"Son of a bitch."

The flashlight beam jerked straight up, and the door slammed.

What if the squeaking were baby owls? A mother owl…her mind pictured the sharp, hooked beak and long talons.

Ann didn't know whether to laugh or cry. He was gone, but now she was in this attic with who knew what. She lay very still. If it starts flying around, I'll faint. I can't take much more of this.

She heard the man cursing as he went noisily down the stairs. In a moment the kitchen door banged—then, the back door.

He'll go now…no…he's reacting to the owl…he's just trying to make me think he's gone.

Suddenly wings flapped over her, very near. Then silence.

Had the owl flown through a hole in the eaves?

She was aware of the windmill again, but she didn't hear cars on the highway. The luminous dial on her watch showed 2:30. Her mind ran over all the possibilities again, and her imagination began to conjure up horrible scenarios…murder, rape, perversion, drugs.

She resolved to stay where she was for three hours. Then it would be growing light. If she heard nothing more, she'd risk going out.

She listened…only the windmill. Relaxing a little, exhaustion overwhelmed her. She dozed off.

She drifted back to consciousness sometime later. Her mind began to replay the events of the night. A nightmare? No. She was stiff and cramped. It felt as if she was lying on a board. It was all too real.

She slowly realized that it was morning. Faint light was creeping through cracks around the edges of the roof. Birds were chirping. It wasn't dark enough for her luminous watch dial to be effective. She half-guessed the time was 5:40.

She listened for a while, hearing only the windmill. Wes and Sue weren't due back till 3:00; Bill wouldn't return until evening. She could stay cramped up here till 3:00, or chance that the intruder was gone.

She had developed a sense of the rhythm of the country sounds, and heard nothing out of the ordinary. She raised up slowly and began to crawl stiffly and carefully over the planks. Just as she reached the door, the creatures began squeaking again. Without hesitation, she pushed open the door and scrambled out as quietly as her fear would allow.

She eased across the floor to the open closet and peered in. She opened the bedroom door gently. She considered checking all the rooms and dismissed the idea.

He might still be around. Best to get away quickly.

Drawing courage from the daylight, she descended slowly to the first floor, and went quickly down the hall to the bathroom, locking the door.

When she had flushed the toilet, she scrubbed her hands, but decided to forego anything else. She pulled her dirty clothes from the hamper, dressed quickly and went cautiously into the kitchen. Through the door she could see the porch screen dangling next to the open locks. Bill's horse stood quietly in his pen.

Breathing a sigh of relief, she pulled her keys from her pocket as she crossed to the kitchen sink. Her throat was parched, and she reached for the glass on the counter.

"I'll take those keys now."

The glass shattered in the sink as she whirled around. Her mind registered a switch-blade, glistening as it reflected light from the door where he stood.

"I'll take a glass of water, too. Only I want ice water."

"It's there, in the refrigerator," Ann said.

"Come over here and get it."

As she moved hesitantly toward him, she watched his eyes. Cold and gray, they swept her from head to toe.

As she passed, he stepped behind her. Grasping her upper arm tightly, he placed the blade of the knife between her shoulder blades.

"Listen carefully."

His voice was hard.

"Don't move quickly. Don't try anything, and you won't be hurt. All I want is your car. Now, get the water."

She went to the refrigerator and took out a pitcher of water. Returning to the cupboard, she got a large glass, filled it shakily, handed him the glass and stepped back.

As he watched her over the rim of the glass, Ann studied him. He was about 30, 5'11", with neatly trimmed dark hair. He was unshaven, with smudges on his face and hands. His clothes were stained and rumpled. With a shave and fresh clothes – without the knife and cold, gray eyes—he could pass for a clean-cut yuppie.

"Another," he said, handing her the glass.

"I'd like to pour myself some," Ann said.

"Be my guest," he replied, "but be careful."

When they had finished the water, he said, "Now, the car keys."

Surprised at her willingness, Ann surrendered the keys.

"All right. I'm going to tie you up and take a shower. I roamed around in the brush some yesterday, and need to clean up before I go. Then we'll have some breakfast."

Ann's heart sank.

"You should just go. I'm expecting people."

"Right," he smirked. "I've been watching this place since late yesterday afternoon. My car broke down not far from here. You came along just as I was ready to leave. I checked out that trailer . . . no one's there. I heard you and the cowboy talking when he left. He and the trailer guy are both gone until later this afternoon. Plenty of time. Sit down in the chair in front of the sink."

How can he be so casual? Is he running from the law? A drug runner? I don't care. I just wish he would go.

Keeping an eye on her, he backed up to the kitchen door, opened it and reached down to pick up a coil of rope.

Coming back, he ordered, "Hands behind your back."

He stopped and stood there looking at her.

Her flesh began to crawl.

"You're going with me."

No...no...oh, please, God...no.

"WHY?"

"I have business in Mexico. It occurs to me that a couple of tourists going over for the day would not arouse suspicion."

"You don't need me. Cleaned up, you'd look like an everyday yuppie."

"That's not an advantage if I'm alone," he said. "You are going with me. After I shower and shave, you'll shower and put on clean clothes. You don't look much better than I do right now. A little dusty in that hole, was it?" he smirked. "Hands behind the chair."

He bound her arms and legs to the chair quickly, anchoring her in place by running the rope through the old-fashioned double fixture on the sink and knotting it again at the chair.

"Sit tight. I won't be long."

He stopped and studied her with eyes that made her feel naked.

"You're not bad. Well, Mexico will be time enough," he said at last.

He turned and went into the hall.

Ann shuddered. She listened as he climbed the stairs and closed the bathroom door. He had just made her decision.

Knife or no knife, I have to escape...no way I'm going to Mexico with him. Once we got across that border, no telling what would happen. What if the Mexican police arrested him? Would they believe I wasn't with him?

She'd heard about people being thrown into Mexican jails mistakenly and being there for years. And the way he had looked at her meant only one thing. She had to get loose.

She waited for the sound of the shower and then struggled to work her arms up and out of the ropes. Instead, the ropes worked up above her elbows.

Water began to drip freely from the wainscot ceiling above the back door. The shower curtain...he did not have it inside the metal shower stall. There was always at least one flood at every family gathering. Water would drip from the ceiling, and someone would charge up the stairs and bang on the bathroom door, shouting for the culprit to pull in the curtain.

Thinking more clearly now, she remembered seeing the sharp vegetable knife that was kept in the front of the silverware drawer. She sat with her back to the sink . . . the drawer just to her left. She twisted her lower left arm around and bent it out to the side. The edge of the drawer was an inch away from her outstretched fingers.

She scooted the chair toward the drawer until she was able to ease it open. Pushing against the ropes until her arms felt raw, she struggled blindly to get her fingers into the drawer. At last, she felt metal against her nails. Scooping with her fingernails, she brought up a potato peeler, a baby fork, and at last, the knife.

The shower was still running. She brought the knife to her side and worked the blade beneath the ropes. Sawing doggedly, she made slow, steady progress.

The shower stopped.

After she had sawed through two loops of rope, it began to loosen.

She shook frantically at the ropes until she was able to raise them over her head, loosen the part around her legs, and step free.

She went quickly and quietly to the end of the table. A spreading puddle of water lay directly in front of the kitchen door. Stepping over it to the door sill, she gripped the door jamb and leaned toward the metal chairs beside the refrigerator. As she pulled one out to obstruct the door, the others shifted and clanged against the refrigerator.

The door above opened. His feet pounded on the stairs.

Ann pushed the screen door open and jumped off the porch.

He'll catch me if I run toward the highway. Throwing open the gate to the horse's pen, she ran toward to the adjoining cattle pens.

There was a loud crash from the house.

Her booby trap had worked.

Spooked by the commotion, the horse snorted loudly, and ran out the open gate.

Ann climbed the fence and stole a look back toward the house.

He was standing on the porch, rubbing his hip and searching. He wore only a pair of jeans. The knife was in his hand.

For an instant, Ann froze.

It must be 8:00 a.m. Traffic's picking up on the highway...trucks going back and forth from the border...a plane to the north...the world is passing by...and I'm running for my life.

From his crop duster north of the ranch, Bill detoured and scanned ahead to check on his horse. He was uneasy—she was spooky lately. He knew Wes and Sue were gone for the day, and Ann was due in yesterday; but, he didn't know what she knew about horses.

Good thing I flew over, he thought, peering ahead at the mare out in the open field. As he dropped down, he saw a man jump off the back porch and run out the gate.

"That guy has a knife in his hand," Bill said to no one. "What in thunder is going on down there?"

Out of the corner of his eye, he caught motion in the cattle pen. Ann...running!

"Good Lord. I'll have to put down in the field."

The man had spotted her. He was coming out of the yard.

Ann jumped down into the crowding pen and ran to the doctoring chute, now overgrown by branches from a mesquite tree. She pushed at the branches, scraping her arms. The ends of the tree branches slapped back at her as she pushed through into the squeeze chute.

I don't hear him running...he's climbing the fence.

As she cleared the branches, the dipping vat yawned two feet beyond the end of the squeeze chute. With luck, he'd rush out the end of the squeeze chute and fall into the dipping vat. She crouched down, snatched a stick from the ground, and slung it into the dipping vat. If he fell in, she'd have a little more time to work her way back to the highway and flag down a car.

Crouching, she crept back along the side of the squeeze chute, obscured by the brush.

"Damn."

Flailing through the branches, he spotted the dipping vat ahead. She was nowhere in sight.

Stunned, he glimpsed the sides of the squeeze chute just before they snapped shut, pinning his arms to his side and digging the edge of the knife into his leg.

"Aaaaaaah."

Bill heard the scream as he jumped from his plane. Pulling a pistol from under the seat, he started running.

Ann had all her weight on the lever that controlled the chute. Blood ran from long scratches on her right arm.

"My God. let me out of here. This knife is digging into my leg."

Ann lifted her head, but kept full pressure on the lever. It should hold. I'll have to trust it or stand here till someone comes.

Just as she eased off on the pressure, she heard Bill.

"What in tarnations been goin' on here? Are you all right?

His head poked out of the mesquite branches covering the first chute.

"Oh, Bill. Am I glad to see you. I saw a plane a minute ago, bu...I didn't hear you land."

"Well, I'm not surprised. You can let go of that thing. He's not goin' anywhere."

Thankfully, Ann released the lever. Her arms were leaden.

"He broke in last night, and it's been a nightmare ever since. He was going to take me to Mexico. I suppose we should get him out of the chute. The knife is digging into his leg."

"You sit tight here. I'll get a rope."

As she waited, tears of relief and exhaustion streamed down her cheeks.

❀

Ann padded down the hall in her pajamas and went into the kitchen.

"Feel better after your bath?" Bill asked. "Sit down and I'll tend to your arms. Sure you don't want to see a doctor?"

"No. I'll just be sore for a while. The bath really helped."

"Did you find out anything about him?" Ann asked.

"Yeah. Sheriff said he was wanted for embezzlement back east. Got tangled up with the wrong crowd and was sent down here to make some kind of dope deal in Mexico. Had a pile of money in that bag he was carryin'. Found his car in the brush just a little ways past the ranch. Guess he'd seen it as he passed, and it was the closest place when his car broke down.

"Anyway, you are one lucky—and smart—little lady. I thank the good Lord you kept your head. There's just no tellin'....."

"Let's not even think about it," she shuddered.

"The sheriff wants a statement tomorrow," Bill continued, "but no hurry today. Get some rest. I hope you won't be staying at the ranch alone anymore."

"Not for a while," Ann agreed. "But, you know, the ranch means a lot—good times, good memories. It makes me furious to think some mixed-up kook could drop down from nowhere and ruin it all in one day.

"I'll stay with Wes and Sue, but I want to work here during the day. I don't want this to be my first memory when I think of the ranch."

***

Shirley K. Wright, 84, is a native of Des Moines, Iowa. After graduation from high school where she became interested in writing, she worked for two years as Associate (traveling) Editor for a retail trade journal. She married Edward V. Wright, Jr., and moved with him to his native Texas where in collaboration they wrote two books, *Todos Santos*, ISBN 978-1-4634-1226-5 and *Branches*, ISBN 878-1-4018-7271-0, published by Authorhouse. The couple reside in Coppell, Texas.

PETIT FOURS

Jolie Caldwell

It was a long time ago—sticky hot the way it gets in the summertime in the Tennessee mountains. Charlene was just there temporarily; Bobby was selling Bibles to poor people to make enough money to go back to college in the fall. A recruiter came around to MSU telling all the college boys how they could make buckets of money in the summer selling $50 Bibles to poor folks in Appalachia for $5 a week. The Bibles were huge white ones with gold edged pages and color pictures of a blue-eyed Jesus. There was also a place in them to write births and deaths and marriages which seemed a strong selling point to the mountain people.

Bobby thought selling Bibles in Tennessee sounded better than cooking hamburgers at the Frostop the way he did other summers. At least it would be a change, and he wouldn't smell like grease all summer. So he signed up.

Bobby and Charlene met at a spring-fed swimming hole, Potter's Point, when Charlie was thirteen and Bobby was fifteen. Bobby swam up under Charlie's inner tube and knocked her off. The water was icy in spite of the boiling Mississippi sun.

"Hey, there. I didn't mean to turn you over."

Charlie smiled shyly and got back on her inner tube with what she hoped was gracefulness. She was small and brown eyed; she was always told her eyes were her best feature which made her hopefully apply lots of sea green eye shadow. She had on a black bathing suit she got at the beginning of the summer at Belk's where her grandmother worked. Her mother didn't like it.

"Charlie, you take that thing back. It's too old for you."

She didn't. She just hid it and never let her mother see it again.

Bobby must have liked it, though. He stayed there hanging on to the inner tube chattering away. Charlie sitting in the middle trying to look older than thirteen, flat chested, the pink of her sunburn contrasting strongly with the blackness of the taffeta-looking, too old, bathing suit. "Where do ya go to school?"

"Pleasantville High."

"Yeah, I go there too."

"What grade are you in?"

"Ninth."

"Yeah, I'm in the eleventh."

"You come here much?"

"Yeah, when I can get a ride out here."

Bobby dazzled Charlie. He was nice looking—slightly built, but very athletic and well-formed. He could do back flips. Bobby won the math award in high school one year and he drove a roaring black rattletrap, a Ford convertible with a black top. Charlie could always hear him coming from a couple of blocks away, plenty of time to run to the mirror to smear on Tangee lipstick in the natural shade.

Bobby and Charlie dated steadily from that summer on. Bobby was Charlie's first boyfriend. He was wonderfully attentive. It was that third summer that things got interesting and they ended up in Tennessee. Bobby just finished his freshman year at MSU; he was studying accounting. Charlie just finished her junior year in high school. She was studying piano and Bobby. Music was pretty much the thing that absorbed Charlie the most until Bobby came along. After Bobby, it was Bobby first and playing the piano second. Even so, playing something just right made Charlie feel breathless. That Tennessee summer she was on the verge of playing concert repertoire, the fiery Chopin, which her teenage heart adored, instead of the predictable waltzes. In fact, she was given, as a solemn and special gift,

The Fantasy Impromptu, to work on over the summer, the Tennessee summer.

It was Mrs. Greenberg's carrot—a taste of what was to come with discipline and practice. It was nice of Mrs. G. to give her that piece since Charlene was a slacker that year in keeping up with her practicing. Mrs. G. knew when to bring out the carrot, the inducement to suck you back in to the soul satisfying highs of addiction to music. The other thing was that Mrs. G. wanted Charlie to get some experience playing in contests so she entered her in a competition at Sophie Newcomb College in New Orleans. The winner got to play the first movement of a concerto with the college orchestra.

Charlie and her mother got up early the morning of the contest. After coffee they dressed and went by to pick up Mrs. G., the little Russian lady Charlie lucked into for a music teacher. Mrs. G. weighed 100 pounds and still spoke with a charming accent though she came to the States as a child during the Bolshevik Revolution. She was trained as a youngster to play concert repertoire and was expected to be a concert pianist. Delicate health precluded such a life and she ended up in Charlie's little southern town married to a merchant. In Pleasantville, she was the unquestioned superior of any other piano teacher. She gave music lessons to students she felt had some possibilities, or who inclined at least to practice and to not slaughter the music. She was an absolute perfectionist about everything including music. She taught as she had been taught—scales and exercises as the basis of technique—every lesson began with a scale and arpeggio. Some children went to the first lesson with Mrs. G. and never ventured back. Charlie loved her. The sentiment was returned.

The drive to New Orleans took about three hours in the Plymouth. Charlie's mother and Mrs. G. were making pleasant conversation in the front seat, Charlie sitting in the back trying not to think of what was coming. When they found the campus, it took awhile to find the right building. They parked Old Feeble and walked over to the music department. The auditorium was dark except for the dimly lit stage with the piano in the middle of it. The judges were sitting near the front in the audience. Other contestants were sitting sprinkled around the vast auditorium with their parents and their music teachers.

All Charlie could think of when her turn came was the buzzer. The judges had a buzzer they used when they had heard enough. From the minute she began to play, her heart pounded loudly in her ears; the sound coming from the piano sounded as if it were coming from a great distance, and had nothing whatever to do with her. Her slender hands shook so badly, she couldn't hold them on the keys.

About two pages into the Haydn, she got the buzzer ZZZZZZZZZST—like the sound of an electrical shock. You were supposed to stop and wait for the judges to tell you the next thing they wanted you to play. Nothing registered for Charlie after that. When her turn was over, she lurched from the piano bench and off the stage shaking with relief to get away. Mrs. G. and her mother were waiting solemn-faced where she left them a few minutes earlier. They walked out of the auditorium together.

"Don't worry darlink; this was the first time. You have to get use to the contests. Next time will be better. You will see."

Of course, Charlie didn't win. The judge's remarks came a week or so later. Mrs. G. read them to her; the only positive thing said was that she was well coordinated.

Bobby left in early June that summer for the Bible selling job in Tennessee. Charlie followed a few weeks later. Charlie, her mother and Bobby's parents all drove to Tennessee together in the Ross's air-conditioned Ford. They were married in a little church in Tennessee. Charlie wore a pale green borrowed suit with a flowered blouse; it was Aunt Sukie's. Bobby had his graduation suit to wear.

The honeymoon was just one night at a mountain inn since Bobby had to get back to work selling Bibles right away. He needed the money for fall tuition. They boarded that summer with a widow lady in a big white two-story house out from town in the territory Bobby was working. They had a bedroom upstairs and kitchen privileges. The landlady stayed gone during the day most of the time so Charlie was there alone with the whole house to herself. Charlie was sort of afraid of the landlady.

It wasn't that there was anything wrong with her, it was just that Charlie never was away from her Mother and family too much before that summer.

"Just make yourself at home, honey. You can use the kitchen anytime you want to."

"Thank you, Mam."

"Just make sure you leave it clean."

It was a spacious sun lit kitchen on a back corner of the house. You could see a corn field out the window over the sink.

"I can't stand a dirty kitchen. The roaches just take the place over if you leave food out."

"Yes, Mam."

The landlady was a strong looking middle-aged woman who wore lace-up hushpuppies and clip on sunglasses over her regular glasses.

The summer days drifted by in a warm lazy haze. Charlie would wait till Bobby and the landlady left in the morning and then she would slip downstairs and watch TV stretched out on the landlady's green damask couch. The room was dark and cool. She only got up to fix herself a coke and a mayonnaise sandwich for lunch. She knew the landlady wouldn't like her eating sandwiches on the couch. Whenever Charlie heard the landlady's station wagon coming up the gravel drive, she jumped up, turned off the TV and ran upstairs to her room. The landlady would come in, put her hand on the warm TV and laugh out loud at Charlie for being so shy. Charlie would just stay up in the room reading and looking out the window till Bobby came home. She missed her piano and her Mama. She slept a lot.

Mainly out of boredom but also because she was practicing to be a good wife, she decided to cook a big dinner for Bobby—the landlady was out of town so she didn't have to worry about running into her. The dinner turned out OK but Charlie decided it wasn't worth doing any more because there such a mess to clean up. The frozen spinach cooked down too much and burned before Charlie smelled it and turned it off. It stuck to the landlady's Farberware pot. Charlie cleaned it up the best she could and hid it on a bottom shelf, way behind the other pots and pans. Bobby didn't say much about the dinner, one way or the other. He was tired from being out all day selling Bibles. It had been a good day though; three big Bibles and half a dozen small ones. One of his customers sent him home with fresh corn, tomatoes and cornbread. Mountain people in that little town lived pretty much the way their grandparents did and they scraped up $5 a week for a beautiful Bible. It was the only luxury in what was often no more than a shanty.

Charlie lived in absolute terror the last couple of weeks of the summer partly because of the burnt Farberware pot, but also because of the landlady's petit fours. There was a beautiful box of little one-inch petit fours on the landlady's dining room table. Charlie saw them every day when she came down to watch TV. She decided to take the lid off the box to see if the real thing looked as pretty as the picture on the lid. They were beautiful—24 chocolate covered petit fours with little green icing leaves and pink flowers.

Charlie knew she shouldn't but she couldn't help herself. She took out a petit four from the middle of the box and took a bite off the bottom and then carefully put it back in the box. By the end of the last two weeks, all the petit fours had their bottoms eaten off, but if you just took off the lid and looked at them, they looked perfect and beautiful. Bobby and Charlie left in August to go back home.

❧

Jolie Caldwell is retired after a long and successful career in financial services, which took her from Florida to Texas to New York City for the last years of her career. She began as a secretary and finished as a mid-high-level executive running corporate training and development for a major brokerage firm. She is also the mother of a son and a daughter, four grandchildren, and a cat. She lives in Dallas with her husband of many years, Ralph Perry.

PRESSURE

Raymond Chatelin

Those hours spent together. So fragile, those moments—the joy that seemed at once solid yet transparent. The delicate hand attached to Cheryl's fingers, the body that seemed to gain its strength from the energies that flowed from mother to daughter. How had the time passed?

Even then, during the crushing ordeal when the world seemed to be collapsing around Cheryl, seeming to press upon her chest, Cheryl believed the two of them would survive it. The love, the sharing, the unsaid things would transfer from one to the other and firmly implant within the body chemistry, unrestrictive, permanent.

"No!"

A once lilting voice that sang when it spoke now reduced to a barbed instrument of battle. Like a claw pulling at nerve endings, it was a voice that now only pained. Not like before, those times that Cheryl now spent her nights remembering.

"I won't go," said the voice, shrill, harsh. Nothing gentle now, tinged by an edge of desperation.

"You have to go," said Cheryl, softly.

"I won't."

"I won't argue with you any more, Janine. You know you have to go and you know why."

"I don't care."

"Your father has custody every other weekend, alternating Christmas and two weeks during the summer."

"I hate New York."

"It doesn't matter."

"You don't care about me. All you want is to get rid of me for two weeks."

"That's not true," said Cheryl, forcing her voice to remain calm.

"It is."

"I love you very much. You know that. Your father loves you as well. Everything that happened between us has nothing to do about the way we feel toward you."

"Then why do you want me to leave? I don't want to go."

"We don't have any choice."

"That's what you always say. Dad said I didn't have to go if I didn't want to."

"He never told me that."

"He said it to me. He said that he didn't ever want me to go unless I really wanted to. And I don't want to go with him to New York. I don't like it there."

"It's only for two weeks."

"I won't go," whined Janine.

Child, thought Cheryl, you know nothing about the pressure that corrupts your life, those that suck the strength from your muscles. No, nothing to you is permanent, rather a simple choice, a momentary consequence. The decision is made, the action completed and nothing is left to make demands. It's nothing to you in the long run, everything to me.

The kitchen, bright in its yellow paint, the shimmering reflections from the brilliant sunlight on the far side of the room streaming through the glass sliding door that opened onto the small patio—they seemed like yet other pressure upon her weakened spirit. The warmth of the room and the brightness outside seemed a conspiracy against the bone-deep chill that was always with her lately.

The divorce was not a particularly ugly one. It had in fact, been so disgustingly civil. Its end was like a creeping tide, slowly making it felt, then suddenly closing the last piece of visible land in its liquid grasp. At first, there was nothing specific, nothing that overpowered. There was just that creeping tide of doubt. That's what had really drained the fight from her. The doubt had rid her of the life force she thought she had.

How slowly concepts die, she had discovered. Even to the end she held out hope until the lawyers, the courts, the psychiatrists had taken everything away—husband, love, marriage, self respect. All replaced by a need to survive.

"Mother?"

"Yes, Janine?"

"What if I do some extra work around the house? I'll do the dishes and even the floor if you ask. I'll be good. I promise, really I do, not to give you trouble. Not like before."

Cheryl stared at the badly acted look of innocent sincerity that smeared across her daughter's face like an insufficiently defined fresco. Turpentined emotion freeze-dried in a plaster face. It was the substitution of reality with a model born of escape into a world of television cartoons, a fantasy humbleness siphoned from automobile and soap commercials.

"Don't do that, Janine."

"What," asked the whining voice, becoming more treble with each question? The ten-year-old eyes sparkled like a cat exciting itself while chasing its prey. It was less conversation than competition. The voice had become so patterned that its owner now thought it only natural.

"Don't pretend. You aren't very cute. You know it only irritates me."

"But mother, I'm only being nice to you," squealed the voice, taunting, probing at the open wound.

"Stop that I said!" The anger rushed out in a thunderclap of energy. Janine, startled by the force, jumped back from the edge of the kitchenette table where she had been leaning toward her mother. She looked at her mother, the child's face flushed. Cheryl took a sip of her tea.

"I'm very tired, Janine. There have been many things on my mind lately. I didn't mean to shout, but you know I don't like having you pretend that you feel things."

"Like what, mother?"

Cheryl stared through her daughter and for a brief moment saw the youth that had seemed to disappear from the child's countenance.

The child never spoke of the battles. Sometimes Janine would sit in the corner and watch. Other times she could hear them from the bedroom. They were contests of control.

And the child had well absorbed the primitive means of communication like a dry sponge set to drift, thrown aimlessly off the end of a dock into a briny sea.

"You know why I really want to stay, mother?" asked Janine.

"No," replied Cheryl.

"Christine is having a party in the middle of when I'll be away and I don't want to miss it."

"There will be other parties, Janine."

"Not like this one."

"Yes, just like this one. Perhaps better ones."

"Christine's mother said this will be the last one. She'll be 13 next year and her mother says that's too old to be having parties."

"Thirteen-year-olds have parties, too."

"She'll never have another one again and I'll be the only one who misses this. It's important to me, mother. I have to be there. It's very important."

"It's very important that you go with your father, Janine."

"If you make me go, mother, I'll take off. I'll leave."

There! Just for a second. What was it Cheryl saw in the child's contorted face? Fear? Something else? Yes, a child's fear, terror.

"I mean it. I'll take off and you won't find me."

It was a birthday party for Janine when she turned five. It was a fine party and for a while the tensions that had become so much a part of Cheryl's daily existence seemed to melt into the company of friends, family, and children. That soft powdered blue dress Cheryl had bought for Janine's party hung upon the child like a declaration of love. The child was a tribute to the marriage, the bond. Janine seemed perfect and the party brought them closer. The child was the best of them that day. Now that memory seemed to have been compressed into a mere blink in time—memories left out in the sun to bleach white.

"Why don't you want me to stay?" insisted the voice.

"I simply don't want you to disappoint your father. I have no choice. Your father can make it difficult if you stay."

"If you could, you'd let me stay?"

"Yes," said Cheryl, knowing the lie.

"I don't like visiting grandmother. She makes me feel funny."

"How do you mean?"

"She keeps calling Gail. I don't like that."

"She's your father's wife. It's awkward for everyone."

"Yes, but he's nicer to her than he ever was to you, mother."

It was the look in the child's eyes that gave her away. Behind the wide look of innocence was the sense of pleasure in knowing she had scored in her battle with the adult in front of her. A look of triumph, of knowing your opponent is incapable of comeback. Why, thought Cheryl, was every word from the mouth of her child designed to make her bleed, to inflict the pain it always did?

"Dad said he'd like to take me to Hawaii someday."

"That's good."

"Maybe next Christmas, Dad says. That's the Christmas he takes me, isn't it?"

"Yes."

Always, the competition, Janine playing two adults against one another not out of spite nor even revenge, but because of a need for tangible evidence of her importance.

"I really have made up my mind, you know."

"About what?"

"About not going, mother." The face was pugnacious, the stance in the doorway defiant.

"I thought we had been through all of that."

"You didn't believe me when I said Dad would give up the visit if I asked him."

"Perhaps he was just being nice."

"He said he meant it."

"It's the party, isn't it? That's why you want to stay? Because you don't want to miss that party."

"That, too."

"What else, then?" asked Cheryl, brushing her stringy strawberry colored hair from the front of her eyes. She needed a session with the stylist. Perhaps tomorrow, she thought.

"I just thought you might want me to stay," Janine said in a gentle, pathetic voice.

"Of course I want you to stay," lied Cheryl.

"I thought I could keep you company."

How much was the truth, Cheryl asked herself? Had Janine been playing this game so long that she could no longer separate reality from fancy?

"I appreciate that, Janine. I really do."

"I can talk to Dad. He listens to me. I can call him and explain there's a party I want to go to and he'll understand. He will. You don't know him like I do. He'll do it if I ask."

"And if he doesn't, Janine? If he says he won't?"

"Then I'll go. Please mother," pleaded the desperate voice. "Let me try."

"Yes, Janine. You can try," said Cheryl.

Nightfall.

There used to be comfort in watching the darkness slowly envelope the inside of the house. Like a tranquilizer, it numbed the emotions, banishing the anger and stilling the flow of energy from her body. It was a time of truce, when the conflicts in her mind could be called to a halt. She respected the night, then, when she could breathe the temporary innocence the sweet smelling night air heavy with the scent of Lilacs brought with it.

Now the darkness meant something else. It now allowed time for the mind to race, to anticipate what the sun and the necessities of daytime would bring. The darkness had become only a connector, not an interlude, between stretches of time. All the days seemed linked now like an unending chain. Time was no longer a buffer. It merely pressed upon her with a constant forewarning of urgency.

She rose from the sofa and left the stillness of the living room, walked to Janine's room and looked in. The child was sleeping, but restless. Like me, thought Cheryl, wanting reprieve from the constant pressure of battle. But, even in sleep there was no escape.

Cheryl took out the telephone book she always placed in the drawer just below the wall phone and began fumbling through the pages, her hand visibly shaking. Stupid, she thought. Like a schoolgirl calling a date. Why the butterflies in the stomach, the nervous heart palpitations?

The number. She had never used it before. Everything went through the lawyer. Why had that happened? Why couldn't they talk to one another when there was something to discuss?

One ring. Two. Please be home. Three.

The line was broken in the middle of the fourth ring.

"Hello," said a gentle woman's voice at the other end.

Cheryl hesitated. "Hello?" it repeated in a questioning tone. Even the question sounded soft. When was the last time Cheryl had heard a voice so gentle? When was the last time her own had sounded like that?

"Yes," said Cheryl at last. "Is Frank there?"

"Who' s calling?"

"Please tell him it's Cheryl."

A pause. "Just a minute, Cheryl. I'll get him."

A muffled voice in the background. Then only silence and the quick rush of air as the receiver was taken hand to hand.

"Yes?"

"It's Cheryl, Frank. I want to talk to you."

"We shouldn't be talking without our lawyers."

"Forget the lawyers for once, Frank. I just want to talk. I need your help."

"There's no more money."

"I know."

"You're getting the maximum of what I can afford to pay. I'm not behind."

"I know that, Frank." Cheryl closed her eyes tightly. It was always a confrontation. "It's about Janine," she said.

244

"Something's wrong?" asked an urgent voice.

"Not in the way you think. She doesn't want to go with you. She wants to stay. A party, I think, and she plans to call you in the morning."

"Okay, so she doesn't have to go. I'm not going to force her. You didn't have to call me about that." Anger was creeping steadily into his voice.

"No, you don't understand, Frank. I don't want her to stay. You have to take her. I need the break, Frank. You don't know how much I need to be by myself. I have to be able to think."

"I'm sorry, Cheryl. If she doesn't want to go, I won't force her."

"You bastard. I need the time. Take her. It's your turn," she yelled into the mouthpiece.

The receiver at the other end clicked in a defiant climax, cutting off Cheryl's last words and leaving her holding a telephone connected to no one and nothing. She leaned against the wall having difficulty catching her breath.

A door closed. "Janine," called Cheryl in a startled voice? "Is that you, Janine? Are you awake?"

There was no reply. Cheryl looked toward her daughter's room, to the closed door. Had a breath of air shut it? But the air was still.

"Janine," she called softly into the darkness. "Were you listening?" Only the silence answered. Cheryl turned and sat on the sofa in the darkened living room. Perhaps if she closed her eyes and leaned back. Yes, the darkness would relax her, as it used to, wiping out some of the pressure. The insistent pressure.

***

Raymond Chatelin was previously with *The Province* newspaper in Vancouver, British Columbia, as an arts writer, travel columnist, television critic, and features editor.

THE NEXT DAY

Greg Doering

At nineteen years old I turned my life over to the Marine Corps. My quest for manhood and needing to leave home were strong motives. I was surrounded with romantic notions of old war movies and war stories growing up to guide my choices. I was going to be taken anyway; therefore, I had to avoid the inevitable 1-A draft status hanging over me and make my own choice.

It was May of 1968 and the hard reality of my choice was that now I had no choice. In late 1967, I struggled to survive boot camp and was lifted by the hope of becoming a truck driver instead of an infantryman. But in April 1968, I was assigned to an infantry battalion motor pool belonging to Second Battalion Ninth Marines when arriving in-country Vietnam. The consequences from the February Tet Offensive by the North Vietnamese left the battalion depleted and caused me and four other new personnel to be transferred to the infantry.

I was attached to the command post (CP) of Fox Company with the first platoon mortar squad. Because I had a vehicle license, I drove a small utility vehicle M274 that looked like a go kart with a flatbed to haul gear on, nicknamed a mule. Through the process of learning to become a mortar man, I drew close to my teachers and new friends: Tom, the skinny ammo humper and wheeler dealer, Lucky the California surfer athlete with cunning survival skills, BB the wire-rimglassed, bearded deep-thinking gentleman. Vick was a quiet black man and our squad leader who spoke with gentle wisdom and authority. In the few weeks we spent together, I developed a kinship trust and acceptance into the ways of an infantry mortar squad, and was given my own nickname, Motor T.

I went to bed one night with stories buzzing of possible field operations involving our unit. The next day, Lucky, Tom, Vic, and BB had all their gear gathered together ready to saddle up and leave. With backboards packed with 60mm HE mortar rounds, backpacks and all the field gear a mortar squad required neatly set up in the mortar pit, I could hear Sgt. Klein and the Gunny yelling at me to get my ass down to the CP. My immediate feeling was wondering where my squad was going, and why wasn't I going with them. I loaded up the mule with my gear and headed down to the CP to load up Sgt. Klein and the Gunny's stuff with about fifteen cases of beer to haul. I slid around the corner of the CP bunker and yelled up to Tom when Klein went back inside.

"Hey Tom, check this out!" Tom knew what to do and quickly took a case back up to their bunker. When we arrived at our new CP bunker, I was asked to explain where the missing beer went.

"Honest Gunny, some of the beer must have fallen off the mule between here and Ca Lu."

The Gunny didn't really seem to care, because at the new CP they had a huge fortified sleeping bunker and command center with a whole pallet of "PBR," Pabst Blue Ribbon, and all the ice they wanted. The new CP bunker was located high above the airfield at LZ Stud, just down the road from Ca Lu, overlooking a fuel depot. The road outside the bunker led down to the motor pool I was previously attached, located off to the right, and below the fuel depot.

When I traveled to the motor pool, I would sometimes stop and jump on the thick black fuel bladder that felt like walking on a giant water bottle. I could get a wave going and jump up to see the airfield below to my left, and motor pool below.

After the beer inventory situation was all figured out, Sgt. Klein led me over to a couple of makeshift pup tents made from ponchos to meet my new squad from second platoon. Sandy, the squad leader, was introduced by Klein; as I stuck my head in to say hello, I was greeted by that look of being a total outsider. It was starting to rain so Sandy told me to come on in. I looked around while sticking my head in the door and was trying to figure out where I could fit. There was a big black guy, Ricks from Virginia, and the fair skinned red-blonde crewcut Sandy from South Carolina, and Joe Bell, the dark-haired guy from Brooklyn or Queens, with the thick NYC accent. Warner from Michigan, who was in the hooch next door, stuck his head out to greet me.

Warner, who seemed a little friendlier, said, "You must be Motor T, we heard about you from Sgt. Klein." They all joined in a laugh.

Sandy, who had begun bickering with Klein about beer rats, turned and told me to stay with Warner. Warner stepped out to greet me, as I scratched my head trying to figure out what beer rats were.

"I'm Warner, Chester is okay." Beer rats were a daily ration of two beers per troop per day, I was told by Warner.

I heard Joe in the background. "Hey Warner; be nice to this FN new guy, he's got wheels, maybe we can finally score a ride to the BX." We had finally gotten a mobile Base Exchange that rolled in once a week, but only stopped way below on the main entrance road.

Ricks joined in the banter. "Yeah; hey Warner, you can introduce him to your rubber bitch!" Great, I thought; what the hell is a rubber bitch? I am not going to ask, knowing I had to start over with a whole new bunch of clowns. At least I had an idea of how a mortar squad functioned, and that it was intertwined with a weapons platoon. I still had to ask Sandy what happened to Vick's squad.

Sandy was straightforward and serious. "It's our turn to rotate out of the company's weapons platoon and travel with the CP, and Vick's squad will replace us." I was good at pretending things made sense, and nodded. Warner showed me where to put my gear and told me I should stay in touch with the guys in the motor pool to help get supply stuff they couldn't get. Warner explained that lots of the gear they had was World War II and Korea leftover crap; even some of the

C-rats are World War II "K-rations." The guys in the rear know where to get the good shit, Warner explained.

I had to leave my mule parked outside the CP and go back and stay with Warner. The best way to pass time was to sleep and try to ignore the guns in the distance always firing H&I rounds into the hillsides with the four deuce batteries on the tanks, or the 106 recoilless firing from outposts, or the artillery batteries doing fire missions. I was trying to adjust to noises that were friendly, including Warner's snoring. Joe would throw rocks at our tent and yell at Warner, "Shut the fuck up, Warner!"

Later the next morning, I was called into the CP. We had a new first Lieutenant, Lt. Pierce, "the firecracker man," he was called. Pierce was going to be our Artillery Forward Observer. I couldn't tell he was an officer when he asked me a question. "You're the guy with the Motor T MOS?"

"Yes sir!" I said.

"I got a job for you; see that big box?" Pierce said.

"Yeah; I mean, yes sir!" I blurted back.

"Just call me Lieutenant."

"Yes, Lieutenant," I managed to mumble.

The Lieutenant went on to explain that inside that box was a very sophisticated piece of equipment called a Starlight Scope, or NOD Night Observation Device. I was told it was a top-secret piece of equipment.

"What's it do?" I had to ask.

"We can see the Gooks at night almost like daytime, as long as the stars are out." I was told to take it up to OP Texas, down past the motor pool and around the corner from the ammo dump, just up the highway a piece. OP Texas was a short distance across the highway and up a steep hill I had seen before, that was overlooking the valley with a clear view of the LZ stud landing strip.

I loaded the box onto my mule. Wow, I was impressed with $12,000 worth of gear sitting on my mule. I was given a 45-caliber service revolver with which I was to protect the box.

"This box is worth more than you are, private; guard it with your life!" The Gunny and Lieutenant both barked at me.

"Yes, sirs!" I was rolling my eyeballs inside my head as I pulled away.

As I drove by the huge black fuel bladders below the CP, there were a bunch of tanker trucks in line. I thought about jumping on my favorite trampolines, but I noticed some officers in the distance looking my way, so I proceeded to stop by motor pool instead. As I made the turn past the fuel bladders, I could see the ammo trucks offloading at the ammo dump. I was dying to explore over there but needed to stay focused. I finished catching up with the guys at the motor pool, and began traveling back down the road to my destination. I looked up at the hills above the main entrance of the base to my right, and noticed some unfamiliar explosions occurring in a sequence, almost like they were walking their way toward my location. I looked left at the airfield, and could see that three caribou C-130s had landed and troops were running out the backs. I heard a buzzing, whirring scream of rockets flying over my head, and could see them exploding on the airfield. I heard screaming and chaos off to my right, followed immediately by the sound of more rockets coming off their launchers. I cranked on the emergency brake, and as the mule was bouncing to a sideways stop, catapulted off my right foot from the mule and hit the road with my left foot, and dove into a drain culvert ditch on the side of the road. WHAMM! The concussion made the earth jump around me with small pebbles and sand peppering my face. My body was lifted up, completely rotated while in the air, and then smashed back face down into the floor of the drainage culvert. I was sure I was dead, and remember thinking, wow this is what it's like to be dead; this is really kind of peaceful. I wonder if angels or God or someone will talk to me...I heard someone screaming at me. "Get your ass over here, Marine!"

I wasn't sure I wanted to leave the quiet peace I had found as I abruptly heard again, "Marine, get your fucking ass over here!" I felt the wind had been knocked out of me, and my ears, mouth, and nose were full of dirt. I opened my eyes, and through the cordite gunpowder grey cloud, mixed with red dirt, I saw another Marine dragging a wounded Marine into a group of rocks near me. I crawled over like a crab racing to hide under the rocks on a beach as a series of rockets hit the ammo dump a couple hundred yards away. Shrapnel began falling like rain in chunks so big I could hear them hit the ground like small pieces of bricks. Meteor debris was what my imagination conjured up as I watched the chunks fly through the air, whistling by with smoky trails. I could hear more rockets flying over our heads, as I sensed we were no longer the target, because of all the explosions on the airfield. The ammo dump continued to burn with small explosions. There was nothing we could do for the wounded Marine who died in the sergeant's arms; he said he would take care of him and told me to get back to my unit. The guy who was hit had been next to the outhouse, which had taken a direct hit. The rocket that nearly hit me landed just behind a huge rock about ten yards from where I dove into the ditch. I checked out the big hole in the side of the rock, and the half of the rock that was blown away, saving my life.

I headed back up the road to get back to my unit as ordered, just as another volley was on its way toward the fuel dump. I could not believe my astonished eyes as one rocket hit a fuel truck, creating a fireball explosion going way up into the air. I felt a twang of worry, and hoped the rockets would not hit the bladder of fuel, because not too far behind was where my new squad was camped out. As I headed up the road, seabees' bulldozers were backing off their flatbeds, with people running around moving other tankers out of the way as a river of jet fuel began heading across the road toward the motor pool. It spilled into the drain culverts and then split into so many directions across the road there was nowhere to go. I abandoned the mule and the NOD and ran towards the motor pool. Corporal Muir, who was in charge of the motor pool, was in rare form that day as a brave and compassionate person, taking charge and directing people what to do. Jeeps were being used for ambulances with stretchers tied on the front and back, driving the wounded to the battalion aid station with the

Med E-Vac helicopter pad. Muir handed me a shovel to dig a trench to divert the burning fuel away from the motor pool, as off in the distance I could hear the Phut! Phut-Phut-Phut of another volley on its way. One rocket hit the mess hall, another hit between us, and another hit the seabees hooch. We had nowhere to hit the deck, because of the rivers of fire everywhere. We just kept digging. "Charlie," the enemy's nickname, had dialed in on the airfield and hit it with at least fifteen more rounds until we heard massive outgoing rounds from our guns; finally, we were hitting back.

We got the fuel turned away from the motor pool and diverted it back down into the drain culvert where I had taken refuge minutes earlier. "Keep your head down, Doering," Muir said.

I shook Muir's hand. "See you later, Corporal Muir."

Upon my return to the CP area, it was good to find my new squad intact and unscathed by the estimated 90-rocket barrage. Everyone was okay except that "Cuddles," our XO, Executive Officer/ paper shuffler had been killed. He had been laying out sleeping at the flight line bunker waiting for an outbound flight to Da Nang. He was headed to Hawaii for R&R to meet his wife and kids, and then to rotate back to the States for duty. I felt bad the way they laughed about it when they told me, and I regret not recalling his name, but I know I can look it up. The Gunny and Klein were experienced old war horses from previous combat, and had learned to handle loss with cynicism. The lieutenant, firecracker man Pierce, laid into me for not delivering the NOD. While I was being chewed out, the Gunny noticed I was pale as a ghost and stepped in between us, and told the lieutenant to go inside and have another beer. "Yeah! I almost got killed three or four times down there," I told the Gunny.

"Have a beer, Doering, and deliver the NOD tomorrow." Gunny allowed me to step inside the bunker and sit back in the corner out of the way, and feel safe for a while. I finished my beer while sharing my experiences and listening to all the chatter. There must have been three to four cases of empty cans piled up in a 55-gallon barrel in the corner. I marveled at all the activity: there was a big map on the wall with names of the NVA units and their projected activities around us, with lots of communication gear; Ringy-Dingy land line, or Lima-Lima phones that had a hand crank on the side to ring outgoing calls connected to a switchboard for base communication. There were PR 25 radios, the portable backpack size carried in the field being used to communicate to the Fox Company Platoon positions. Outside the bunker next to my mule, there was a Com Jeep with some Radio Units affixed surrounding the back seat with a huge antenna protruding off the back. I definitely got an overview of a grunt company command center's operations that day.

For the moment, I could reflect on the experiences I had. I was soon told we would be reactionary forces to support the fourth marines being over-run on hill 512. So now the only focus I could have was to try and imagine what was to happen the next day.

❧

Greg Doering is a 68-year-old retired dental laboratory technician. Writing became part of his healing journey during counseling sessions occurring over more than a 20-year period. This story is an excerpt adapted from his finished, but yet unpublished work of a memoir titled *Honor and Indignity-Diary of a Marine 1967-1969.*

The Pack

Derry Sampey

So here I am, a grown man, curled up under my bed with my hands over my face like a kid hiding from closet monsters. You'd be under your damn bed, too, if what just happened to me was happening to you.

It started out like all our other nights, with me at my end of the couch watching sports on TV and tipping back a few brewskis. Per usual, my wife was at her end, digging through a stack of mail order catalogs to find something else she could buy. But every damn ball game kept turning into what announcers like to call pitchers' duels, meaning nobody's scoring any runs. So I started flipping channels, and stumbled on one showing what looked like a pack of junkyard dogs on steroids hauling butt through some woods and yammering to wake the dead.

Right away, my wife looked up and squealed, "Oh, I wanna watch that! Leave it there, okay?"

I figured if I humored her for a couple of minutes, she'd get bored and go back to her catalogs. Boy, was I wrong! First, the announcer started carrying on about some kinda crazy scientists who live out-doors and spend their lives studying wolf packs. Then a dude with long hair and granny glasses popped up. Turned out he's one of the scientists, and he went on and on about how much humans can learn from a bunch of mangy wolves he called "loyal, highly intelligent animals."

"He's kidding, right?" I said to my wife.

But she was staring real hard at the screen and paying me no mind. So I got up and went in the kitchen for another beer, which I figured I was gonna need if I had to listen to some guy telling me how he's best friends with a pack of cold-blooded killers.

I was hoping she'd get bored with all the wolf garbage and I could start flipping channels again. But when I got back and looked around for the clicker, she had it. So I put out my hand and said, sweet as pie, "Lemme see that a minute, okay?"

But she said, "Uh-uh," and stuck the thing behind her back.

Well, that did it. "Gimme the damn clicker!" I said real loud, and grabbed at it.

Right away, I heard a bunch of snarling, and the TV screen filled up with gray snouts and red eyes. Then, god-awful howling noises blasted from all eight speakers.

My wife growled, "Git him!" Then she howled, too!

Now, I'm under our bed, wishing I'd slammed the damn door harder when I ran in the bedroom. But it's too late now, 'cause something with breath bad enough to gag a maggot just dragged itself in beside me and is poking a cold, wet nose in my neck. I know a real man would open his eyes and see what it is. But I'm hoping if I keep mine shut, I won't have to watch what happens next.

***

Derry Sampey is a former newspaper reporter and has also been writing flash fiction for some time. In addition, he edits fiction for a variety of authors around the country.

WAITING...

Tom Boone

The dog sat and waited for her people to come home. Much of the time her eyes focused down the road in the direction in which the family had left, their car packed and pulling a rented trailer. Though the dog did not know this, the people had no intention of returning. They had everything they owned in the trailer and had moved on. They—the man, the woman and the two children—scarcely glanced back at the ramshackle house they left behind, and at the dog, which was a costly nuisance at best. Besides, the dog was really not theirs; she was a stray they had discovered skulking around back in the early spring. The dog had stayed on, unapproachable but always nearby, and always alert to any human movement outside the house. The woman surmised the dog, a female that appeared to be only a two or three years old, probably had been abused, though she could see no visible signs of injuries. The woman based her assumption on the fact that the dog would not let anyone touch her, not even the children. The dog would drop her head and shy away, her tail between her legs. Even the food that the woman instructed the children to leave on the porch was not enough to gain the dog's trust. The children, a boy and a girl, took turns each morning pouring dog food into a heavy clay bowl on the porch and retreating into the house to watch the dog through a window as she came to eat. If they waited on the porch, the dog would not come.

Every day during the week, the people were gone from the home, the man and woman to their jobs and the children to school. But the dog was always there waiting when they came home, wagging her tail from a distance and seemingly happy to see them. Still, she was not a part of the family. When the children asked why that was, the woman told them the dog probably had been abused and, because of that, was afraid of people. After the family moved out with their belongings, the dog went about her usual routine, sleeping, exploring the area around the house and trotting back and forth to the lake nearby. Several times a day she checked the spot on the wooden porch where the bowl had been, hoping someone had left some food. Through the tall grass that surrounded the yard, she had beaten a path to the lake that lay some two-hundred yards from the house. Now that summer had come, she followed the path several times a day to drink from the lake. Then she would return to her position near the road where she could see her people coming when they returned home. She waited expectantly, alertly, certain that at any moment the old pickup truck would rumble into view and relieve her anxiety. And her hunger. While water was plentiful, food was scarce now. At least it was scarce near the house. Perhaps there was food elsewhere, around the bend of the road or across one of the grassy fields that lay in all directions. But to go in search of food would take her away from her vigil, and she might miss her people when they returned. So she stayed, waiting. Her people had been gone two days now.

The dog was mostly black, with a white blaze across her chest and two white front feet. Her rear feet were mottled white as well. She weighed perhaps 25 pounds and possessed a pair of healthy eyes, alert ears and a long tail, which at first she waved back and forth rapidly whenever a car approached. Eventually the tail wagging stopped entirely and she merely watched the cars whiz past her. Even so, she knew the next car could be the one bringing her people home. Two more days went by.

The morning of the fourth day she could stand the hunger no longer, and she left her sleeping place on the porch of the house and, instead of taking up her usual position near the road, she crossed to the other side and began a search for anything she might eat. There was a small area of houses not far away where people stayed some-times. The houses overlooked the lake and could be reached by a short, winding road that cut off of the main road and disappeared through an electrically operated gate into a wooded area. The dog could not see the houses, but she sensed they were there, for cars traveled into and out of the wooded grounds regularly, and occasionally she had seen people walking up the lake road and onto the main road. Where there were people, there was bound to be food.

The dog knew she could bypass the gate easily if she wanted to. But did she want to? Yes and no. Hunger had driven her this far, but she was anxious about what she might encounter should she venture past the gate. She had been hurt by people before, and she could be hurt again. It was better not to trust anyone, anything. So she sniffed the air and paced back and forth in front of the gate, then turned and trotted away. Her hunger was not yet strong enough.

On the fifth day, the dog sat at her vigil as usual. By scouring the side of the main road, as well as other narrower roads she encountered, she had found the remains of small animals that had been run over by cars. She devoured them, hair and all, sometimes vomiting the meal up almost as quickly as she could swallow it. She felt herself getting weaker, yet she remained confident in the surety that her people would return any moment. And so she waited.

On the sixth day she discovered a small plastic sack of garbage someone had thrown alongside a side road she had searched the day before. The sack had not been there then, but it was here now. Hungrily she tore through the plastic and found inside enough edible waste to take away the hunger pangs entirely, though only for a very brief time. She licked her chops and backed away from the sack and its remaining, inedible contents, finally turning and, reluctantly, walking away. A few minutes later she came back to inspect again the site of what had been her most satisfying meal since her people left. There was nothing more in the sack that she could find to eat, so she left it and trotted off toward home.

It was the following day that a car stopped near where she sat. Immediately, her tail began to wag. Were these her people coming home? She stood alert, watching, as a man she did not recognize got out of the car and walked toward her carrying something. Frightened, she bolted away and stopped behind a bush about 60 feet away. Cautiously she peered around the bush at the man, who put something on the ground and then returned to his car and drove away. As she watched, the car turned onto the road leading to the lake houses. She was able to see the gate swing open to admit the car, then slowly swing closed again when the car was out of sight. She wondered what the man had put on the ground.

Hesitantly, the dog approached, head down, nose alert for any whiff of danger. Circuitously she neared the object on the ground, circled it, sniffing the air. She stopped and looked around her, but in no way could she sense anything to cause her fear. The man had left a small plastic bowl on the ground, and in it was some food. She smelled the food and felt her mouth fill with saliva. She grabbed up a morsel and retreated with it several feet away, her teeth crunching down on something that tasted good and familiar. She swallowed it and returned to the bowl, but again cautiously, as if this bowl of food might be a trap. Another bite convinced her that this was not a trap at all. She looked all around her, then ate the food in a few gulps, pausing again to scan the area around her. When she finished, she licked her chops and backed away. Then, as before, she cautiously inspected the bowl again in case she had overlooked something. Satisfied, she turned and trotted off down the grassy trail to the lake. Full at last, she returned from the lake and took up her position, lying in the weeds and dirt near the road, and waited for her people. Each time a car passed, she rose to a seated attention, hopeful. No one stopped.

The following day, the man in the car returned, and this time he brought with him from the car a sack of food that he poured into the plastic bowl. Again the dog retreated until the man was gone. When she determined it was safe to approach, she did so and, once again, consumed the bowlful of food. Then, satisfied, she took to her post.

"Here's the deal," Bob said, "I don't want a dog, any kind of dog. I don't want that dog. But I feel sorry for the thing, so I'm feeding her.

I can't do that forever, though." He looked around at the other people assembled in the living room of his lake house. Everyone nodded. "I also don't know what to do about her," Bob continued. "Any thoughts?"

"I hear you," Steve said. "I don't want another dog either, but I think we should try to do something."

"I guess the owners just went off and left her there?" Janine, Steve's wife, said. "I can't believe someone would do that."

"The thing is, she won't let you come close to her," Bob said. "She runs off."

"I'd be afraid she's gonna get hit by a car," Les said. "She just sits there. I've seen her."

"That's the only place I've seen her," Janine answered. "She just sits there waiting for that family to come back."

"And of course they won't," Bob said.

Bob's wife, Angela, said, "She must have been abused at some point, to act that way."

"Probably," Les said. "Sounds like it, the way she won't come near you."

"She's a nice little dog," Bob said. "But I'm afraid she's going to starve to death or get run over."

Les's wife, Audrey, posed another possibility: "She could wind up pregnant, and then we'll have a bunch of puppies to deal with."

There was silence for a moment while all considered Audrey's scenario. Steve spoke up: "Well, you're right. I supposed we could try to catch her with a net or something." He looked around at the others. "Anybody have a net?" There were some chuckles. "Or we could tranquilize her somehow. Don't we have animal control officers out here?" No one knew the answer to that, so Steve said, "Maybe the sheriff's office could shoot her with a tranquilizer dart."

"Or maybe a vet in town could help us," Les said. "Put a tranquilizer in some meat and give it to her. The vet could make sure we have the right kind of stuff, and the right amount."

The group talked some more but came up with no more viable solutions to the problem.

"Okay," Bob said at length, "I'll call the vet and see what kind of advice he can give us, and see if he can help us do whatever we need to do."

⁂

The woman was driving the pickup, and the two children sat in the back seat. It was Saturday morning, and the three of them had been traveling for nearly 30 minutes since leaving their new home. They had stopped at a market/gasoline station where the woman made a few purchases, and now they were entering territory that was neither pleasing nor displeasing in its familiarity. As they followed the curving road, the old frame house with its peeling paint, still vacant, came into view ahead. The woman slowly pulled the car to a stop at the side of the road, noticing first a "For Rent" sign stuck in the ground in the front yard. Except for the sign, everything appeared as it had two weeks before when they left with the trailer full of furniture. She was happy to be living away from there now, away from that house, from that area near the fancy lake houses and the fancy people that lived in them. Beside her on the front seat was a grocery bag, and she took from it a small sack of dog food, looking around at the house and yard with growing apprehension. The dog was nowhere to be seen.

"I don't see her anywhere," the boy said.

"Me neither," his sister said.

They all exited the car and stood looking around before shutting the doors, making a loud noise as a signal to the dog, should she still be around. On the ground nearby the woman saw a small plastic bowl turned upside down in the dirt. She walked over, picked it up and examined it. She supposed that someone had been feeding the dog. Good, she thought. The children walked up to the house and climbed the two steps to the porch, then got down and circled the house, at length calling to their mother that the dog was nowhere around. They returned to the road and their mother. At that moment the dog appeared at the head of the grassy path to the lake.

The dog stood stock still, head high, eyes bright. She stared and rec-

261

ognized the three people. Her people. The woman and children stood frozen and stared back. It was for only an instant that they remained like that, locked in each others' gaze, before the dog let out a sharp yelp and charged. Never had the woman or the children seen the dog behave in such a manner, and instinctively they knelt down to greet the black and white streak of lightning that was speeding toward them. The dog tore across the yard and hurled herself into their midst, landing with such force that she knocked both children backward onto the ground. The woman laughed and the children joined in as they tried to fend off the dog's affectionate greeting. The dog licked the little girl's face, then turned to the boy, then back to the girl. The woman lowered herself to one knee, laid aside the bowl and instantly became the third target of the dog's delirious joy. The dog began licking her hands and arms, her tail wagging furiously, then spun away and again revisited the children. Laughing, the children rolled on the ground, the dog first atop one of them and then the other. While the dog and children were occupied with their happy reunion, the woman returned to the car to retrieve the unopened sack of dog food. But before she could reach the truck, the dog left the children and bounded to her, jumping and whirling in an excited and happy dance. When she opened the pickup's front door, the dog bounded inside and sprang from the front seat to the back seat and back again, over and over. On their feet now, the children ran to the truck and scrambled inside. Before getting inside, the woman glanced around at the house and yard where they had once lived and was thankful again they were no longer living there. Her eyes fell upon the empty plastic bowl she had laid on the ground, and she circled the truck to pick it up again. She figured that someone from one of the fancy lake houses probably had left it there. They could afford to part with a little bowl like this, which would make a nice water bowl for the dog, she thought. She returned to the car with it, got in and they all drove away.

"The children missed you," the woman said to the dog as she drove. "So I told 'em we'd try to find you." She turned to smile at the children in the back seat, who were petting the dog and allowing her to lick their faces and arms. "They want to name you Bootsie," she said.

"Because of your four white feet!" the little girl squealed.

"How's that sound to you?" the woman said.

The dog had never felt such magic in her life.

Bob made phone calls to his neighbors to tell them the dog had disappeared.

"Coyote got her, maybe," Steve said. "That wouldn't surprise me."

"Maybe someone stopped and picked her up," Les said, before adding quickly, "Naahh, that's impossible. Nobody could have gotten that close to her."

"Steve thinks maybe a coyote got her," Bob said. "Could be."

"I don't know," Les said. "Coyote sounds likely."

Bob agreed. Coyote. But from then on he couldn't help but wonder occasionally whatever happened to that little plastic bowl. He searched all around but never found it.

Tom Boone, 77, is a retired newspaper writer who loves dogs.

Young people think they are so smart. But if you took away all their devices for communication, they would be lost. We, on the other hand, can talk or an hour on any subject, barely taking a breath.

—Barbara Mott
92-year-old author

Contest Judges

James R. Callan...

...took a degree in English, intent on writing. But when that did not support a family, he entered a Ph.D. program in the field of mathematics. Upon graduation, he worked as a research mathematician, and later as vice-president of a database company.

He has received grants from the National Science Foundation, NASA, and the Data Processing Management Association. He has been listed in *Who's Who in Computer Science,* and *Two Thousand Notable Americans.*

When his children were grown and self-supporting, he returned to his original love—writing. For two years, Callan wrote a monthly column for a national magazine. For six months, he wrote a weekly column that appeared in newspapers in four states. Callan has published four non-fiction books, two on the craft of writing (at the request of a publisher) and two on computers. But his primary interest is in mystery and suspense novels. He now has eleven books published. These include two in the popular Father Frank cozy mystery series, and two in the successful Crystal Moore Suspense Series. The third Crystal Moore Suspense is due out in 2017. All of his books have been published in print, seven are also published as e-books and four have been published in audio.

One of his mystery/suspense books ranked as high as number seven in its category on Amazon. The audio version of another book rose as high as number six on the Books in Motion list. He has had shorter works published in five anthologies. His twelfth book, a suspense, is scheduled for publication in 2017.

In addition to writing books, Callan gives workshops on various writing and publishing topics in Texas and Mexico.

For fourteen years, Callan served as director of a respected writers' conference. He has belonged to writers' groups in Texas, Missouri, Oklahoma, and Puerto Vallarta, Mexico. He and his wife split their time between homes in east Texas and Puerto Vallarta. They love to travel and have visited all 50 of the United States and six of the seven continents, missing only Antarctica. They have four children and six grandchildren.

All books in all formats can be purchased on Amazon. Visit the Amazon author page for James R. Callan at: http://amzn.to/1eeykvG.

Jane Giddan...

...is Professor Emerita of the Department of Psychiatry, University of Toledo Health Sciences Center and a Fellow of the American Speech-Language and Hearing Association. A retired speech-language pathologist, she has specialized in language development and disorders, child mental health, and autism and is co-author of numerous articles and books including *Autistic Adults at Bittersweet Farms, European Farm Communities for Autism,* and *Childhood Communication Disorders in Mental Health Settings.* With their three grandchildren in mind, she and her husband, Norman, have written children's books including *Grackles of Green Grove Protect Their Land* and its translation, *Los Zanates de Valle Verde Protegen Sus Tierras.*

With childhood pal, psychologist Ellen Cole, she blogs at 70candles.com and at Huff/Post50, and has conducted a series of conversation groups throughout the U.S. for women near or in their 70s. Their book, *70 Candles! Women Thriving in Their 8th Decade* (Taos-institute.net/70candles) is about this incredibly rich era in women's lives.

Norman Giddan...

...is a retired clinical psychologist and writer living with his wife, Jane, in Carrollton, Texas. His novels have been made into screenplays and *Two Sweeties* was a finalist for the Ariadne Prize. Recent novels include *The Bogus Killer* and *The Rat Murders,* along with a collection of novellas, *Five Tales.* He is a stove-top short order chef, loves time with his grandchildren, works hard in yoga, and has traveled in North America, Europe and the Caribbean.

Ann Howells...

...was born and raised in the Chesapeake Bay area of Maryland. She graduated from Shepherd University cum laude with double majors in Biology and English and worked in cryomycology research at American Type Culture Collection in Rockville, Maryland. In fact, her first publication appeared in the scientific journal, *Mycologia:* "The Effects on Fungi of Freezing at Ultra-Low Temperatures" with Dr. Shuh-wei Hwang.

During the 1970s, her husband's work with the U.S. Treasury kept her, her husband, and two children on the move, primarily up and down the East Coast. Then, in 1979, the family arrived in Carrollton, Texas. Here she taught oil painting classes both in a local store and the city's recreation program.

By the mid-eighties her interest in poetry, which waned after college, resurfaced. In 1990, she joined Dallas Poets Community, a workshop and service group, and has served on its board since 2000 (four years as its president and many more as secretary or treasurer). She joined the staff of *Illya's Honey* poetry journal, becoming its managing and poetry editor in 1999, and recently moved the journal to a digital format (www.IllyasHoney.com). In 2001, Ann was named a "Distinguished Poet of Dallas" by the city.

Her chapbook, *Black Crow in Flight,* is from Main Street Rag Publishing, 2007. *The Rosebud Diaries,* a limited-edition chapbook, is from Willet Press, 2012; it is now out of print. *Under a Lone Star,* her first full-length book, illustrated by J. Darrell Kirkley, is from Village Books Press, 2016. A chapbook, *Letters for My Daughter,* was released just two months later from Flutter Press, and yet a third publication, *Cattlemen and Cadillacs,* an anthology of Dallas/Ft. Worth poets which she edited, was released by Dallas Poets Community Press in the summer of 2016. Ann's own poetry appears widely in small press and university publications (over 300) both on-line and print, including such journals as Borderlands, *Concho River Review, Little Patuxent Review, Spillway, THEMA,* and a variety of anthologies including: *Goodbye, Mexico* and *The Southern Poetry Anthology, Volume VIII: Texas* (both Texas Review Press) as well as *Pushing the Envelope, Texas Weather Anthology,* and *Great American Wise-Ass Poetry Anthology* (Lamar University Press). Other poems appear in Canada, Australia, England, Ireland, Scotland, Wales, Germany, Nepal, Thailand, and Israel.

Ann's work occasionally places in competitions, including two firsts. She serves on advisory boards and panels for various literary organizations and is often solicited as a judge for poetry and chapbook competitions. She has done radio and television readings and interviews (Writers Around Annapolis) in connection with her chapbook: *Black Crow in Flight* (Main Street Rag, Editor's Choice 2007). She has been four times nominated for a Pushcart, twice in 2014, and two times for a Best of the Net. Ann enjoys attending poetry conferences and festivals within Texas and beyond, both as a spectator and a participant. When she is not writing, editing, traveling, or submitting her work, she enjoys photographing Texas courthouses.

***Under a Lone Star* and *Letters for My Daughter*:** http://www.amazon.com/Ann-Howells/e/B01D3RNONU/ref=sr_ntt_srch_lnk_1?qid=1474593395&sr=1-1

***Black Crow in Flight*:** http://mainstreetragbookstore.com/?product= black-crow-in-flight\

Leslie Ligon

As the mother of two young men, Leslie Ligon has learned more about being flexible and responsive than she imagined possible— even at the height of her dance career. Years of dealing with difficult news, emergencies and relatively long-term difficult situations with at least outward aplomb have shaped her ability to handle herself as a voice talent.

Leslie earned a Bachelor of Science with a mass communications major and a minor in dance. The discipline learned in dance technique and journalism/editing classes has proven to be an invaluable base of support.

Throughout many years of performing in local and regional theater, working as a magician's assistant, and teaching ballet, she also worked as an administrative assistant, secretary and receptionist at such companies as Fina Oil and Gas and Dr Pepper/ Seven-Up, and, at Southern Methodist University and Texas Christian University. She also worked in several capacities at a Dallas talent agency and two local recording studios (where my interest in voice work was initially piqued).

After returning as an older student, then, graduating college, Leslie worked as a free-lance writer/news stringer (Ft. Worth Star-Telegram) especially keen on grant writing and helping others with grant applications; the highlight of her arts grant writing career was spent working at The Kennedy Center as assistant to the director of the National Initiative to Preserve America's Dance (NIPAD) during the launch of a three-year Pew Grant funding program. Following that position, I worked as associate development director of the Van Cliburn Foundation.

The last 20 years have been filled raising two sons, and, as the owner and designer of the world's first line of fashion jewelry featuring braille (2010 Smithsonian/Cooper-Hewitt People's Choice Award, and American Printing House for the Blind Best Use of

Braille award). She learned to read and write braille, and utilized her dance background to help teach orientation and mobility— and later, white cane travel—to her older son.

In 2014, she returned to her performance roots in voiceover work, where her stage performance, writing skills and love of reading culminate in the job of voice actor.

Barbara Morris, . . .

. . . 87, is a pharmacist and advocate for balanced lifelong growth and productivity. She publishes the online *Put Old on Hold Journal* and has written several books on managing the aging process. Her most recent book is *The Expert's Guide to Strut Your Stuff!* available on Amazon in paperback and on Kindle. She recently acquired her real estate license in keeping with her belief that we are never too old to learn, grow and be productive. She is affiliated with Teles Properties, specializing in high-end luxury homes.

Barbara lives in Southern California with daughter Pat, son-in-law Bob and two rambunctious corgis, Lola and Sam, rescued from the local shelter. Visit www.BarbaraMorris.com to learn more.

Amazon paper link: https://www.amazon.com/gp/product/15024284 74/ref=as_li_qf_sp_asin_il_tl?ie=UTF8&camp=1789&creative=9325&creativeASIN=1502428474&linkCode=as2&tag=putoldonhold-20&linkId=7KNGXM6ZIDABQQZ2

Amazon Kindle link: https://www.amazon.com/gp/product/15024 28474/ref=as_li_qf_sp_asin_il_tl?ie=UTF8&camp=1789&creative=9325&creativeASIN=1502428474&linkCode=as2&tag=putoldonhold-20&linkId=7KNGXM6ZIDABQQZ2

Put Old on Hold Journal **link:** http://www.PutOldonHoldJournal.com

Riva Nelson, . . .

. . . MA, MS, PhD, is a retired Clinical Psychologist and former Associate Clinical Professor at the University of California, San Francisco. She had a private psychology practice for more than 30 years.

In addition to teaching and supervising graduate level students in psychology, she taught in the Division of Behavioral Science, Ethics and Professionalism in the School of Dentistry at UCSF. She lives in the San Francisco Bay Area and spends time in New York, beautiful Sea Ranch, California and Paris (whenever possible). She is the recent bride of a semi-retired criminal law professor and between them they have four sons and six grandchildren.

Most of her hands-on writing and editing experience has been in the nonfiction realm, that is, primarily psychology and teaching. However, her ever-enduring love of the written word in all forms led to her second and most recent career as an audiobook narrator and producer. She has narrated a number of books of all genres, both fiction and nonfiction—including the narration of a cookbook for Paleo desserts, an academic text of Rabbinic Tales and a weight loss guide. Most of her narration, however, has been of fiction including mysteries, literature, romance, etc.

Dr. Nelson believes the art of audiobook narration begins and ends with a profound respect for the art and craft of the writer. Before a mic is ever turned on, audiobook narration begins with a comprehensive and respectful reading of the book with an ear exquisitely tuned to the writer's intent and voice. If perceived and understood correctly, the narrator becomes merely the conduit, the respectful, non-intrusive voice of the writer. The narrator's only goal and measure of success lies in allowing the reader (or listener) to hear the words of the writer clearly and without personal embellishment, as if the writer were whispering directly into the reader's ear.

Catherine Ortiz'...

...writing career harkens back to the eighth grade when she won the Knights of Columbus Essay Contest. The topic was completely open, and she was the new kid in school, something she was accustomed to as a military brat.

Catherine wrote about exactly that: what it was like being "The New Kid." She did not think it was particularly well-written, but apparently several of the nuns did, and that was the beginning of putting pen to paper and, later, hands to the keyboard.

On completing her bachelor's degree in English, Catherine was hired to teach EFL (English as a Foreign Language) classes at Gulf Technical College in Bahrain for a year. After that, she bought a one-way ticket to Spain, where, in spite of not having a job, speaking very poor Spanish, and limited to meager savings, she spent the next quarter century. It was 25 years that would forever change her.

Her first writing job was cobbling together weekly movie reviews for Guidepost, the English language magazine for ex-pats in Madrid. She also wrote the occasional feature story or satirical piece, the latter of which suited her inherently sarcastic nature.

One prophetic day she went to the office to turn in her weekly copy, and the typesetter asked if she wanted part-time work doing proof-reading for EFL textbooks. As a poor EFL teacher, she wanted work doing just about anything. And that turned out to be the first step in many involved in textbook production over the next two decades: writing recording scripts, directing recordings and photo shoots, working on post-production for audio and video ancillary materials, writing stories for EFL textbooks (K-12 and adult), and eventually working as a senior project editor for a multinational publishing company.

The final stepping stone in her writing experience was the jump to English-Spanish translations. While in Spain, she translated two travel guides for the Ministry of Culture's Everything Under the Sun series. On re-patriating to the U.S., she did a joint translation with her husband for the government project, "Free to Grow." Her most recent translation project was her first literary venture: *Told from the Hips,* a collection of short stories by Chilean author Andrea Amosson (original title: Cuentos Encaderados, ©2015) which recently won second place in the International Latino Book Awards for fiction work in bilingual editions. (URL: https://www.amazon.com/dp/0692377905/ref=rdr_ext_tmb)

Currently, she works as Coordinator of the Lower Level Spanish Program at the University of Texas at Arlington, where she earned a master's degree in Spanish. In her spare time, she is working on her own short story collection based on her years in Spain. And she has ideas for English-Spanish bilingual books for children, such as stories in rhyming English and Spanish.

This is Catherine's idea of fun. She just wishes she could draw.

www.ingramcontent.com/pod-product-compliance
Lightning Source LLC
Chambersburg PA
CBHW032037080426
42733CB00006B/114